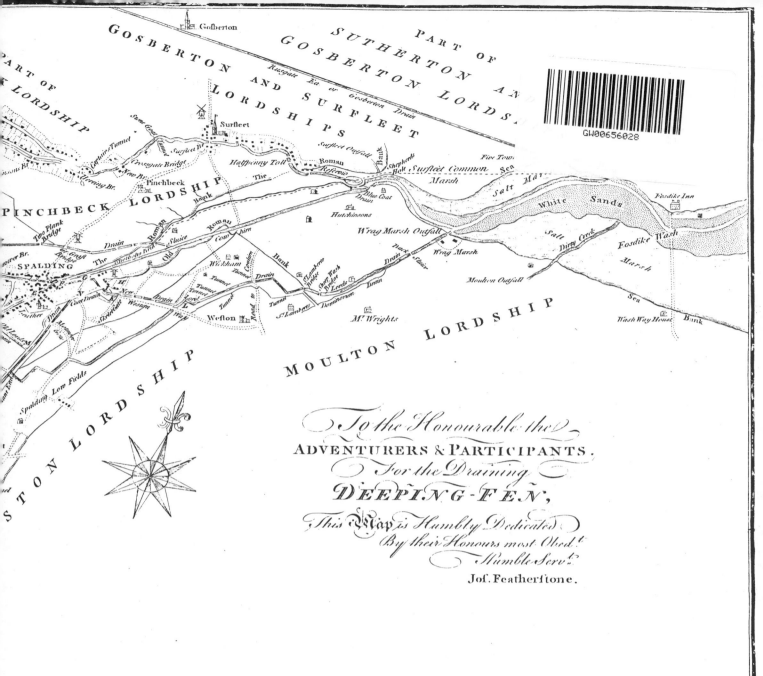

PART OF SUTHERTON AND GOSBERTON LORDS.

GOSBERTON AND SURFLEET LORDSHIPS

PART OF LORDSHIP

PART OF LORDSHIP

PINCHBECK LORDSHIP

SPALDING

MOULTON LORDSHIP

STON LORDSHIP

To the Honourable the
ADVENTURERS & PARTICIPANTS,
For the Draining
DEEPING-FEN,
This Map is Humbly Dedicated
By their Honours most Obed.t
Humble Serv.ts
Jos. Featherstone.

A. Stop Sluice on the Forty Drain

B. Ditto on Hills Drain

C. Two Sluices at Hills Drain Outfall

D. Six door Sluice and Locks

E. The High Brid.

F. The Draw Bridge and Tunnel under the Welland

G. The place call'd the Timber Yard

H. Fulney Hall

I. Chapel Hill

K. Ash Close

L. Pear tree Meadow

M. Gangoats

N. The place where the House stood belonging to Mr Chas. Stevens, &c.

1. A Timber Bridge on the Westload

2. A Single Arch ditto of Stone

3. An Arch over ditto of Stone

4. The Navigable Lock into the Welland

The Different Lengths of the several Rivers & Drains.

	M	F	C
The Old Welland from Spalding Locks to Brother House	4	4	000
The Welland from Spalding High bridge to the Outgang near the East end of James Deeping	13	2	900
The River Glean from Baston Hedge to the Reservoir	14	7	200
Horse-gate Roft to it. Outfall into Langtoft Roft	7	5	500
Black-dike Roft to its Outfall into Horse-gate Roft	5	7	000
Langtoft Roft from Langtoft hedge to the Outfall of Hills drain	7	0	100
The Gravel Drain to the Counter Drain	1	7	146
The Counter Drain from Gravel Drain to Pode hole Sluices	7	6	300
The little West load to Monks House	1	1	000
The Great West load to its Outfall into Welland	1	3	000
The Eighteen feet Drain	1	4	000
The Forty feet Drain from Hills Drain to Monks House	0	6	000
Vernatts Drain from Pode hole Sluices to its Outfall	4	0	000
New Drain and Lords Drain to Wrag Marsh Outfall	6	6	600
The Welland from Spalding High bridge to the Reservoir	5	0	000
Hills Drain from the upper Engine to the Outfall	0	4	000
Raisons Dike from Deeping Bank to the South Drove & the Old Division from the South Drove to Baston Bank	5	7	000
Cloot Dike from Deeping Bank to the South Drove	1	0	000
The North Drove Dike	3	6	660
The South Drove Dike	4	6	240
Miles	99	4	336

The Different Lengths of the several Banks, Viz.t

	M	F	C
The East Bank or Country Bank from Spalding High bridge to Brother House	5	4	000
Deeping Bank	13	2	900
Baston Bank from Dove-hirn to Baston hedge	7	7	200
The North Bank of Glean from Dove-hirn to Gutheram Coat	2	2	300
Dozens Bank from Dove-hirn to Winsoever Bridge	3	2	100
Hanthorn Bank from Winsoever to the Outfall of Hills Drain	0	6	700
The Bank on each side of Hills Drain to the upper Engine	1	0	000
The Gravel Bank	1	5	866
The Counter Bank	7	6	000
The Sixteen feet Bank from Clarks Corner to the Glean	0	4	000
The Banks on each side the Vernatta's Drain	8	0	000
The Banks on each side of New Drain & Lords Drain	13	5	200
The Bank on the South side little Westload	1	0	500
Miles	66	6	766

ASPECTS
of
SPALDING VILLAGES

in words and photographs by
Michael J. Elsden

Front Cover: Photograph of osiers being prepared for the basket makers. Cowbit Wash.

Front and Rear endpapers: A Map of Deeping Fen by Joseph Featherstone, 1763.

Dedication

To my grandchildren Alice and Ian hoping that they learn to appreciate
the importance of preserving our past for future generations.

Author:
Michael J. Elsden

Published by:
Bookmark
The Crescent, Spalding

Produced by:
Elsam Cross & Co.
Printers
London Road, Spalding

ISBN: 0953958205

Printed in England

2000

Contents

Acknowledgements

During my research in the last few years many people have kindly given me their attention and supplied information, both written and verbal. To recall all of them and list them is not possible, but I thank them most sincerely.

I wish to thank the Council of the Spalding Gentlemen's Society for allowing me access to the archives. Among the many items available it has been a privilege to reproduce some of the photographs of Moulton that were taken by the late Rev. J. Russell Jackson (Vicar of Moulton 1866 to 1899), and some of the scenes from Cowbit Wash taken before 1900. These early photographers with their plate cameras worked hard to get their pictures.

In particular I would like to thank Mr. Norman Leveritt (President of Spalding Gentlemen's Society) for his help and encouragement, and also the members of the Society, who have often pointed me in the right direction when looking for information.

Finally I must thank Christine Hanson of Bookmark for having faith in my work, and my wife who has tolerated me leaving notes and photographs lying around the house.

Foreword

So often people are heard to say that the countryside in the Fens around Spalding is flat and uninteresting. This is not true. You can find much of interest, and you don't have to look very far. Every village church is different, and although many of the public houses have closed down, there are still quite a few that are attractive and interesting. Traces can still be found of some of the village railway stations, although the tracks have gone. It is still possible to recognise the old crossing gate houses despite them having been given face-lifts by their present owners. Look hard and you might still find and old "Paddy Hut" although they are no longer occupied by Irishmen. Many drains criss-cross the fens, and despite pollution they still contain plenty of wildlife. The heron can often be seen at the waters edge looking for fish, and at dusk the owl can be seen flying low along the dykes searching for its supper. Quite a few farmers are re-planting hedge-rows, and this can only help to increase the wild life.

The next time you pass through one of our local villages, stop, park your car, and have a walk round. You will be surprised how interesting these villages can be. Visit the church grave yard, and read what is on the grave stones. Many a story can be unravelled, and some villages still have a school with school house.

No, the countryside around Spalding and its villages is far from uninteresting, start looking and you will be surprised what you find. Our villages have much to offer.

Michael J. Elsden

Cowbit

Cowbit

Poor Cowbit next uplifts her head
Oozing from her watery bed;
And little else one sees, indeed,
Except a chapel thatch'd with reed.
And Wellands stream, with sedges crown'd
Where surging waves so much abound,
That oft the farmers hopes are drown'd
And all around one nothing sees
But miry bogs and willow trees.
These scenes, which were a sight forlorn
Are now improved by fields of corn.

Cowbit

Cowbit is a small village and parish, on the east side of Deeping Fen. The main road (A1073) from Spalding to Crowland follows the course of the Barrier Bank which was erected under an Act of 1666 to protect the South Holland Fen from the waters of the River Welland. The Barrier Bank and Wash Bank was constructed east of the river, and the intervening space known as Cowbit Wash is nearly a mile in places and extending 20 miles from north to south serving as a reservoir for surplus water in times of flood..

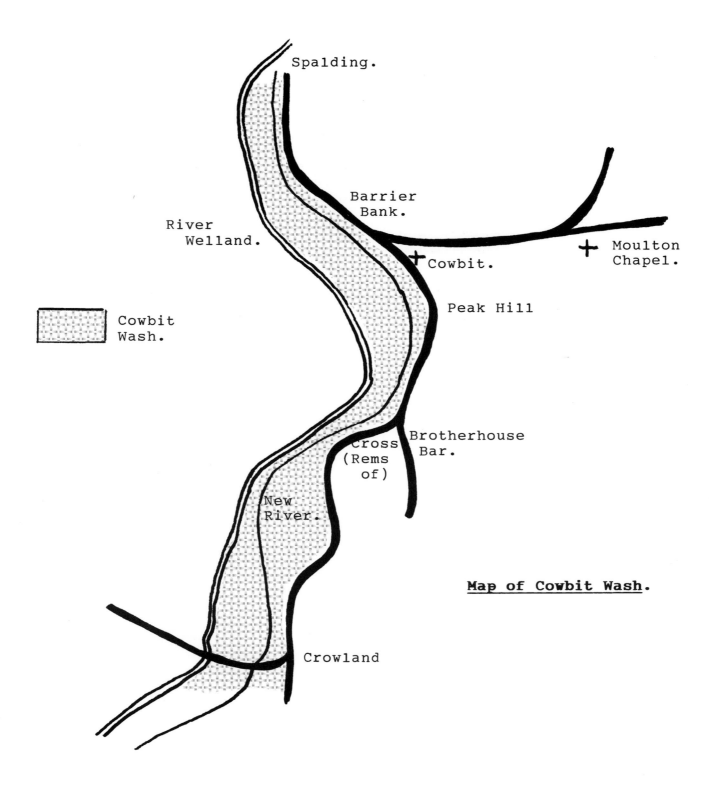

Map of Cowbit Wash.

Trades and Business people in Cowbit in 1937

Atkin, Hy, smallholder, Barrier Bank.

Batterham, Abraham, cowkeeper.

Batterham, Frank R., smallholder, Cape Entry.

Batterham, Mildred (Miss), dressmaker.

Bell, Norman Goodman, smallholder.

Blue Boor Inn (Fred Newman).

Boon Jn. Harry, smallholder.Boston Coal Co. Ltd. Station.

Braybrooks H. K., bulb grower, Croft House.

Braybrooks, Jas., farmer, Barrier Bank.

Braybrooks, Jn. T., farmer, Fair View.

Brown, Wm., boot maker, Rose Cottage.

Bull Inn (Tom Pepper).

Crampton, Jn., smallholder, Barrier Bank.

Crosstock, Sidney, smallholder.

Culpin, Samuel, bulbgrower, Floralton House.

Drury, George, smallholder.

Drury, Wilfred Edward, smallholder, Peak Hill.

Dun Cow Public House (Wm. Lane).

Elwes, Jn., smallholder, Barrier Bank.

Flowers, Edith E. (Mrs.), grocer.

Harrison, Frederick, smallholder, Drain Bank.

Hickman, Fred, smallholder, Barrier Bank.

Highham, Joseph, cycle dealer.

Higham Nellie (Mrs.), shopkeeper and post office.

Hodson, Isaac, smallholder.

Holden, Jn. J., cycle agent.

Holmes, Harold J., cowkeeper.

Howlett, Albert G., farmer.

Kendall, Thos., smallholder.

Lake, Herbert, Edward, farmer, Drain Bank.

Lindsay, Frank, farmer.

Newbon Hy. & Son, miller.

Parkin, Jn. C., smallholder, Ash Tree Farm.

Parrish, Jn. Thos., farm bailiff to R. H. Tointon, Bellesmore Farm, Peak Hill.

Pearson, Harold, farmer.

Railway Hotel (Wm. Rt. Wright).

Read, George Edwin, cowkeeper, Barrier Bank.

Rippin Daniel, cottager, Peak Hill.

Sansby, Walter R. smallholder, Barrier Bank.

Skells Bros., bulb growers.

Smith, Rowland Walter, dairyman, Barrier Bank.

Stainsby, Christopher, farmer.

Stainsby, Jn., smallholder.

Tye, Percy Geo., smallholder, Drain Bank.

Tyrrell, Austin Bird, farmer.

Tyrrell, Parker, dairyman.

Print of St. Mary's Cowbit in 1842.

The church of St. Mary is an ancient structure in the Perpendicular Style, consisting originally of nave and south porch, built probably by Prior de Moulton of the Benedictine Priory of Spalding about the year 1200. In 1486 a chancel and an embattled western tower of stone was added by John Russell, Bishop of Lincoln containing a clock and bells. The church was restored in 1882, at a cost of £1,500 when the thatched roof was replaced with lead, and the flooring relaid with wooden blocks. New seats were also fitted.

Cowbit Church photographed in 1999.

Cowbit Church from a painting by Hilkiah Burgess, 1820. Spalding Gentlemen's Society collection.

For over 160 years Cowbit had a Methodist Chapel which stood next to the Barrier Bank at its junction with Parkin Road. The first chapel is thought to have been built about 1820. In 1902 a piece of land was purchased next to the original building for the purpose of building a new chapel, and the older building was converted into a Sunday School. September 1983 was a sad day for the Methodists of Cowbit, because the chapel had to close down. The reason for this was that the offices of church steward, property steward, and secretary to the church council could not be filled. Cowbit chapel was in the Spalding Methodist circuit, and the last minister to have care of this chapel was the Rev. John Smith. There is still a Methodist congregation at Cowbit, but the majority now go to the chapel at Moulton Chapel.

Barrier Bank and the Methodist Chapel about 1920.

The Firing of a Royal Salute at Cowbit.

In years gone by the Cowbit punt gunners were very loyal. The West Elloe Magazine of September 1902 gave the following account of the Coronation Day celebrations for the Coronation of King Edward VII together with the Firing of the Royal Salute:–

"Coronation Day. Our Committee carried out their original programme with great success, and we are sure their efforts were appreciated by all the parish. The day began with a certain amount of gun-firing and various decorating, and at 1.30 p.m. the church was crowded for the Special Coronation Service. Then the programme was carried through; all passed off most pleasantly and everybody seemed to have a happy time. Heartiest thanks are due to the Committee and Tea-makers for all the trouble they so kindly took; the tea tables looked very inviting, and everybody must know what a lot of work that alone means. We congratulate the gunners on the excellent time they kept in the Royal Salute, and the splendid volley with which they ended up. When it grew dark we did our best with fireworks and coloured lights to show the rest of the world where Cowbit was, and we hope that everybody saw."

Punt Guns being used to fire a Royal Salute at Cowbit.

Yachting on Cowbit Wash.

Cowbit Wash was well known for ice-skating, but when the ice had thawed people then took the opportunity to race sailing boats over the vast expanse of water.

Newscutting 3rd March, 1900.

Boating on Cowbit Wash. Yesterday's Unique Regatta.

A hasty arranged regatta on Cowbit Wash last Saturday afternoon was, despite unfavourable weather, so well attended that the committee resolved upon bringing off a second yesterday (Thursday), and, the weather being all that could be desired, a great crowd lined the banks for a long distance nothing of the kind having been seen there in memory.

Four events were on the card, but a good deal of delay ensured at the start, the gun not being fired until half-an-hour after the advertised time. The course was about three quarters of a mile in length, being from near Lock's Mill as far as the osier bed, and there being during most of the afternoon a strong northerly breeze, the sailing boats ran down and tacked back.

Newscutting
Yachting Over His own Land (Cowbit).

The Wash at Spalding, Cowbit and Crowland, was flooded and Dr. Frank Husband-Clutton had the unusual experience of yachting over his own land at Crowland. The only means of communication between Crowland and Deeping Fen was by boat.

Racing sailing boats on
Cowbit Wash.

Wildfowling

The Cowbit Wash Wildfowler was a hardy breed of person making his living from the wild environment of the flooded wash. Until the construction of the Coronation Channel around the outskirts of Spalding in the 1950s a flooded Cowbit Wash was a common site in winter. Earlier this century before the River Welland had been widened, and cleaned out, flooding was more common still, and records show that in a bad summer the Wash could be flooded on and off for most of the year. This was not very helpful to the farmers who grazed this land and cropped the hay in summer.

Attempting to gather hay on a flooded Cowbit Wash 29th July 1912.

14

Cowbit

Punt gunning was a popular form of fowling on the flooded Wash. A gunner would launch his fragile "shout" punting it across the water until he sighted birds in the distance, then using paddles he would stealthily approach his prey. At the same time crouching over his huge punt gun he would charge it with powder and shot ready to fire on the unaware ducks and geese.

In earlier times the "Big Bertha" punt guns were home made from water pipe, and accidents with these rather lethal weapons was common.

("Shout" is a local name for this type of punt that was used on the inland waters of Cowbit Wash. For tidal waters that are rougher a better finished, and stronger boat with some decking was used.)

Punt gunners stalking their prey on Cowbit Wash. Early 1900s.

When the frosts came and turned Cowbit Wash into England's best skating ground, the fowler often reaped a rich harvest by mounting his punt gun on to a sort of sledge. To the front of this was fitted a screen of reeds. The gunner knelt at the rear of the sledge and pushed himself along with two iron-shod sprits. When the gun was fired the sledge would shoot backwards quite a way over the ice.

Punt gun mounted on sledge.

Above: Clearing ice ready to launch the punt.

Below: Two local wildfowlers with their "shouts". In the background can be seen Cowbit village and the church.

Cowbit

Possibly the most fascinating form of wildfowling was luring the birds to destruction by means of decoy plovers, and then pulling a net over them. A live plover was used as a decoy, a practice which is no longer legal. The plover was tethered to a padded iron plate by his feet, and balanced upon an iron upright so that by pulling a cord the bird could be swung up and made to flap its wings, at the same time the wildfowler took shelter behind his screen, and made the well known pee-wit calls. The nets were set and the ropes from them taken behind the screen of canvas and twigs, where the wildfowler would hide, hands on the ropes ready to pull, at the crucial moment, a strong pull necessary to bring over the nets, and the captured birds being taken from the nets and carried home.

Plovers being set as decoys.

Setting the nets.

The decoy-man behind his screen.

Winter scene on a flooded Cowbit Wash.

17

Above & Below: Cowbit Wash flooding over the Barrier Bank in 1947.

The Cultivation of Osiers at Cowbit.

The frequent flooding on Cowbit Wash made the cultivation of most crops very difficult, but one crop that did grow well were the beds of osiers.

Osiers are a particular type of willow that was used for basket making. A portion of Cowbit Wash was fenced off so that osiers could be cultivated without hindrance from grazing animals. Sets about 12 inches long, and having a number of buds were taken from older trees, and pushed into the ground. Stock collected and planted in the winter was ready for growth in the following spring. Three years after planting, the first osiers could be cropped, and if well managed the same stock could be cropped for anything up to 50 years. Cropping took place in the winter when the sap had gone down. There were three types of rods. The green rods were used for making hurdles, and were not treated before use. Brown rods were left to dry in the atmosphere, and were used mainly for furniture. White rods were the best quality rods. These were stored in water from when they were cut in the winter until May. The stems were then pulled through an iron device called a brake which gripped the bark as the wood passed through, and stripped it off revealing the white rod. This job was usually done by the women folk and the children who were paid by the bundle. The last basket maker to use osiers grown on Cowbit Wash was Mr. Thomas Aistrup of 3, Double Street, Spalding, who when he died in January 1944 was the oldest basket maker in Spalding. He had been making baskets for 78 years. Mr. Jason Draper Wright of 15, Double Street, Spalding was the last basket maker in the town, and he ceased trading in the 1960s.

Plot of cultivated osiers on Cowbit Wash.

Women and children working on the osiers.

Women and children stripping the rods.

Men bunching the osiers.

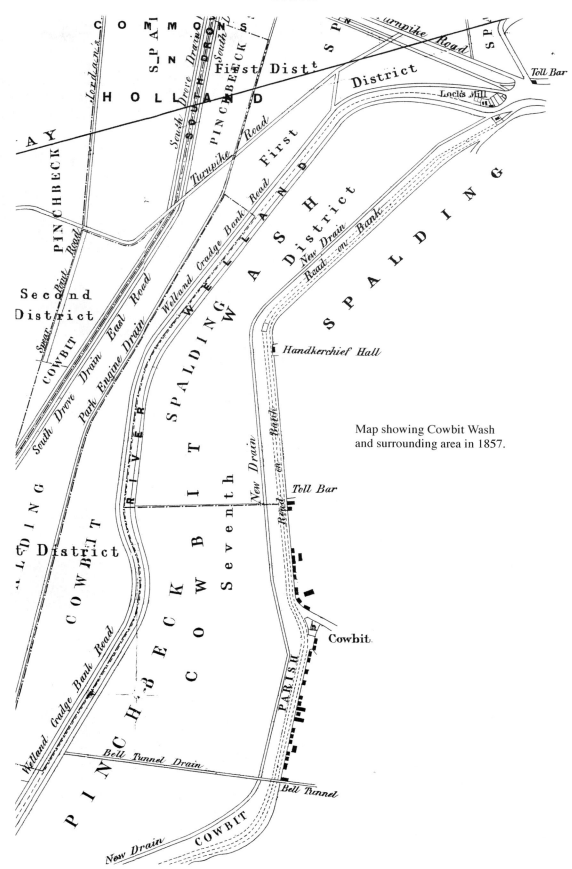

Map showing Cowbit Wash
and surrounding area in 1857.

Cowbit Station.

The 1st April 1867 was a great day for the people of Cowbit when the Great Eastern Railway opened their line from March to Spalding, providing the inhabitants with an easy way of getting into Spalding for the shops and market. This also provided the farmers with a means to transport their crops. The March line terminated at Spalding, until in 1882 when a joint running agreement with the Great Northern Railway extended the line to Lincoln. In 1928 the Whitemoor Marshalling Yard at March came into use, and this led to a further increase in traffic. After the second World War use of the railways began to decline and eventually on 27th November 1982 the line closed down completely.

The scene at Cowbit Station about 1900.

Newbon's Mill, Cowbit.

Erected in 1798 the original mill was slightly lower than the later one. It is thought the mill had an extra floor added about 1814, probably to enable the sails to catch more wind. The mill was powered by the wind until the mid-1930s when it was converted to be powered by engine, and finally electric motor until it closed down in 1969.

When wind powered, the mill had four patent sails driving three pairs of stones, two grey, and one French.

Newbon's Mill, Cowbit, from a sketch by G. W. Bailey.
Spalding Gentlemen's Society Collection.

22

Above: The Blue Boar public house, Cowbit. This stood on the site where Thorpe's Garage now stands, Barrier Bank.
Below: The Blacksmith's shop that was situated next to the Blue Boor.

Snippets from what the papers used to say.

September 1st 1804.

About seven this morning, a very alarming fire was discovered in the roof of Cowbit Church, co. Lincoln, occasioned by a person shooting at a flight of starlings; but by the prompt assistance of the inhabitants of the village it was fortunately subdued without doing much injury.

March 1828.

On Monday the 24th advanced in years, Mr. Thomas Hall, farmer of Cowbit. The deceased was a person of eccentric habits, and a friend of vermin. Upwards of sixty rats have been seen feeding at one time at his pig-troughs; and for several years he has had a manure heap in his yard which he constantly kept as a hot-bed for snakes, several of which at the same time have been seen creeping about his premises with the greatest confidence, no one being allowed to disturb them.

May 22nd, 1869.

An Odd Fish.–A fisherman plying his calling on the 22nd May in Cowbit Wash, a fresh water lake some miles from Spalding , was startled when opposite the vicarage by a monstrous living thing rearing itself out of the water. No fish had ever before been seen in these shallow waters, and the question arose – whence did it come, and how did it get there? The villagers were called together and took counsel. To capture the monster alive was an impossibility, and they accordingly shot at it – one bullet penetrating the head. After this they entangled it in a net, and conveyed it on wheels to Spalding, when it was found to be what was once considered a Royal Fish – a sturgeon. It was eight or nine feet in length and weighed 200 lbs. It must have been brought up from the German Ocean by the tide, floating up the Welland through Spalding. It would afterwards have to pass through the doors of the "locks". How this was managed it is difficult to conceive; but it is one of the wonderful events of 1869 that farms and green fields usually covered with stock at this seasons, should now be so flooded as to afford swimming room for a sturgeon of this size. The poor men showing it will realize a handsome sum of money.

5th July 1869.

Cowbit Wash – This extensive and valuable track of grazing land (recently under water) is now luxuriant with vegetation, and fodder sales are announced to take place in a few days. Scarcely three weeks have elapsed since a Royal Sturgeon was caught in the Wash, and in the course of a few days the scythe will be in full operation, and haymaking very general.

October 1871.

Cowbit Wash. – The low-lying tract of land near Spalding known as Cowbit Wash is now under water. Some of the occupiers have had their fodder (the course hay grown in the Wash) floated away and many of them have lost the eddish or aftermath through not having stocked or sold in time. The Wash land was covered with an abundance of grass and herbage, which will now be worthless. The grazing season this year has been a short one for Wash farmers – not more than four months.

January 1872.

Cowbit Wash – This large tract of land is now under water, and has the appearance of a large inland lake. The scour of the Welland from the "freshes" is great and will much improve the outfall.

Cowbit

April 1873.

The Wash – For a year and a half Cowbit Wash, containing nearly 3000 acres of land has been flooded with water. The whole of last summer's crop of grass was lost, and the occupiers had a sorry time of it. The Wash is now dry, and promises, after its 18 months soaking, an enormous crop of fodder and grass. It is about 20 years since the calamity of a continuous summer flood happened; and it was followed by a long series of seasons of abundance for Wash farmers, so we trust the same result will follow the late exceptionally wet season.

July 1873.

Cowbit Wash – A considerable portion of the land in Cowbit Wash is again flooded, entailing a very serious loss upon the occupiers. Some of the land has been mown, and the fodder cannot be got out of the fields. That such a thing should occur when the ditches on the land on each side of the Wash are almost dry is a most disgraceful thing in a district which is renowned for its drainage works. The Wash land pays five shillings and fourpence an acre drainage rate, and under present management a thunderstorm will drown the land and bring ruin upon a large number of small and poor occupiers.

January 4th, 1877.

Spalding – The Floods. The continued heavy rains which have fallen during the past fortnight throughout the hilly country surrounding the fens have caused an immense flow of the overplus water seawards. Cowbit Wash has for some time past been partially flooded, but it now presents the appearance of a vast lake or inland sea. During the fresh breeze which prevailed on Sunday and Monday large numbers of people congregated upon the barrier banks to witness the surging billows which were dashing up the inclines and which broke against the locks bridge, sending volumes of spray many feet into the air. Several boating excursions have been made in the Wash, and on Saturday last Mr. Tye's steam launch "Petrel" proceeded to Crowland, a distance of about ten miles, over fields which in the summer are stocked with hundreds of beasts, horses and sheep. One or two narrow escapes from drowning have occurred by the capsizing of the narrow, flat-bottomed punts used for fowling. The high tides on Monday and Tuesday last caused considerable inconvenience in the low-lying parts of the town. The water rose to the level of the road and entered many of the houses bordering upon the river at Pigeon-end, and the Sheep-market and Crescent were partially flooded on Monday night and Tuesday morning by the water forcing its way through the sewers. The tide on Wednesday morning was again strong, and holding up the immense volume of fresh water running down the Welland raising the water sufficiently to again inundate the Sheep-market corner and a portion of Station-street.

July 1877.

At Cowbit on the 12th the Foresters court Gunners Delight, No. 1107, held their annual festival at the Dun Cow Inn. Mr. Beales, photographer, of Spalding was in attendance to take the portraits of the members with their officers and band in uniform. A good substantial dinner was provided by host Armstrong; Mr. Oldman the medical officer, presided. £51 has been added to the funds and twelve new members were made last year.

May 1878.

Cowbit Wash flooded. – The heavy rains which have fallen of late have brought down an immense body of water and the Wash is like a vast lake several feet deep in water. This is the fourth year in succession that the Wash has been flooded in summer, and the crop of grass and fodder more or less destroyed. The loss to the occupiers by the present flood may be estimated at from £5,000 to £6,000 and to make things more unpleasant they will have to pay the annual drainage rate of 7s. 6d. per acre.

Above and below – Cowbit Wash flooded.

Cowbit

June 1880.

Cowbit Wash – The whole of last summer this extensive tract of land was under water (except a few fields on the highest part), and the occupiers were unable to either mow or graze. For some weeks past the Wash has been dry, and the growth of the fodder has been prodigious, the flag, thus early in the season being 4 feet in height. With fine weather the occupiers will this year obtain the most abundant crop known for a long time.

May 1881.

Cowbit Wash – Now the water is off, the land presents a curious sight, and thousands of wild birds may be seen upon it. Fortunately the Wild Birds Prevention Act stops the shooting which would otherwise take place.

May 1881.

Another Sturgeon – For several days previous to Thursday the 28th inst. a fenman named Atkin knew there was a big fish in the New River which runs through Cowbit Wash, and he was intent with the assistance of another man upon catching the illustrious stranger. On the afternoon of the above day the capture was effected but not until the "Royal Fish" had made a gallant and desperate effort to escape his pursuers. The sturgeon is believed to have come up the Welland and entered the Wash during the last flood; it measured 8 feet and 9 inches in length, and weighed nearly 14 stones. It was cut up and retailed in the town at 6d. per pound.

October 1881.

In the village of Cowbit the inhabitants seem to have a very lazy and tranquil time of it. For three months there has not been either a death or a wedding in the parish. Unless this sort of thing ends the bells of the beautiful church will be getting rusty.

December 23rd, 1883.

An accident of a singular and painful character occurred at Cowbit on Sunday last. The large tract of land facing the village, known as Cowbit Wash, is usually flooded in Winter, and many of the inhabitants keep little boats for shooting wildfowl and for going across the Wash to other places in the vicinity. On Sunday last two young men (cousins), John George Batterham, aged 21, and John Batterham, aged 24, had been across the Wash to Deeping High Bank to see some relatives, and were returning about three 'o clock in the afternoon in their boat. The usual way of propelling these boats is for one man to stand up and push it along by a "sprit" (a pole having a spike and hook at one end). The two men had proceeded safely across, and were on what is known as the slipe close to Cowbit village and very near to their home, when the boat was suddenly overturned in a deep pit. A woman on the bank saw the mishap, ran into a neighbouring cottage, gave the alarm, and immediately several of the villagers hastened through the shallow water, but before they could reach the spot both men had disappeared, and about an hour elapsed before their bodies were recovered. The greatest excitement prevailed; nearly every inhabitant having been attracted to the spot to render assistant or watch the distressing scene. The cause of the accident would doubtless be that when the boat reached the pit, which was concealed by the surrounding water, the sprit failing to strike ground, the man lost his balance, and the little long and narrow boat toppled over.

May 1884.

The Welland and the Wash. For several years past the owners and occupiers of the land in Cowbit Wash have complained bitterly of the state of the River Welland from Locks Mill upwards, which from being almost grown up, has failed to carry off the upland waters even after a moderate rainfall, and in consequence the water has overflowed into the Wash. Summer after summer the greatest portion of the Wash land (about 3,000 acres) has been valueless owing to continued floodings; fine crops of fodder and hay have grown, hundreds of acres of hay have been mown, and before it could be got in rain has fallen and it has floated away. We are glad to say that the Wash Trustees have at length arranged with the Welland Trustees to undertake a portion of the necessary work for remedying this evil. A contract has been entered into with Mr. Westmoreland of Kirton, for cleaning about two miles of the river and depositing the soil taken out upon the bank called the Cradge Bank between the river and the Wash, thus at one operation deepening the river and raising the bank. If this work be carried out for several miles up the river the Wash would never be drained except in time of flood.

April 1885.

Cowbit Wash – The greater part of this tract of land was unexpectedly and rapidly flooded on Sunday and Monday last by a volume of water from the high country in consequence of the very heavy rains which fell in Leicestershire last week. As we have had in effect no rain in this district for a considerable period the sudden overflow of the banks of the Welland seemed to surprise even the Cowbitites. That the Wash should be flooded from the recent rains in Leicestershire, after such an exceptionally dry winter and spring, shows that the Welland is very far from being a proper and sufficient outlet for the upland waters.

March 1887.

Annoying a Magistrate – At Spalding petty sessions, on Tuesday, John Peake, of Cowbit, a farmer and butcher, was charged by the Rev. J. T. Dove, J.P. , Vicar of Cowbit, with being the driver of a horse and cart on Barrier Bank, Cowbit, and by misbehaviour hindering and interrupting the passage of Mr. Dove on a carriage (a tricycle) on Saturday evening February 26th – Defendant denied the charge – . Mr. Dove stated that while returning home, between 7 and 8 o'clock, on a tricycle, when about three-quarters of a mile from Cowbit Wash a cart driven by the defendant drove past him. After this the cart was driven across the road in front of complainant and pulled up, interrupting his progress. Complainant then turned his machine to the other side of the road, when defendant repeated his action. He asked the driver which side of the road he wanted, but received no answer, so he went to Cowbit. Defendant, however drove on in the middle of the road and kept alongside the tricycle, causing complainant to ride at the side of the road, which was very rough. This continued during the remainder of the journey. Further misconduct was alleged later on that evening, defendant telling Mr. Dove it was time he went to bed to get his sermon prepared for the morrow. Witnesses were called who stated that on the Saturday night defendant told them he had been having a game with the arm-chair man, meaning the Vicar. On the same evening he also admitted to the policeman that he had been annoying Mr Dove, and said he could not help doing so. He appeared to have had some drink, but was not intoxicated. Defendant made no real explanation of his conduct or defence to the charge, and the case was ultimately settled by defendant apologizing to Mr. Dove, and promising not to repeat the annoyance, and paying costs of 22s. 6d.

November 1887.

Breaking up a Club. – The old Friendly Societies – bred and born in the public-house – which have not husbanded their resources and provided for the traditional rainy day, are destined to disappear from off the face of the earth. The temperance men of the present day object to the compulsory pint or a three penny fine on club nights. The young labourers and mechanics prefer the Foresters or Oddfellows, with their smart regalia and chances of promotion to official dignity, to the hum-drum routine of the old clubs. Hence the later dwindle in numbers as time rolls on and eventually break up. The latest instance in this neighbourhood took place at Cowbit last week. The Gunner's Delight Club was established just 50 years since, and having become reduced in numbers to 20 and in wealth to about £40 it was agreed to celebrate its jubilee by dividing the money and breaking up the club.

July 1893.

Property and Grass Sales. – At Cowbit, near Spalding, on Tuesday evening, Messrs S. & G. Kingston, auctioneers of Spalding, sold a large quantity of hay in Cowbit Wash, and owing to the scarcity of keep exceptionally high prices were realised. A considerable portion ranged from £5 to £6 per acre, whilst some went as high as £6 17s. 6d. per acre

Copy of Advert.

To Brewers – Freehold Property To be Sold by Tender.

Railway Hotel, Cowbit, close to station and three miles from Spalding.

The house has 10 rooms, and there are convenient Outbuildings and 4A.2R.1P. of first class Arable Land in splendid condition. – Tenders to be sent in not later than Feb. 1st, 1894, to John Bradley, Abbey Holme, Abbeydale, Sheffield.

Railway Hotel, Cowbit, 1952.

February 1st 1895
Lincolnshire Skating Association.

A youth's race was brought off on Cowbit Wash yesterday week, when nearly 40 competitors entered, including some promising skaters. The match was won by W. Pickering of Cowbit, after a keen contest with G. Pawson of Gedney Hill. Batterham of Cowbit was third.

An open match on the Wash, organised by the Lincolnshire Association, in which James Smart, the champion; Lindahl, the Norwegian, Fred Ward and the pick of the Fen Skaters competed, was brought off on Saturday afternoon, in the presence of about 2,000 spectators. The proposal had been for a straight mile, but owing to the thaw which set in this had to be altered, and the race was decided as a mile with three turns. The ice, owing to the thaw, was in poor condition. Smart and Lindahl were drawn together, and a very exciting race resulted. For nearly the whole distance the men were level, but the champion drew away slightly towards the close, and won by about three yards.

Results.

1. James Smart.   4. P. Tyrell.
2. H. Lindahl.   5. Housden.
3. Fred Ward.   6. Aveling.

December 1895.
The Proposed Enclosed Skating Ground on Cowbit Wash.

The Lincolnshire Skating Association held a meeting at their headquarters, the White Hart Hotel, Spalding, on Monday night, to further arrange for the proposed enclosed skating ground on Cowbit Wash. It was reported that the consent of the Crowland and Cowbit Drainage Trustees would be requisite and that a special meeting of that body would be called to consider the scheme. It was arranged that the Skating Association should appoint a deputation to wait upon them, and also upon the owner of the ground, which is 40 acres in extent, with a view to arrange a lease for seven or ten years. It was also stated that the ground could be flooded by a tunnel from the River Welland, which would save pumping operations. The proposal is to form a limited liability company, and very fair promises of support were made.

January 1896.
The proposal to form an enclosed skating ground on the Wash at Spalding has collapsed for the present season, owing to the owner of the land selected (Mr. James Tointon) having withdrawn his consent. In all probability, however, the project will be taken up another year. Should frost set in, there will be good skating facilities, as the Wash at Cowbit and a considerable area of land at Spalding is flooded.

April 1860.
Mary Lawson, aged 50 was charged with stealing liquor, value 11s., the property of James Smith, of Cowbit. The jury acquitted her of this charge, but found her guilty of stealing the bottle, and the court sentenced her to two months imprisonment with hard labour. Mr. Torkington of Stamford, appeared for the prosecution. The prisoner was defended by Mr. Percival.

March 1861.
Fire – On Tuesday morning last, a fire broke out at the Dun Cow, at Cowbit, and the fire engines were sent to the place, accompanied by Blinkhorn and Co's portable fire engine. There was no need of either, for the fire was confined to a small outhouse, and was extinguished before the engines arrived.

Deeping St Nicholas with Deeping Fen

Deeping St. Nicholas.
(Littleworth and Hop Pole).

Deeping St. Nicholas situated in the middle of Deeping Fen, which was at one time nothing more than a large mere, or lake, at the bottom of which grew and accumulated the aquatic plants which afterwards formed the peat of which the surface of most of the land is composed.

Deeping Fen lays between the rivers Welland and Glen and was bounded by the coastal ridge on the north east and the higher ground on the west.

In 1846 the lands in Deeping Fen were made into an ecclesiastical parish under the name of Deeping St. Nicholas, and a church was built. Ten years later in 1856 this was also made a civil parish under the powers of an Act, with provision for the maintenance of the poor, who hitherto had been provided for by the Adventurers of the free and taxable lands.

Map of Deeping Fen.

View across Deeping Fen.

32

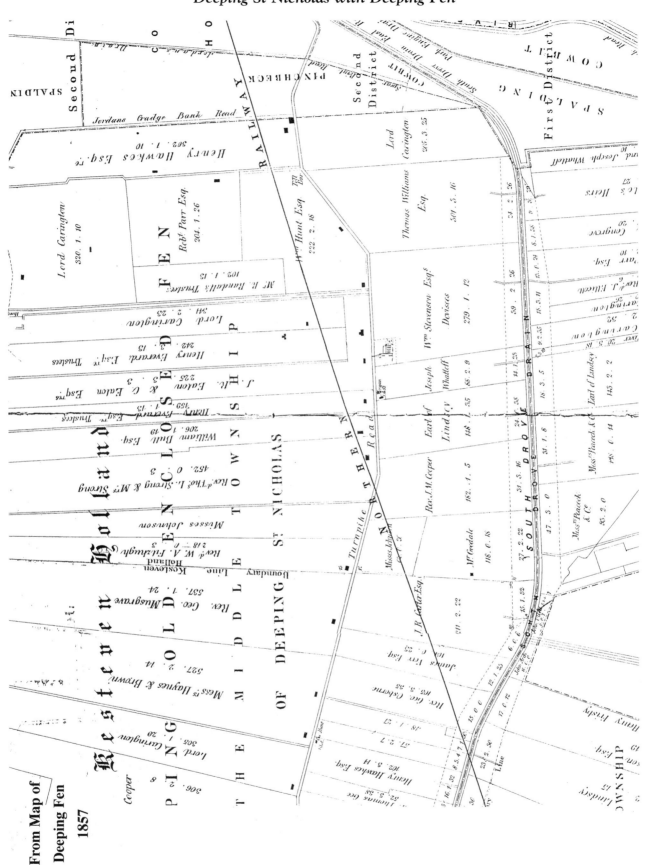

**From Map of
Deeping Fen
1857**

Deeping Fen in the 18th century

In the 18th century, and before the creation of the parish of Deeping St. Nicholas, Deeping Fen was a far different place as the following article illustrates:–

From Spalding to Deeping St. James, on each side of the road, called Littleworth Drove, stood a large quantity of wind engines or water mills, to drain off the water that stood on the farms. In the year 1763 an Act was passed to form a Turnpike Road from Spalding to Deeping St. James, and the said mills were moved a short time after to the bottom of the farms, but since have been taken down, being quite useless, on account of the steam engines at Pode Hole. In the year 1766 or 67, due to the pressure of the water against the River Welland Bank, it broke, and gulled a large hole by the side of the bank near Mr. Robert Parr's farm, 131 feet deep with a sound gravel bottom. The cropping upon all the farms in the Fen was entirely drowned, and continued so, all the winter following, and when the frost broke up, the ice sawed several mills down by the half-way. On 20th February 1799, the bank broke between Spalding and the Four-Mile-Bar, and again drowned the Fen, and formed another gull or deep hole. The month of March, 1773, was remarkably hot and dry, so that the farmers could scarcely get their land ploughed. The horses and men sweated so much, they got in their cropping and it began to look prosperous, but in the month of May following there came a downfall and drowned every acre in Deeping Fen.

Windmills along the North Drain, Deeping Fen, 1825. Watercolour by Hilkiah Burgess. (Spalding Gentlemen's Society Collection).

Map of Deeping Fen, 1857 showing the GULL that was formed in the 1760s near Mr. Robert Parr's farm.

Gull or Deep Hole that was formed by the water when the river bank burst in the 1760s.
Now used by a private fishing club.

Littleworth Drove, Deeping Fen from a watercolour by Hilkiah Burgess, 1828. (Spalding Gentlemen's Society Collection).

The Four Mile Bar Public House, situated on Deeping High Bank. Photographed 1948.

Trades and Business people in Deeping St. Nicholas in 1937.

Barnett, A. R., Tolethorpe House.
Stainsby Rev. Herbert Henry M.A. (vicar)
    Vicarage.

Commercial.
Adcock, Leonard & Leslie, farmers.
Atkin, Harry Russell, smallholder, Owens Farm.
Atkinson, Lucas, farmer, Deeping High Bank.
Atkinson, Thomas Hardy, farmer,
    Deeping High Bank.
Birch, G. F. & Son Ltd., farmers.
Bishop, William H., wheelwright.
Blue Bell Public House, Albert Maplethorpe.
Branton, Walter George, smallholder.
Brewster, Samuel, smallholder.
Brittain, George T., farmer, Lonsdale House.
Burrows, Charles A. E., farm bailiff to William
    Dennis & Sons Ltd., The Beeches.
Carter, Albert H., farmer, Bar & Park farms.
Chappell, Albert Edward, farmer.
Chappell, Reginald W., wheelwright.
Clayton, Walter, farmer.
Coleman, Arthur, smallholder.
Cook, Sheddle, smallholder.
Cornwall, Fred, smallholder, North Drove Bank.
Cornwall, Jnr., smallholder.
Dennis, William & Sons Ltd., farmers &
    landowners.
Ellis & Everard Ltd., coal merchants,
    Railway Station.
France, Charles, butcher.
Gandy, Jarvis Kilham, farmer.
Grooby, Rt. & Wltr., Little Duke Farm.
Halfway Inn, John W. Kettle.
Harrow Inn, Alfred T. Browning.
Ivatt, George E., smallholder.
Ives, George, smallholder.

Jackson, George, smallholder.
Jackson, Herbert, smallholder.
Jackson, William, smallholder.
Mann, Thomas, smallholder.
Maplethorpe & Brakes, smallholder.
Miller, William Seth, smallholder,
    North Drove bank.
Munton, F. S., farmer, Hop Pole farm.
Neal, Sydney, farmer, The Poplars.
Noble, Thomas, smallholder.
Oatsheaf Public House, Albert Hare.
Perkins, Fred & Sons, saddlers.
Perkins, Fred, smallholder.
Pick, Thomas Arthur, farmer.
Pick, Thomas Raymond, farmer, The Chestnuts.
Plough Public House, Edward Barnatt.
Pocklington, Albert Ernest, farmer.
Posey, John William, smallholder.
Preston, Arth. Cecil, farmer, Oak Tree Farm.
Reynolds, William Henry, smallholder,
    Willow Tree Farm.
Richardson, Thomas Frederick, farmer,
    The Hollies.
Richardson, Thomas Henry, farmer & landowner,
    Church & Hedge farms.
Steele Jsph, (Mrs.), smallholder.
Stennett, William, smallholder, Willow Tree Farm.
Taylor, Edward, smallholder, Willow Tree Farm.
Tinsley, Henry Cole Cyril, farmer.
Vauplew, Frank A., shopkeeper.
Watts, Robert Knowles, farmer.
Webster, Jsph. Ernest, smallholder.
Wensor, James Arthur, smallholder.
Wigginton, Henry, smallholder.
Woodhead, Bros., farmers, Halfway Farm.
Worth, Sidney, Farmer.

Church

    Prior to the year 1846 the people of Deeping Fen had to travel five or six miles if they wished to attend a parish church. In 1845-46 a beautiful church was erected at a cost of £4,000. It was the magnificent gift of two individuals, lately residing at Stamford, Messrs. William and Nicholas Clarke Stevenson (brothers). William, the survivor, by deed dated 25th May, 1844, three days before his death, secured the sum of £4,000 for the purpose of building this church, £5,000 for the endowment, and £200 for repairs to be vested in the Ven. T. K. Bonney, Archdeacon of Leicester, as trustee. The church which is situated close to the turnpike road leading from London to Spalding, was commenced on the 18th August, 1845, when the foundation stone was laid by James Stevenson Esq., and was consecrated by the Bishop of Lincoln on the 24th July 1846.

It was erected from the designs of Mr. Chas. Kirk of Sleaford. It is in the late Decorated style, 84ft 6 inches long, 37ft. wide, the Nave being 42ft. high. It consists of a Nave, North Aisle, Chancel with a small Vestry attached to its north side, and tower and spire occupying the second bay of the north aisle from which it projects its whole width; the lower storey serves as a porch, and on its west side is the principal entrance. The tower, being unconnected with the fine high-pitched roof of the nave rises to a height of 113ft 9 inches.

In 1889 forty three years after the building of the church the Vicar issued a circular stating that he proposed to erect a new organ in the parish church. The present instrument he said was wholly unsuitable for the musical parts of the service. The new organ will contain fourteen speaking stops with swell, pedal organ, open diapason, bourdon and three couplers. The parishioners and all friends were invited to assist in raising the desired sum.

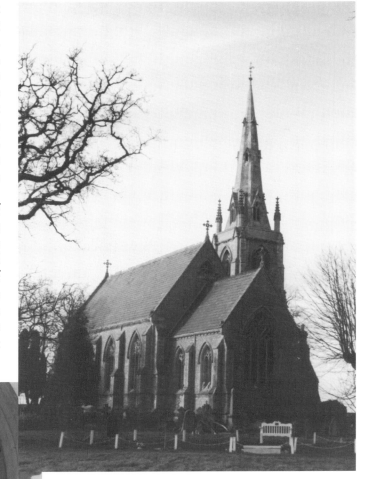

The fund raising for the organ must have been successful for on the 6th June, 1890, the new organ was officially opened by Dr. Turpin, Mus.Doc., organist of St. Brides, London. Services were held at 3 p.m. and again at 7 p.m. At the afternoon service the sermon was preached by the Lord Bishop of Lincoln. A Public Tea was provided in a marquee at five o'clock and the tickets for this event cost 9d. To assist people attending this event the 2.29 p.m. express and the 10.12 p.m. mail train from Spalding to Peterborough made an unscheduled stop at Littleworth Station for the occasion.

The altar and chancel of the church of St. Nicholas at Deeping St. Nicholas.

The Church Sunday School.

During the year 1899 a new church Sunday School was built for the church of St. Nicholas at Deeping St. Nicholas at a cost of £130.

The church Sunday School built in 1899.

Littleworth Mission.

Standing close by the railway crossing, the Littleworth Mission, built in 1896 will always be associated with the zeal and generosity of the late Mr. Robert Smith, farmer, and prominent member and deacon of the Spalding Congregational Church, who, impressed with the need for greater spiritual facilities for the residents of Deeping St. Nicholas not only gave the land, but erected at his own cost the Mission House and subsequently added thereto a schoolroom. Here for many years Mr. Smith conducted a vigorous and successful work.

The Littleworth Mission has been closed down many years and today the Mission House is converted into living accommodation.

The Littleworth Mission House, photographed in 1994, now used as living accommodation.

The Primitive Methodist Chapel.

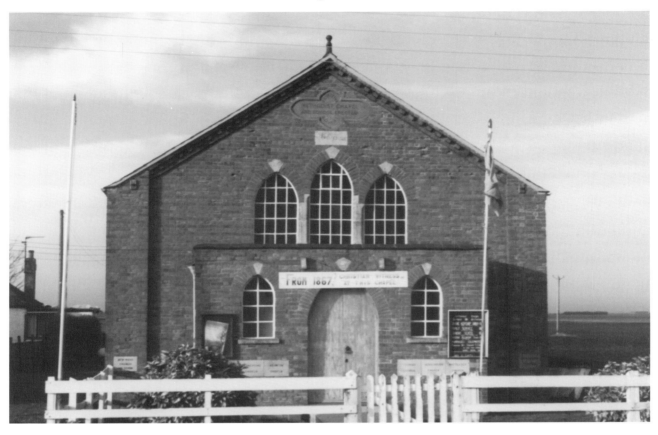

In 1867 the Deeping St. Nicholas, Primitive Methodist Chapel was erected, the site for which was given by the late Mr. James Haynes of West Deeping Fen.

The chapel was demolished and re-erected in 1922.

The Deeping Fen Toll-bars.

By 1876 Toll-bars had nearly disappeared from the Spalding area. The only ones remaining being those across the old coach road through Deeping Fen. Those bars belonged to what was called the Littleworth Turnpike Trust, and unfortunately the trust was heavily in debt, money having been borrowed over the years on bonds or mortgages. A number of Deeping Fen farmers attended a meeting of the trustees, and complained of the inconvenience and expense of the bars, and of the unequal way in which occupiers in the Fen had by the bar system to contribute to the maintenance of the roads. Mr. Samuel Kingston acted as spokesman at the occasion, and from the meeting it was discovered that the question of the renewal of the powers of the trust to continue the tolls was to be brought before a committee of the House of Commons. The farmers alluded to at once determined to present a petition to the House against the proposed continuance, and also against a proposal which the road trustees had decided to make to the House of Commons that the bondholders should receive 5 per cent, for the next 20 years as compensation and in full discharge of the existing debt, and such money to be raised by a tax upon the lands in Deeping St. Nicholas and Pinchbeck for the repairs to the road known as Littleworth turnpike which extended from Spalding Highbridge to Deeping. The petition was prepared by Mr. H. H. Harvey and presented to his Parliamentary agent. Mr. Calthrop appeared before the committee to represent the turnpike trust.

Deeping Fen Toll-bar house.

The committee's decision was as follows:–

1. That the trust be not required to expend any more money in the repair of the roads.
2. That no further interest be paid to the bondholders.
3. That the salaries and incidental expenses of the trust shall not in future exceed £25 per annum.
4. That the bars may be continued until 1st November, 1878, and no longer.

Therefore a little more than two years saw the removal of the last of the pikes around Spalding.

Littleworth Station and the Railways.

The railway first came to Deeping Fen in the 1840s when the Great Northern Railway Co. laid the track which passed through Deeping Fen crossing the Turnpike Road next to land owned by the Rev. J. M. Cooper on whose land Littleworth Station was then built. At this time the parish of Deeping St. Nicholas did not exist, so the station was called Littleworth, and that is why the station had a different name to that of the village. It was not until 1856 that Deeping St. Nicholas became a civil parish.

The land in Deeping Fen at one time was of 'little worth' because of the poor drainage, and it is a fair assumption that the name of Littleworth was so arrived at because the land in the area was of little worth.

Littleworth is no longer a station, but the locomotive shed still stands, and the station entrance and booking hall is now used as offices.

Littleworth Station booking hall and entrance (now used as offices).

Littleworth Station
locomotive shed.

The Deeping St. Nicholas Potato Railways.

The soil in Deeping Fen is excellent for the growing of potatoes, and earlier this century potatoes were the main crop that was grown. During the winter months the weather often made it difficult hauling the potatoes from the fields to the main roads or railways. This problem was overcome with the introduction of the light railway to the farms.. The most prominent potato producer and the biggest user of light railways was W. Dennis & Sons who farmed 2,000 acres in Deeping Fen. By the year 1916 they had installed a 2 foot gauge light railway which extended to almost 11 miles in length around their farms, serving, The Shrubbery, Pickworth's Farm and Goose Hill Farm. From Goose Hill Farm this light railway met up with the national railway network, just north of Littleworth Station level crossing where a potato warehouse was built.

The other farms in the Fen that also had railways were:–

Tongue End Farm – about 2.5 miles.

Sixscore and Little Duke Farms – about 1.3 miles.

Carters Farm – just under 1 mile.

Victoria Farm – 1.3 miles.

Hedge Farm – 2 miles.

Bottom Farm – 1.75 miles.

East Reach Farm – almost 2 miles.

Vine House Farm – 2 miles.

Caulton Farm (also known as Worth's Farm) about 3.3 miles. By 1950 all these light railways had gone out of use and today the only obvious landmark left in the potato warehouse close to the Littleworth railway crossing.

The potato warehouse adjoining Littleworth level crossing.

The Half Way House, public house, Deeping Fen (about 1950).

The Oat Sheaf Inn, Deeping Fen (Photographed March 1948).

The Harrow Inn, Deeping St. Nicholas, 1950. The little shop coming in the right hand side of the picture was the butchery business of Alfred Browning.

Supply of Drinking Water for Deeping St. Nicholas.

Today we turn the cold water tap on and draw pure clean water that you can drink with safety, but before 1894 the people of Deeping Fen had to rely on what rain water they could catch in various receptacles or saved in wells sunk in the ground.

In December 1893 a local newspaper records the evidence given to an inquiry held by a Local Government Board Inspector, and two following articles record the progress of the inquiry, and finally the satisfactory conclusion:–

December 1893.

Water Supply – At Deeping St. Nicholas near Spalding on Wednesday, Mr. R. Walton, C.E., Local Government Board's Inspector, held an inquiry with respect to a complaint of the alleged default of the Spalding Rural Sanitary Authority to provide a proper water supply for the parish. The Rev. W. Benson, the Vicar, who had taken a prominent part in the matter, produced an analysis of water used for drinking purposes. It was certified to contain a large number of animalculae from half to three-quarters of an inch long, and a microscopical examination revealed innumerable living organisms. Such water was absolutely injurious if used for drinking purposes. The drinking water, in many cases, was stated to be stored in paraffin barrels. It was proposed that the want should partly be met by sinking artesian wells. Against this it was stated that the parish was one of the healthiest in England, that during five months there had not been a single death, and that to provide water for such a widely-scattered population would entail a scheme costing a hundred thousand pounds. The Inspector adjourned the inquiry for particulars of the number of houses for which the water was wanted, and the distance from which it was now fetched.

Early in 1894.
The Water Supply of Deeping St. Nicholas.

Mr. Rienzi Walton, Local Government Board Inspector held an inquiry at the Board School, Deeping St. Nicholas, on Friday, as to the water supply of the parish. A statement was submitted which had been prepared on behalf of the Rural Sanitary Authority, from which it appeared that out of 231 dwellings in the parish 85 were without a special water supply. The Medical Officer admitted that the supply should be improved, but it was stated by the Sanitary Inspector that Deeping St. Nicholas was better off as to water supply than Weston, Moulton or Cowbit. The Rev. W. Benson, who had prominently interested himself in the matter, read a letter from the South Lincolnshire Fen Water Company, in which it was suggested they might take the matter up, but it was doubted by those present whether the capital would be raised. Mr. Benson as an alternative scheme, produced plans of works to supply Littleworth Drove – the part of the parish most in want – by making an artesian bore and laying a main along the drove. The total cost was estimated at £1,800, which it was proposed to raise by loan. The inspector will report the result of the inquiry to the Local Government Board.

July 1894.

Boring for Water in the Fens. – Information has been received at Spalding that boring operations at Deeping St. Nicholas, some five miles distant which have been in progress for the past three months, have been successful, and that a splendid supply of water, about 40,000 gallons per day, is the result. The work has been carried out by the South Lincolnshire Fen Water Company, the contractor being Mr. Sykes, of Bankside, London. The bore extends to a depth of 285 feet, water being tapped in the limestone. Hitherto there has been no water supply in the parish, and the Vicar taking up the matter on behalf of the poorer parishioners, the Local Government Board recently held an inquiry into the matter. Geologists attach considerable importance to the finding of water in the Fen district, and as a result, boring operations are likely to be commenced at other places in the Spalding district.

Harvest Riots in Deeping Fen.

Life was not always tranquil in the country. In August 1882 the local newspaper reported a disgraceful scene:–

In Deeping Fen drunkenness, lawlessness and rioting have been prevalent amongst the harvestmen, until matters have arrived at such a pitch as to be a disgrace to a civilized land. As usual, when high prices prevail, the men have been insubordinate and reckless to a degree. Very few Irishmen have come into the Fen, but even these few excited jealousy, and "rows" have been of frequent occurrence. On Sunday afternoon last there were several disgraceful scenes: a number of men went into the premises of Mr. Joseph Shepperson, one of the oldest and most esteemed farmers in the district, pelted his men with large stones and brickbats, and created a great disturbance. On Sunday at midnight a gang of desperadoes went upon the farm of Mr. John Holland, another much esteemed agriculturalist, broke open the tool house, armed themselves with forks and other weapons, and then proceeded to lay siege to the granary, in which some Irishmen were sleeping. There was an alarming riot; the inmates of the house were all aroused, and but for the firmness and tact of Mr. Holland and his household some serious consequences must have ensued; as it was some of the men were hurt, and one had a fork run through his wrist. On Monday morning a number of policemen were dispatched into the Fen to arrest the ringleaders and prevent further disturbances. None of the marauders were however captured, but a publican in the Fen was summoned to the petty sessions on Tuesday for permitting drunkenness in his house on Saturday night the 19th. Notwithstanding the evidence by the police, and that of a labourer named Cooper, who admitted having had seven or eight pints before dinner, and being a wet day he was in and about the two public houses drinking from half-past nine in the morning to nearly ten at night, and was twice turned out, until at last the police took care of him, yet the publican triumphed through the defence of an able advocate and the witnesses whom he brought forward.

This report however was not accurate and the next week the story was corrected:–

Spalding – The Harvest Riots in Deeping Fen – In last week's paper we stated that the stone pelting on the Sunday afternoon was on the premises of Mr. Jos. Shepperson, whereas it was in the adjoining farmyard. The night riot upon Mr. Holland's farm was not where he resides, but upon his other farm, and was even more serious than we described. The lock on the tool house door was forced; then the men broke into the barn, and finding they could not get into the granary where the Irishmen were sleeping, they attempted to stab them through the floorboards. One man was actually stabbed in this way on his foot, and another on the wrist before the attacking party quitted the premises. Since this affray there has been less drinking, and no further disturbances.

Snippets from what the papers used to say.

April 1894.

The death is announced of Mr. William Hunt, formerly a leading agriculturalist, of Deeping St. Nicholas, near Spalding. He was the owner and occupier of a large farm in South Lincolnshire, commenced life as a farmer, with a fortune of about £20,000, but, owing to reverses, at the time of his death was one of the pensioners of the Royal Agricultural Benevolent Institution. Mr. Hunt, who was an active member of several drainage trusts, died at Woodstone, near Peterborough, at the age of 81.

August 10th, 1891.

Deeping Fen. – Sheep and Horses Killed by Lightning. – Four horses and several sheep were killed by lightning during the storm on Monday afternoon. Two of the horses and three sheep belonged to Mr. G. Waltham, and were on his farm at Deeping Fen, and the other horses were the property of Mr. G. Darley, of Mill Green, Pinchbeck. The crops have been very much laid by the storms, and the harvest prospects are not so good as a few days ago. Unless fine weather returns the outlook for the farmers will be serious.

August 30th, 1893.

Destructive Stackyard Fire near Spalding. – On Wednesday afternoon a destructive fire occurred on the premises of Mr. Porter, an extensive farmer at Deeping St. Nicholas near Spalding. A stack of straw containing 50 tons, sold to go away the same day was reduced to ashes, as also were a stack of new oats, the produce of 16 acres, and the buildings. Nearly 100 fowls and ducks were roasted alive. The damage amounts to several hundred pounds. Three stacks of wheat, worth £600, narrowly escaped destruction. The fire was caused by a boy playing with matches. The Spalding Fire Brigade, owing to insufficient appliances, were unable to cope with the fire, which burnt until a late hour in the evening.

1892.

Deeping St. Nicholas. – A series of five lectures on ambulance work are being given at the Hop Pole by Dr. Benson of Market Deeping, and are well attended.

Last week Mr. H. Donaldson, secretary to the Technical Instruction Committee of the Kesteven County Council, was present and expressed himself highly pleased with the manner of conducting. The classes are very popular and the average attendance is 75.

October 1886.

Novel Harvest. – A Deeping Fen farmer, tired of waiting for the disappearance of the flood, was on Sunday last busy fetching his corn out of the field with a boat! The recent flood had abundantly proved the defective state of the drainage works for Deeping Fen. For several days after the great rainfall the occupiers were compelled to keep their sluices closed to prevent the water from the outfall drains running on to the land, and on some of the lower farms nearly a week of fine weather elapsed before any water could be run off. At Pode Hole a centrifugal pump was set to work to assist the fixed engines, but all combined were for some days apparently of little avail against the enormous body of water they had to contend with; and it is certain that a large outlay, and further taxation must be resorted to before this great tract of land can be made safe against such rainfalls as have been experienced of late years. Every day this week the water has fallen rapidly.

March 14th, 1788.

John Wilson executed at Lincoln for the murder of William Mason of Deeping Fen. At the place of execution he addressed the populace, persisting in his innocence. He said, "I think it very hard in the health and strength I am in to come to this for nothing. I leave behind me a weakly tender wife, and I shall not wonder if the shock killed her in two or three days. I suffer innocent as a child, as God is my judge, and God forbid I should die with a lie in my mouth."

Fleet

Print of Saint Mary Magdalen church, Fleet. 1842.

Fleet.

The village of Fleet with Fleet Hargate is a large parish 2 miles east from Holbeach. Fleet Hargate was situated on the road between Holbeach and Long Sutton, but some years ago a new road was built to by-pass the traffic away from the village, allowing the population a much quieter life. The name "Fleet" means a salt water creek, and this must have been how the village came by its name, because the Fleet Haven flows from the N.E. corner of the parish, out to the foreshore and into the Wash.

Before the axeing of the railway between Spalding and Kings Lynn the village had its own station. Fleet was never a busy passenger station, but it was linked with the Fleet Light Railway. This railway system was often known as the "potato railway" because this is one of the main crops that it transported. The first section was built about 1910 by the Worth family who farmed extensively in the area. In the beginning the Light Railway just served some farms north of Fleet Hargate, linking them with Fleet station. It was a completely new system when it was first installed. By 1920 there was about 2.75 miles of track between Old White House Lodge and Fleet station. By the early 1930s the track extended to nearly 13 miles. From 1921 there was a connection made with the system in the Gedney Dawsmere area that was owned by J. H. Thompson Farms Ltd. enabling them to haul trains over the Worth's track to reach Fleet station.

The parish church, dedicated to Saint Mary Magdalen, is an ancient building, of stone in the Early English, early and Late Decorated and Perpendicular styles. It has a nave, chancel, and north and south aisles, and is noted for the peculiarity of its tower which is separated from the rest of the church by about 4 yards. The tower is square, with embattlements, surmounted by a fine spire, in all about 120 feet in height.

In the village is also a baptist Chapel that was founded in 1690, and rebuilt in 1876.

Engraving of Fleet church showing the tower separate from the rest of the church.

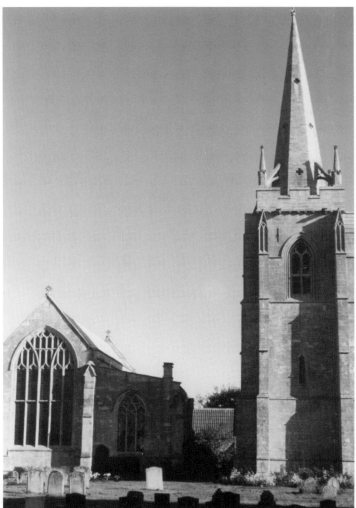

The church of Saint Mary Magdalen, Fleet (Photographed 1999).

Trades and Business people in Fleet in 1937.

Ambrose, Rt. Wm., smallholder.
Baker, Alfred, farmer, Church End.
Baker, Arth., farmer, Kingston Lodge, Millbank & Fleet Fen.
Bateman, Geo. F., farmer.
Bennett, Wm. A. & Rt. A., farmers, Church End.
Bettinson, Jn. Chas., farmer, Fleet Bank.
Bollons, Ernest, smallholder, Fleet Fen.
Bollons, Jn., farmer.
Bolton, Alfd. Hy., farmer, Fleet Road.
Bowling Green Public House (Geo. Powley).
Brumble, Chas., smallholder, Fleet Fen.
Bull Inn (Benj. Cropley).
Bycroft, Rd., smallholder.
Caban, Charles, fruiterer & flower agent.
Chapman, Chas. Hy. & Adlard, farmers, Marsh Lane.
Clarke, Wm. & Son, coal merchants, Station.
Cooper, Chas., farmer.
Coupland, Ephraim W., builder, Church End.
Coupland, Saml., smallholder, Millbank.
Crooked Billet Public House (Arth. E. Wilson).
Crosby & Sons, grocers & post office.
Dickerson, Bernard, farmer, The Chestnuts.
Dickerson, Harold, farmer, Fleet Fen.
Dickerson, Sidney, smallholder.
Dickerson, Wm., farmer, Proudfoot Lane.
Drury, Thos., farmer, Elder Lodge, Fleet Fen.
Electric Filling Station Ltd., Motor Garage, Fleet Road.
English, Harry, bulb grower, Hocklegate.
Ettridge, Jn., farmer, The Limes, Fleet Road.
Fish, Jn. G., farmer, Haycroft Lane.
Five Bells Public House (Geo. Fitch), Fleet Bank.
Fletcher Bros., fruit growers, Pyke Dam Lane, Fleet Fen.
Franks, Harry & Son., builder.
Green, Alfd., farmer, Millbank & Bensgate Lodge.
Greenwood, Geo. Edwin, shopkeeper.
Halgarth, Alfd., poultry farmer, Onslow House.
Halgarth, Arth., fruit grower, Laurel House.
Halgarth, Bert., farmer, The Rookery.
Halgarth, Frederick, jun., farmer.
Halgarth, George, cottage farmer.
Halgarth, Jas., fruit grower, Fleet Road.
Halgarth, Wltr. J., cottage farmer.
Hardy, Chas. Arth., farmer.
Harvey, Jn. Edwd., farmer, Hocklesgate.
Hilliam, Rt., cottage farmer, Fleet Fen.
Hilton, Jn. R., farmer, Maize Dyke Lane.
Jessop, Arth. Geo., farmer.
Knight, Betsy (Mrs.), cottage farmer, Millbank.

Knight, Rt, farmer, Millbank.

Loweth, Freeman & Son, coal dealers.

Manton, Jsph., farmer, Bank House, Bensgate Road.

Manton, Wm., farmer.

Marshall, Robert M., bulbgrower & market gardener, Wood Lane.

Mastin, Rufus. Wm., farmer, Fleet Fen.

Morris, Alfd, farmer, Millbank.

Morris, Herbert, boot repairer.

Munson, James Adlard, farmer.

Neep, Geo., Ernest, butcher.

New Inn (Jn. Chapman).

Owen, Harry, smallholder, Millbank.

Patchett, Chas. I., farmer, Oak Lodge.

Patchett, Jn. Sharp, farmer, Fleet Lodge.

Pedley, Arthur, baker.

Porter, Frank, smallholder, Bensgate Road.

Proctor, Charles, carpenter.

Proctor, Nellie (Mrs.), district nurse.

Proctor, Saml. Smith, farmer.

Raisborough, Jas. A., builder.

Robbs, Jas., smallholder, Fleet Fen.

Robbs, Wallace, farmer, Church End.

Robinson, Jas., smallholder, Millbank.

Rose & Crown Public House (Chas. Oldfield).

Sells Albt., smallholder, Fleet Fen.

Seth, Edward Scotney, thrashing machine owner.

Seth, Geo. Hy, thrashing machine owner.

Shawl, B., farmer, Fleet Fen.

Smith, Geo. Wm., farmer, Primrose Farm.

Sleight, Reginald, insurance agent, Branches Lane.

Sporton, Geo. Ernest, farmer, Hallgate.

Stanberry Annie (Mrs), haulage contractor, Fleet Fen.

Steam Whistle Public House (Jn. W. Baker), Holbeach Fen.

Stubley, Chas., farmer, Fleet House, Fleet Road.

Sturton, Irene (Miss), farmer, Fleet Road.

Syrett, Arth., bulb grower, Fleet Road.

Tatan, Lewis, bulb grower, Beaver House.

Taylor, Wm., farmer, Hurn Fields.

Thorpe, Fras. Chas., farmer, Cyprus Lodge.

Thorpe, Rt., farmer, Wood Lane.

Towns, Jn., potato grower, Branches Lane.

Wain, Harry, cycle dealer.

Waldock, Fredk., bulb grower, Glenavon.

Walsham, Frank, fruit grower, Ravendale, Fleet Road.

Waltham Bros., farmers, Manor Farm.

Watson, Thos., smallholder, Fleet Fen.

Welch, Jas., farmer, Fleet Fen.

Winterton, Arth., fruit grower, Branches Lane.

Worth, Arth. H., farmer, Hovenden House.

Wright, Bert, smallholder, Ivy House.

Wright, Carden, farmer, Fleet Marsh Farm.

Bowling Green public house. 1950.

Steam Whistle public house. 1950.

Fleet Post Office and Store with the Baptist Chapel on the right, 1918.

William Burgess, Engraver and Baptist Pastor.

William Burgess was born in London on the 13th March, 1755. After being well educated, and displaying a taste for the fine arts he was apprenticed for 7 years at the age of 14 to a Mr. J. Jeune, an engraver in a style called line engraving on copper. Mr. Jeune was an English engraver. His principal work was in book plates and portraits. During his apprenticeship William Burgess fell in love with and married his master's daughter Elizabeth Jeune. He continued to work for and help his father-in-law until his death as he had an abundance of work.

Around this time William Burgess joined the General Baptist persuasion, and this was the cause of an estrangement with his parents, particularly his mother, who was a strict churchwoman. He became noted as a preacher at Mr. Britton's chapel in Church Lane, Whitechapel. In 1787 he was invited to go to Halifax in Yorkshire in the place of the Rev. Daniel Taylor, who was removed to London, but he did not remain there long, for in the year 1791 he was removed to the Pastorate of Fleet, near Holbeach. He had 5 children – 3 sons and 2 daughters.

REVᴰ WILLIAM BURGESS,
upwards of 20 Years Pastor of the
GENERAL BAPTIST CHURCH AT FLEET
LINCOLNSHIRE.
Born March 13ᵗʰ 1755, Died Decᵇʳ 11ᵗʰ 1813.

Reverend William Burgess 1755-1813.

Hilkiah, the eldest son, had at the age of 16 become very good at engraving, and no time was lost by his father in making him proficient in the art. In 1796 father and son turned their labours to some account by publishing views of 12 churches, most of them in Lincolnshire, and not far distant from Fleet. These engravings were very popular and several hundred were sold. Thus encouraged Messrs. Burgess decided to produce three large engravings, one of Lincoln Cathedral and the others of Ely Cathedral and Crowland Abbey. These two were very popular, and many were sold. No other engravings were produced after these. William Burgess's health failed through over-work, he was afflicted with asthma and unable to go far from home.

In December 1813 he caught a cold performing the rites over a friend on a cold day in the Fleet Chapel ground, and after a week's illness departed this life on 11th December 1813 at the age of 58.

William Burgess was much respected in the community and the following report was published in the local newspaper:–

1813.

December, at Fleet in the County, the Rev. William Burgess, in the 59th year of his age, who for upwards of twenty years was the Pastor of a respectable society of General Baptists at that place. His talents as a preacher were considerable; his public services were principally extemporaneous, which he conducted with a degree of fervency and affectionate regard for the best interests of all who attended his ministry. His manners were unaffected and conciliatory; in his domestic relations he was peculiarly affectionate; in his private friendships uniform and steadfast. His moral character was without a stain. His loss was severely felt by his family, and the society with whom he was so closely connected. It may be said with truth, he lived usefully, and he died happy.

Fleet Church drawn by W. and H. Burgess 1798.

Snippets from what the papers used to say:

November 1811.

Holbeach, Nov. 18th, 1811.

Stolen or strayed, about Tuesday the 12th instant from out-of-a-close-of-land near Doll's Bank, in the Parish of Fleet, in the occupation of Mr. William Stanger, jnr.;

A Dark-chestnut Nag Horse;

If stolen, whoever will discover the offender or offenders, so that he or they may be brought to justice, shall, on his or their conviction, be entitled to and receive a Reward of Five Guineas from the Hundred of Elloe Association, holden at Holbeach; and a further reward of Five Guineas from Mr. Stanger; and if any accomplice will impeach, he shall receive the same Rewards, and every endeavour will be used to procure a pardon. If strayed, whoever will give information where he may be had again shall receive One Guinea Reward, and be paid all reasonable expenses.

By Order

J. Johnson.

Treasurer and Clerk to the said Association.

1823.

To be Sold by Private Contract.

That wonderful fine draught Stallion Colt, Young England's Glory, the property of Mr. T. Manton of Fleet, Lincolnshire, and one of the best bred horses in England: his colour is a rich bay free from white, he is rising four years old, stands 17 hands high, and all over equal in proportion. His sire, that noted horse England's Glory, the property of Mr. William Bingham, of Holbeach Marsh; which horse is allowed by all judges to overshow any horse in England: his dam a favourite brood mare of the said Mr. Manton's by a very noted horse once the property of Mr. Matthew Cooper, of Fleet. Young England's Glory is in high condition, and has proved himself a certain stock-getter. He may be seen any time by applying to the said Mr. Manton, who will give further particulars as to price, &c. &c.

A reasonable credit will be given, if required.

Fleet, February 17, 1823.

May 1871.

A wedding took place in this neighbourhood on Tuesday which was quite a novelty in its way: the son of a cottager of Fleet took to himself a wife, and it being a fine day five donkeys were harnessed out to convey the wedding party through Holbeach to Whaplode and back; and to crown the whole, the party put up for refreshments at host Hargrave's, at the Crown Inn. It has been suggested that possibly the number of donkeys might exceed five!

1828.

Crane's Charity Lands.

To be Let by Auction

By Mr. Cross.

At the Bull Inn in Fleet, in the county of Lincoln, on Tuesday the 8th day of April next, at 11 o'clock in the forenoon, for the term of Ten Years, from the 6th April, 1828, in convenient lots, and subject to conditions of management.

The several Lands called Crane's Charity Lands, situate in the parish of Fleet aforesaid, containing in the whole 176A, 2R, 33P, or thereabouts, part whereof may be broken up, and the remainder be continued pasture. Descriptive particulars of the several lots may be had at the office of Messrs. Girdlestone, Wing and Jackson, solicitors, Wisbech.

Wisbech, March 26th, 1828.

1896.
Rose and Crown Inn, Fleet, Lincolnshire.

Valuable Freehold Public House, Brewery and Shop for Investment or Occupation. Messrs Hackworth and Abbott are instructed to offer the above for Sale by Auction, at the Chequers Hotel, Holbeach, on Thursday 11th April next at 3 for 4 p.m. punctually.

The fully-licensed Free Public-House contains Bar, Parlour, Tap room, and Five Bedrooms.

The Out-buildings comprise very commodious Stabling accommodation up to 20 horses, and including several newly-erected Loose Boxes suitable for travelling Stallions; also other convenient Buildings.

The Brewery contains a capital Three-quarter Plant including a 12 barrel Cooper in excellent condition, and other fixtures.

Adjoining the Inn is a very convenient shop, well fitted up for a General Business, with a good window facing the Main Street.

The whole is Freehold and stands on 1A. 3R. 26P. of Land, part Garden, and the residue of Pasture, and is excellently situated in the centre of Fleet Hargate, on the main road between Holbeach and Long Sutton. It is now in the occupation of Mr. John Gibson, and possession may be had on completion of the purchase.

For further particulars apply to the Auctioneers, Holbeach; or to
Messrs Coulton and Son.
Solicitors, Lynn.

1799.
Fleet Doles.

The parishioners of Fleet resolved on the 21st December 1799, "That no person who keeps a dog shall participate in the charity distributed there on St. Thomas's Day".

June 1876.

The General Baptists of Fleet in consequence of the unsafe state of their chapel, have resolved that it should be taken down and another built in its place. The foundation stone of the new building was laid on the 7th inst. by Mrs. Ann Wilkinson who, we understand contributed £200 towards the undertaking. A public meeting was held in a marquee on the evening of the same day. The Rev. J. Watkinson, pastor of the church, presided, and addresses were delivered by the Revs. I. Barrass (Peterborough), W. Ordon (Bourne), and J. C. Jones (Spalding), and the Revs. A. J. Robinson, E. Craine, and W. S. Harcourt also took part in the meeting. Messrs. Bateman and Waterman are the contractors at over £900, and already more than £500 has been either given or promised.

1883.

Fleet – Sir, – There passed away from this world, at this village, on the 15th June, a lady who will be missed by the Baptists, and also by other inhabitants of the place. About six years ago she gave several hundreds of pounds to the building of a new chapel. At the interment, however, although she had done so much for the cause, it was rather surprising that none, or scarcely any, of the sect showed their respect by following her remains to their last resting place. Mrs. Wilkinson, who had attained the age of 85, had for years been a liberal supporter of the Baptists. Probably they were offended because she chose to be interred at the Parish Church.
Yours,
A LOOKER ON.

1877.
Fleet School Board – To Builders.

Tenders are desired for the erection of Schools and Teacher's House in Wood Lane, Fleet, near the Railway Station.

The plans and specifications as prepared by Mr. J. H. Dawson, Architect, Sutton Bridge, may be seen at my office in Long Sutton any day between the hours of Ten and Five.

Tenders to be sent to me, marked "Tenders for Schools," before the 21st day of March next. The Board do not bind themselves to accept any Tender.

By Order. Richd. P. Mossop, Clerk.

Long Sutton, 28th Feb, 1877.

Fleet Hargate with the Bull Inn, about 1900.

Fosdyke

The village of Fosdyke with a population of about 450 stands on the A17 road north of the River Welland, 6 miles north-west from Holbeach, and 8½ miles south from Boston. There is a wharf that will accommodate small vessels that come up the river to discharge and load their cargo. Fosdyke is mentioned in records as far back as the 12th century, and in the middle of the 16th century documents name it as a landing place for shipping. By the 1730s the port was handling the imports of coal from the north of the country, and timber from abroad, while the main export was grain. For over 150 years small fishing boats sailed out of the river into the Wash, trawling for shrimps, and the gathering of cockles on the sand-banks when the tide went out. Some fishing boat owners hired out their services to parties who wished to go out into the Wash for a day of shrimping and cockling. The catch was then boiled in a copper on board the boat, giving everyone the chance to feed on the results of their efforts. These excursions were referred to as "going down below". Shipping can only come up the river and out again on the high tide as the water at low tide is quite shallow. In the 1990s the port was still quite busy with handling cargo, but there were no longer any fishing boats using the facilities, and the boat building and repairing yard that once stood on the river side had long since disappeared.

Fosdyke village is divided into two separate areas. One part is centred around the church, and the other around the bridge and river. The area around the church used to lay on the main A17 road, but fortunately for the villagers this part is now by-passed leaving them with a nice quiet community with its modern village hall and fine Victorian church. To the south is the river with its modern bridge carrying the busy traffic of the main road. This area is more industrial with the wharf, row of Custom Houses, and the Ship Inn. In the 1930s the village had four public houses, but now the only public house left is the Ship Inn that has served the community for many years.

Trades and Business people in Fosdyke in 1937.

Allen, Frank, farmer.
Allen, Fred, smallholder.
Birch, G. F. & Son Ltd., corn merchants, Bridge Wharf.
Bryant, John Benedict, pilot.
Burdall, Henry, farmer.
Burdall, William, farmer.
Cannon, Phillip, farmer.
Clayton, Jn. Bloomfield, farmer.
Cooper, Phillip Anthony, farmer.
Cropley, Randolph, motor engineer, Bridge.
Franks, Ezra, farmer.
Franks, Jn. Wm., cottage farmer.
Garner, Wm., cottage farmer.
Harrison, Arth., farm bailiff to Messrs. W. Dennis & Sons Ltd.
Hayes, John, smith, Bridge.
Johnson, Alfd., farmer.
Kitchen, Albert Edward, farmer.
Lawson, Jn., farmer.
Lineham, Jn., fisherman.
Longland, Rowland, carpenter, Bridge.
Moore, George Herbert, farmer.
Moses, Wm., farmer.
Neale, John Thomas, farmer.
New Inn (Jsph Capps), Bridge.
Nix, Sydney, shopkeeper, Bridge.
Old Inn (Jn. Taylor).
Parker, Wm., smallholder.

Rose & Crown Inn (Geo. M. Canty), Bridge.
Ship Inn (Jn. Wm. Simpson), Bridge.
Skelton, Chas. Fredk. Wm., farmer.
Smith, George, bridge keeper & engineer.
Snaith, Fras. Brummitt, shopkeeper & post office.
Sportan, W., farmer.
Stephenson, Fredk, harbour master & supt of Welland drainage.
Thorpe, John & Son, farmer.
Tinsley, Geo, farm manager to Miss I. Sturton.
Moore, Rev. Thomas (Vicar), Vicarage.

The Church of All Saints, Fosdyke.

For several hundred years Fosdyke and the neighbouring church at Algarkirk were both part of the same parish until the 17th century when they officially separated into two parishes. A medieval church certainly had existed in Fosdyke, but little is known about it. In 1755 a new church was erected on the site of the former edifice. Externally the church possessed nothing to attract the attention of the visitor; the interior however contained a beautifully sculptured font, and the tower housed a ring of five bells. In 1868 it was decided to demolish the old Georgian church, and build a new one.

The following newscutting reports tell the story of the building of the new church:–
October 1868.

Fosdyke – The old church of All Saints being insufficient in accommodation, it has been decided to take it down and rebuild a more commodious one. The Rev. Basil Beridge, Rector of Algarkirk, to which this curacy is attached, and who is also the patron, called into requisition the services of Mr. Edw. Browning, Architect, of Stamford, who has prepared the plans. The style adopted is that which prevailed at the commencement of the 13th century. The plan consists of nave, with north and south aisles, chancel, with organ chamber and vestry. The porch, forming the lower part of the tower, is on the south side. The length of nave and aisles is 57 feet 6 inches, and the width 43 feet 6 inches; the length of chancel is 23 feet, and the width 17 feet. The walls are built of bricks, with Bath freestone dressings; the facing bricks are from Grimsby, and specially made 2 inches thick. The roofs are open timbered of fir, and covered with green Westmorland slates. The tower surmounted with a framed timber spire 43 feet high, covered with lead laid in chevron pattern. The nave arcade has circular freestone shafts with moulded bases and carved caps; the arches are also moulded. The seats are executed in pitch pine and varnished; the pulpit, lectern, and desk in oak. The cost of the work will be about £5,000, and the contract has been let to Messrs. S. and W. Pattinson, of Ruskington near Sleaford.

October 1868.

Fosdyke – The proposed new church: – This work has long been talked of, but at last the work has commenced, as the man has started casting the clay to make the bricks. The old church has long since been too small for its inhabitants, so that one much larger is required. We think that we shall be justified in saying that the foundation stone will be laid in the Spring of next year. It is only a little over two years since we had one of the finest schools built here, capable of teaching one hundred and fifty children, and should we get a new church, what we want is five or six old houses pulling down and new ones building, and then we think Fosdyke will be one of the finest places in Lincolnshire.

1869

Fosdyke – The ceremony of laying the foundation stone of the church now being rebuilt, enlarged, and beautified here at the sole expense of the beloved rector, the Rev. Basil Beridge, who performed the pleasing ceremony, took place on Monday, the 27th September. The Rev. gentleman delivered an appropriate address

The church at Fosdyke that was built in 1755 and demolished in 1868.

to the parishioners and work people assembled, the latter being presented with Five pounds, which was divided among them.

Soon after the rebuilding work started concern was shown by some villagers as the next report shows.

1869.

A correspondent, writing from Fosdyke, states that great excitement prevails in the village, consequent on the disturbance of a large number of graves to make way for the erection of the new church. It is said that the total number of graves likely to be interfered with is nearly 100. The work of digging them up commenced on Thursday in last week, and our informant states that at noon on that day there were no less than five coffins exposed to public gaze, while one of the workmen declared that they turned up a skull to which a portion of the scalp and some hair still adhered! The inhabitants residing near the churchyard are apprehensive that fever or some other malignant disorder will break out among them.

Words of consolation soon followed in the next edition of the paper.

The people of Fosdyke have been very unnecessarily deceived by an alarmist who prophesied exhalations from graves about to be disturbed to make room for the improvement of the church. We are assured that no human remains have been or are likely to be disturbed, and that the rumours which have been circulated on that subject are entirely without foundation. The well-known kindness of disposition of the owner of the parish is a guarantee that nothing would be done to hurt the feelings of the inhabitants.

After this upset was put to rest work on the new church went ahead with no more serious problems, and by June 1871 the building was complete. The following notice was published in the local paper.

All Saints Church, Fosdyke..

The consecration of this new church will take place on Tuesday, 6th June, 1871. Morning Service with Holy Communion, at 11 a.m.

The Morning Sermon will be preached by the Lord Bishop of the Diocese, and a Collection made in aid of the Convalescent Home, Mablethorpe. Evening Prayer at 3.30, when the Venerable Archdeacon Trollope will preach, and a collection will be made for the Lincoln County Hospital.

Fosdyke

The Clergy in surplices are requested to assemble at the Schoolroom, Fosdyke, at 10.45 and 3.15 o'clock.

There will be a Public Luncheon in a Tent adjoining the church at 2 o'clock. Tickets at 2s. 6d. each may be had of the Rev. George Shaw, Sutterton; Mr. Bett, churchwarden, Fosdyke; and of Mr. Dingwall, bookseller, Boston; and at the Peacock Hotel.

Consecration of All Saints Church, Fosdyke, which has been rebuilt and enlarged at the sole expense of the Rev. B. Beridge, took place on Tuesday last. The service commenced at 11 o'clock, at which time the church was crowded with attentive worshippers, the number, counted as they walked out after the service, being 711. The Bishop of the Diocese performed the ceremony of consecration, at the close of which morning service was commenced. The Rev. G. Shaw, Curate of the parish, read the prayers.

The Rev. C. A. Moore, of Sutterton, the first lesson; The Rev. John Tunnard the second; the Rev. G. B. Blenkin the epistle; the Rev. B. Beridge the gospel; and the Bishop the Holy Communion. The sermon was preached by his Lordship. After the service about 250 ladies and gentlemen sat down to an excellent luncheon provided by the Misses Jackson, of the Peacock Hotel, Boston. The Bishop presided, and was supported on his immediate right and left by the Rev. B. Beridge, and the Ven. Archdeacon Trollope.

At the consecration of the newly built church Mr. Bett, the churchwarden read to those present a letter that he had received from Rev. Edward Moore, of Spalding, in which the Rev. Gentleman, after expressing regret that he would not be able to attend the consecration service of this day, gave an extract from his church books relating to the parish of Fosdyke which was of such an interesting character that he must read it. It was that in 1752 King George gave instructions for collections to be made in all the churches of that neighbourhood on behalf of the church at Fosdyke, which had been injured by fire, and that the sum collected at Spalding as 8s. 4d. (laughter). Now, if it took King George to raise 8s. 4d. at Spalding what where they to think of the Rev. Basil Beridge, who had erected three churches in the district ? (laughter and applause).

All Saints Church, Fosdyke.

The old font that was originally in the 1755 to 1868 church, with its lofty canopied cover. After thorough restoration this was placed in the west end of the new church, where it still remains in use today.

The west end of the church with the font, decorated for the flower festival, May 2000.

The High Altar and the Chancel decorated for the flower festival, May 2000.

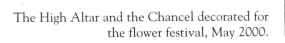

Fosdyke Bridge

Until almost the end of the 18th century the outfall of the River Welland was in a very poor state. The course of the river was not very well defined. Fosdyke Wash came inland nearly as far as Surfleet Reservoir, with the course of the Welland flowing through the middle, and until 1815 there was no bridge over the river. Despite there being no bridge Fosdyke was on the route used by drovers driving their cattle and sheep etc from the north of the country to Norwich and London. The only way across the river was by fording it. This could be done at low tide when there was only a few inches of water in the river. Those wishing to ford the river could find the state of the tide, and the time of low water by visiting the Old Inn nearby. In this Inn was an old long cased clock that besides giving the time of day, also gave the phases of the moon etc., and the time of high and low water. This clock was known as the "Fosdyke Tidal Clock", and is still in existence today. Attempts were made to improve the state of the Welland, when under an Act of 1794 it was improved from Surfleet Reservoir to Fosdyke Wash, but this only served to make the situation worse downstream. The Welland was constantly changing its course, and much danger came from quicksands and tides. This made the fording of the river very precarious for drovers and travellers who were still advised to hire the services of a local guide, who would understand the tides, and know the safest route across the River Welland and Fosdyke Wash.

At a meeting at Spalding on 30th October 1807 a resolution was made to establish a ferry boat at the Fosdyke Inn for the use of travellers passing through the county thus enabling them to avoid the uncertain and sometimes dangerous passage of the Wash. Whether this was brought into being is not known, but three years later in 1810 under the leadership of Sir Joseph Banks a meeting was held at Fosdyke Inn. It was resolved by the gentlemen present that it was expedient to erect and maintain a bridge over the celebrated estuary, Fosdyke Wash to connect more intimately the counties of Lincoln and Norfolk. Mr. John Rennie the well known Scottish civil engineer on the nomination of Sir Joseph Banks, was elected engineer for the undertaking, and Mr. Bower was elected Surveyor. In observing upon the probable opposition of the inhabitants of Spalding to the measure of a bridge over the Washway, Sir Joseph Banks remarked: "With regard to the prejudices of the people of Spalding, the fact is, that if they wish us to go round 10 miles to spend 10d. out of which they would get 10 farthings." This observation applies to the opinion entertained that, in case of a bridge being thrown over the Fosdyke, the road to London from Boston and the Eastern parts of the county, would be better, and some miles nearer by Holbeach & Wisbech, than by Spalding. – Something nearer it certainly would be; and the advantage of getting to the Great North Road, upon which such varied means of conveyance

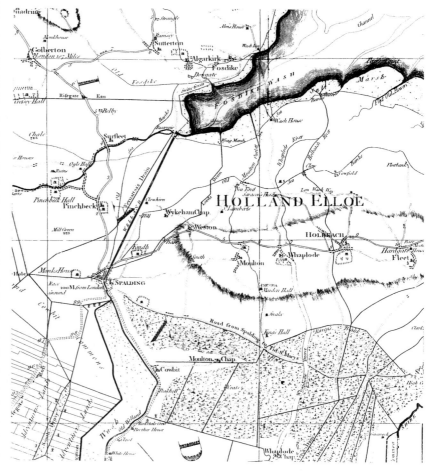

Map showing Fosdyke Wash. (From Armstrongs Map of 1779.)

present themselves, will always ensure a preference to the line by Spalding, Deeping, and Peterborough. The projected bridge, however, would be a work of great public convenience, as being passable at all hours, and obviating the present dangerous conveyance over the Wash.

A committee of gentlemen was formed under the chairmanship of Sir Joseph Banks for the purpose of obtaining an "Act of Parliament"! for erecting the bridge over the River Welland at Fosdyke; approving the plans for the structure; Raising capital for the project, and Appointing contractors to do the work etc.

A plan was produced by Mr. Rennie of a drawbridge, the principle of which was much admired. The length of the projected bridge was to be 265 feet, with a road-way 22 feet wide. It was estimated that a bridge of English Oak of these dimensions would cost £7,000. The calculation for an embankment or causeway required beyond the bridge, along the marsh would be £3,500. To these estimates had to be added the expense of procuring the Bill in Parliament &c. which then would increase the gross amount to about £12,000. The Act of Parliament was eventually granted and Messrs Pacey & Colly of Boston were awarded the contract to construct the bridge which they had hoped would be completed by May 1813, but it was not until 1815 that the structure was ready for the public to use.

The finished roadway rested on a series of oak piles, driven into the river bed. These piles were about 18 inches in diameter, and some of them 42 feet in length. The bridge had three openings of 30 feet, two of 29 feet, and three of 27 feet, leaving a total waterway of 229 feet. The central part of the bridge opened for the passage of vessels, the two sections could be raised vertically by means of a rack and pinion.

Revenue was raised by charging tolls to those who used the bridge, for the Proprietors of the Fosdyke Bridge Company who were solely responsible for any maintenance required.

By 1836 major repairs were needed, and in 1868 it was found necessary to close the bridge to traffic, and the drawbridge was left open for shipping. In 1870 the bridge was taken over by the County who did extensive repair work before re-opening to traffic in 1871. Tolls were still charged, and it was not until 1890 that they were finally abolished.

The condition of the bridge left much to be desired, and in February 1907 the report of the Road and Bridges Committee dealt with a proposal to erect a new bridge over the River Welland at Fosdyke. The Committee were of the opinion that the time had arrived for the County Council to seriously consider the question of erection of a new bridge. This was eventually approved and on March 31st 1911 the new iron structure that was built at a cost of about £17,000 was opened by the Earl of Ancaster.

The new bridge gave good service for many years, but it was eventually too narrow for modern traffic, and it was replaced by the present concrete bridge which was opened in 1990.

Fosdyke Bridge about 1870.

Fosdyke Bridge about 1890.

Fosdyke Bridge in 1985.

Sir Joseph Banks, BART, K.B. (1743-1820) the prime mover to the building of the first road bridge over the River Welland at Fosdyke.

191 Directions for passing Fofs Dyke, &c. 192

The Price of Goods, Cattle, and Paffengers, going over at Auft.and New Paffages.

	s.	d.
A coach, with fix horfes	16	0
Ditto, with four horfes	14	0
Ditto, with two horfes	12	0
A man, woman, or child, each	0	4
A man and horfe	1	0
A fingle horfe	0	8
Beafts, each	0	4
Sheep, per fcorce	2	0
Hogs, ditto	2	6

A Tide Table, directing the proper Times for paffing over Fofs Dyke and Crofs Keys Wafhes, in the County of Lincoln, in the Road from Bofton to Lynn, p. 124.

Moon's Age.		Full Sea.		Begin to pafs over Fofs Dyke Wafh.		Crofs Keys Wafh.		End paffing over. Fofs Dyke Wafh.		Crofs Keys Wafh.	
Days.		H.	M.	H.	M.	H.	M.	H.	M.	H.	M.
1	16	7	0	10	0	10	30	4	15	3	35
2	17	7	48	10	48	11	18	5	53	4	23
3	18	8	36	11	36	12	6	6	21	5	11
4	19	9	24	12	24	12	54	7	9	5	59
5	20	10	12	1	12	1	42	7	57	6	47
6	21	11	0	2	0	2	30	8	45	7	35
7	22	11	48	2	48	3	18	9	33	8	23
8	23	12	36	3	26	3	56	10	21	9	11
9	24	1	24	4	24	4	54	11	9	9	59
10	25	2	12	5	12	5	42	11	57	10	47
11	26	3	0	6	0	6	30	12	45	11	35
12	27	3	48	6	48	7	18	1	35	12	23
13	28	4	36	7	36	8	6	2	21	1	11
14	29	5	21	8	24	8	54	3	9	1	59
15	30	6	12	9	12	9	42	3	57	2	47

For example, if the moon be one or fixteen days old, (which is the day of the change or full) you may pafs over *Fofs Dyke Wafh* from ten to fifteen minutes paft four; and *Crofs Keys Wafh* from half paft ten to thirty-five minutes paft three.

Directions for Passing Fosdyke Wash, and Fees Payable. From: Owen' New Book of Roads, 1792.

Above: Old Inn, Fosdyke about 1950.

Below: The Old Inn now modernised for living accommodation.

Navigation Lamp taken from the 1911-1990 bridge before it was demolished, and placed in the church yard.

COAST GUARD CONTRACT.
To BUILDERS and CONTRACTORS.
TENDERS for the ERECTION of a COAST
GUARD STATION at FOSDYKE, in the county of
Lincoln, consisting of an Officer's House, Four Cottages,
Watch and Store-rooms, Wash-house, and Out-buildings,
will be received at this Office on TUESDAY the 5th proximo.
The Plans and Specifications may be seen at this Office,
or at the Watch-room, Fosdyke Station.
Director of Works Department, Admiralty,
Spring Garden-terrace, London, S.W., April 18, 1874.

This row of cottages was built as a Coast Guard Station 1874-75. Here photographed in 1999.

Fosdyke Primitive Methodist Chapel – First built in 1826 and then re-built in 1861.

Snippets from what the papers used to say.

November 1810:
Severe Flooding.

On 10th November 1810 the whole of the east coast suffered from a calamitous High Tide. None appears to have experienced the devastation more than the premises of Mr. John Birkitt, of Fosdyke. His house and other contiguous buildings, which had been erected almost a century upon the very summit of an inner bank, had long withstood the fury of contending elements, till the tremendous evening which spread desolation over the whole of that unfortunate parish. Alarmed by the presaging storm, Mr. Birkitt attempted to save his stock in the adjacent marsh, but all of his efforts were in vain; the wind being N.E. brought up the tide with redoubled violence; a few minutes had elapsed before the whole of his marsh was a complete deluge: the bank, which for years had stood a faithful barrier, was soon overflowed, and the whole of his property on that side of the intake entirely swept away – hovels, sheds, outhouses, implements of husbandry, all of his hay, every sheaf of corn, 237 sheep, 4 fat pigs &c. to the amount of £2,000 and upwards; and what added to the agonising scene was the loss of a faithful domestic – a servant girl, whose good conduct had endeared her to the family, was washed from the bank by a wave in the sight of her master and mistress, whilst the former was in the very act of reaching forth his hand to save her life, and sank to rise no more. No sooner was the misfortune of Mr. Birkitt made known to his landlord, Joseph Pitt, Esq. of Cirencester, in Gloucestershire, than that gentleman instantly left his house and repaired to Fosdyke (a distance of 250 miles) to alleviate his tenant's suffering. On his arrival he found Mr. Burkitt had begun to repair the breaches in the bank, in which he ordered him to proceed, assuring him that the expense incurred thereon he would cheerfully pay; he next desired him to get the whole of his premises put into repair to his own wish, as soon as convenient: and to enable him to do so, left a sum of money in his hands with strict injunctions on him to draw for more when required. Mr. Pitt then, with that liberality for which he is justly famed generously gave to Mr. Birkitt the whole amount of two years rent: he also relieved some other individuals on the spot; and having expressed a hope that subscription would be made for those unfortunate sufferers who had nearly lost their all, he ordered his tenant to set his name down as a subscriber for £20.

January 1811
High Tide

That very high tides have of late years been more frequent than formerly, along the coast in the neighbourhood of Boston, is demonstrated by the instance of Sunday night last, when, unaided in the least degree by any wind (either then or for a day or two before), the tide rose to an extraordinary height, flooded some streets in the town, and flowed to within six inches of the top of some parts of the sea bank in the parish of Fosdyke, exciting considerable alarm amongst those persons resident near the shore, who lately witnessed its devastating effects when it did actually over flow the barriers.

March 1823.
Sutterton Association for the persecution of Felons.

Absconded, on or about the 12th February last, from the parish of Fosdyke, John Marrat, who is strongly suspected of stealing a Bay Hackney Mare, the property of Edward Ayscough, of Fosdyke aforesaid, in the night of the 9th February last; but which said mare has since been recovered. The said John Marrat is 21 years of age, about 5 feet 8 or 9 inches high, black eyes and hair, rather stout made; has been brought up to husbandry business. When offering the aforesaid mare for sale at Stamford fair on the 10th he wore an under blue coat with a light coloured straight-bodied rough great coat; boots and spurs; sometimes wears a dark brown little coat, with fustian frock over the same.

Whoever will apprehend the said John Marrat, or give information so that he may be brought to justice, shall, on his conviction of the said felony, receive a reward of Five Guineas from Mr. W. Maltby of Sutterton, Treasurer to the above Association.

Fosdyke, 22nd March, 1823.

February 1872.

An Agricultural Labourers Meeting was held at Fosdyke on the 19th, and a club formed for the purpose of Advocating the Nine Hours system and an increase in wages to 3s. per day. 20 members were enrolled. The meeting was attended by 150 men from this and adjoining villages.

November 1871.

Persons whose business calls them to drive from Boston to Holbeach complain bitterly of the state of the road between Algarkirk and Fosdyke Bridge. They say that the road is utterly devoid of hard material, and therefore can never be really good until a different system of booning is adopted. Fosdyke has lately been honoured by the erection of a new church and the construction of a new bridge over the Wash, and its parishioners would do themselves credit and confer a boon on the public if they would appoint a new surveyor to "mend their ways".

May 31st 1894.

    The parsonage grounds at Fosdyke were the scene on Thursday week of a rural fete and sale of work on behalf of the church organ fund, and, notwithstanding repeated showers and other drawbacks, attracted a large attendance of parishioners and visitors from adjacent parishes. The following ladies presided at the stalls: Mrs. Lewis, Mrs. Redford, Mrs. Lamming, Mrs. Smith, Mrs. Bett, Mrs. Wharram and Miss Sparrow. The articles on sale included all kinds of wearing apparel, flowers, ferns, knick-knacks, picture frames, &c. The jumble sale was a great boon to many judging from the rapidity with which bonnets, hats, dresses, boots, &c., were bought and borne off. The Kirton Brass Band played at intervals during the afternoon, and for dancing on the lawn in the evening, the grounds being brilliantly lighted up by Chinese lanterns of varied hues. The sale realised over £30.

Gedney

with

Gedney Hill

Gedney Dawsmere

Gedney Marsh

Gedney Drove End

Gedney Dyke, etc.

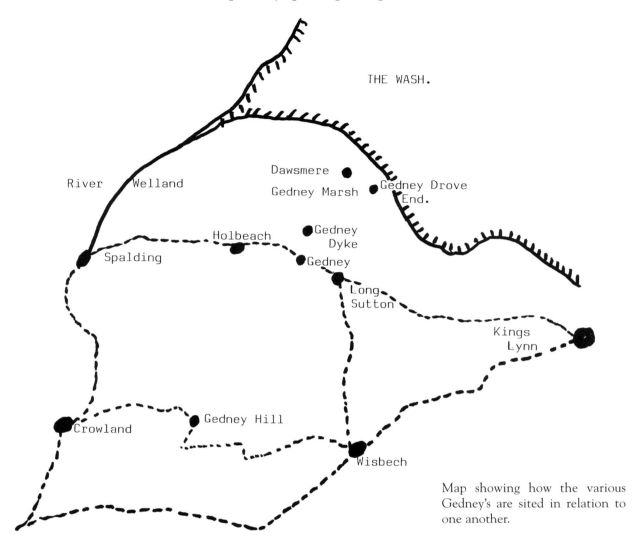

THE WASH.

Dawsmere
Gedney Marsh

River Welland

Gedney Drove
End.

Gedney
Dyke

Holbeach

Gedney

Spalding

Long
Sutton

Kings
Lynn

Gedney Hill

Crowland

Wisbech

Map showing how the various
Gedney's are sited in relation to
one another.

Newcomers to the Gedney area often assume that the "Gedney" villages are all close to one another, but this is not the case as they soon discover. By road Gedney to Gedney Hill is about 15 miles and Gedney to Gedney Drove End is about 6 miles in the opposite direction. Until 1699 this was all contained within the Gedney parish, but in that year Gedney Hill or Gedney Fen End as it was called in those days was separated from Gedney and became a parish in its own right. In 1856 the Gedney parish was reduced in size again, when the parish of Gedney Drove End and Dawsmere was created.

The village of Gedney is situated 2½ miles north-west of Long Sutton, and 3 miles south-east of Holbeach. Church End, Chapelgate and Gedney Dyke are three hamlets contained within the parish which is quite large with some of the dwellings being somewhat scattered although in the last fifty years many more houses have been built in the vicinity of the church. Gedney parish church is a splendid building in the Early English, Late Decorated and Perpendicular styles, dedicated to St. Mary Magdalen. The ancient edifice is remarkable for its spaciousness, and fine proportions making it well deserving of the unofficial title of "Cathedral of the Fens". Standing on the highest ground in the area the building in times past was a grand landmark for travellers. The tower situated on the western side of the nave stands 86 feet in height to the top of the parapet, with a short octagonal spire, and containing bells and a clock. There is a chancel, clerestoried nave of six bays, aisles and south porch. The building is about 160 feet in length exclusive of the tower.

Gedney

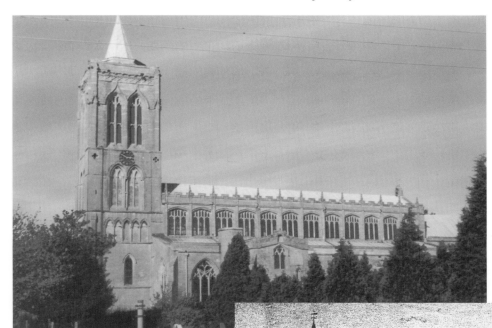

The church of St. Mary Magdalen, Gedney (Photographed 1998).

Print of the church of St. Mary Magdalen, Gedney, 1842.

The church of St. Mary Magdalen, Gedney (Photograph taken about 1870).

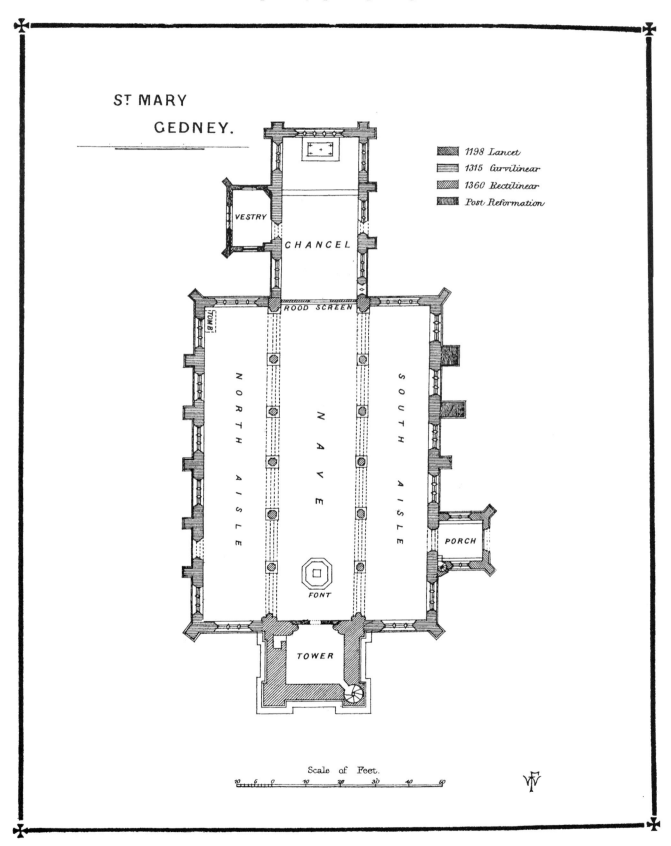

Plan of St. Mary Magdalen Church, Gedney.

Trades and Business people in Gedney in 1937.

Andrew James & Edmund, farmers, Broadgate.
Andrew Geo., farmer, Broadgate.
Anvil Public House (Jim Deans), Gedney Dyke.
Ayres, Walter Frank, Fried Fish Dealer, Gedney Dyke.
Baker, Arth. Albert, farmer, Fen.
Baker, Eva (Mrs.), smallholder, Chapelgate.
Barnes, J. E. (Mrs.), baker, Ramparts.
Bass, Geo. & Claude, farmers, Gedney Dyke.
Bateman, James R., farmer & potato merchant, Crown Lodge, Gedney Marsh.
Bates, Martin, jnr., farmer, Charter Farm.
Bayston, Joseph, smallholder, Middle Drove.
Beba & Sons, farmers, Gedney Marsh.
Belsham, Leonard & Fras. Abraham, farmers, The Lodge, Charters Drove.
Bemrose, Geo., farmer, Gedney Marsh.
Bemrose, Jn., farmer, Gedney Marsh.
Black Lion Public House (Arth. Wakefield), Chapelgate.
Blowers, Marjorie (Mrs.), shopkeeper, Church End.
Brown, Jn. Wm., Brook House, Gedney Marsh.
Butters, Chas. Hy., smallholder, Gedney Dyke.
Chapman Bros., farmers, Broadgate.
Chequers Inn (Geo. Phoenix), Gedney Dyke.
Clarke, Chas. Hy., farmer, Broadgate Farm.
Clifton, B. & D. M., farmer, Gedney Marsh.
Cooper, Fred, farmer, Fen.
Cooper, Wm., smallholder, Gedney Marsh.
Darnes, Chas, farmer, Rampart.
Drew, Jn. Thos., smallholder, Broadgate.
Dring, Alfd. Wm., smallholder, Broadgate.
Dring, Herbert Matthew, fruit grower, Fen.
Dring, John Thomas, smallholder, Fen.
Drury, Wm., fruit grower, Gedney Dyke.
Everard, Edwd, cottage farmer, Gedney Marsh.
Fines, Albt. E., farmer, Gedney Marsh.
Fines, Jn. A., farmer, Gedney Marsh.
Franks, Albt., fruit grower, Church End.
Grant, Edith (Mrs.), tobacconist.
Garner, T. W., farmer, Church Farm.
Green Man Inn (Thos. Hannah), Church End.
Hammond, Walter, farmer & cattle food & manure agents, Gedney Marsh.
Harrison, Rd. T., smallholder, Gedney Marsh.
Hix & Bateman, potato growers, Crown Farm, Gedney Marsh.
Holbourn, George Robert, farmer, Gedney Marsh.
Hollingsworth, Ernest Sidney, farmer, Gedney Marsh.
Howman, George, tobacconist, Victory Hall.
Hunt, Fredk., smallholder, Church End.
Jackson, Chas. F., Cycle Agent, Gedney Dyke.
Jackson, Saml., carpenter, Gedney Dyke.

Jones & Edgley, smallholders, Gedney Marsh.
Jones, Edwd., smallholder, Common.
Kent, Wm., Blacksmith.
Kent, Jsph., Blacksmith, Gedney Marsh.
Kitchen, Wm., farmer, Brook House, Gedney Marsh.
Lynn & Parratt, Cycle Agents.
Mackman, Eliz. (Mrs.), smallholder, Broadgate.
Munson, John William, millers (steam & wind) & agricultural machine owners, Gedney Dyke.
Munson, Misses. Bakers, Gedney Dyke.
Munson, Albt. Hy., farmer, Mill House, Gedney Dyke.
Munson, George, farmer, Garnsgate.
Munson, James Arthur, farmer, Common.
Munson, Jn. Wm., agricultural machine owner, Gedney Dyke.
Neve, Charles Henry, fruit grower.
Norman, Jn. Albt., shopkeeper, Gedney Dyke.
Palmer, Alfred, farm bailiff to W. K. Wright & Son, Red House. Gedney Marsh.
Parratt, Hy. Ernest, Dairyman, Broadgate.
Parsons, Martha J. (Mrs.), farmer, Middle Drove.
Piggins, Fred & Son, grocers, drapers & general dealers & post office, Gedney Dyke.
Pipe & Glass Inn (Wm. Fras. Cannon), Gedney Dyke.
Portor, Alfd., farmer, Boatmere, Gedney Marsh.
Redhead, Susannah (Mrs.), smallholder, Gedney Dyke.
Red Lion Public House (Alfd. Clark), The Rampart.
Schofield, Emma (Mrs.), shopkeeper.
Shepherd, Chas., smallholder, Broadgate.
Simpson, Thos., farmer, Boatmere, Gedney Marsh.
Snasdale, Geo., cottage farmer, Gedney Marsh.
Steel, Frank, farmer, Brook House, Gedney Marsh.
Tagg, Wm., fruit grower, Daffodil Nurseries.
Thacker, Jn. Wm., market gardener, Station Road.
Thorpe, Percy Harold, smallholder, Hurford Gate.
Walsham, Jas., farmer, Clark's Hill, Gedney Fen.
Whatling, Saml., butcher, Gedney Dyke.
Wilkinson, Frank, farmer, Fen.
Wilkinson, Fred, farm foreman to J. E. Johnson Esq., Common.
Wilson, Arth., farmer, Gedney Dyke.

Dawsmere

Ashford, Charles A., blacksmith.
Caudwell, Geo. Farmer, Red House.
French Eliza (Mrs.), shopkeeper & post office.
Slator Albt., farmer.
Thompson, Jn. Hy., farmer.

Red Lion, Inn, Gedney (photographed 1948).

February 1908.

Mr. William Thacker of Gedney, Lincolnshire, a veteran drover of cattle in "the good old days". He is now nearly ninety years of age, and during the past 42 years has been a licence-holder 29 years at the Black Lion Inn, Gedney, and 13 years as landlord of the Greyhound, Sutton Bridge. "Old Bill Thacker," as he is familiarly known, is probably the only drover of his class in the southern part of Lincolnshire. Scores and scores of times Thacker has passed through the Eastern Counties, sixty and seventy years ago, with large droves of cattle, on his way to Norwich, London, and other markets.

The journey to London occupied about four or five days, and the drover or "topsman" as he was known, having got rid of his stock, would walk back into Lincolnshire, and pick up another drove and return to London, Norwich, or some other centre again.

"Bill Thacker" was brought from Norfolk into Lincolnshire as a child, and commenced driving when but a lad.

It was no uncommon thing for a drover in those days to have the care of 5000 or 6000 sheep, and 300 cattle, for ten or twelve days.

Bill Thacker, of Gedney, Lincs.

Gedney Post Mill.

There does not appear to be any evidence as to when Gedney Post Mill was built, but it was referred to as an "old mill" when the last person took over the occupancy. The last occupant was Mr. Herbert Petch of Holbeach. Herbert married his wife Eliza Jane on Christmas Day 1898, and for a short time after their marriage Mr. Petch worked as a baker at Market Rasen and Long Sutton, and afterwards at Gedney where he took over the business at the old post mill. Whilst there he met with an accident on the Coronation Day of King Edward VII, losing part of his index finger on the right hand. They worked hard in this business for nearly 20 years. After eight years there the old post mill was demolished in 1909.

Whilst at Gedney, Herbert Petch was closely connected with public work being a representative on the rural council, a member of Gedney Parish Council, and on the Board of Guardians.

Gedney Post Mill, demolished 1909, from a sketch by G. W. Bailey, Spalding Gentlemen's Society collection.

Photograph of the Old Post Mill at Gedney before it was demolished in 1909.

80

The Reclamation of Land in Gedney Marsh

For several hundred years a battle has been fought to reclaim land from the sea, especially in the marshland areas around the Wash. If successful the prize is very fertile land which in turn gives high yielding crops. The newscuttings of the 1870s relate to one attempt at reclaiming over 300 acres of land in Gedney Marsh.

November 1871.

On Friday last an influential meeting of the holders of common rights in the parish of Gedney (the Rev. Geo. Rogers in the chair) was held at the Bull Inn, Long Sutton, to consider the desirability of inclosing the Sea-marsh. The opinion of those present was in favour of immediate inclosure; but it was resolved that Mr. Edw. Millington should send his report and a plan of the undertaking to each of the proprietors in order to obtain the opinion of all interested.

Eventually after due consideration an application by the Lords and commoners of Gedney was put before Parliament for consent to go ahead with the appropriate works.

Copies of the proposed Bill were deposited in the Private Bill Office of the House of Commons by the 21st December 1872.

The progress through Parliament was fairly rapid and by February 1873 the press reported that:–"The Gedney Commoners Enclosure Bill and the Moulton Salt Marshes Enclosure Bill have been read a second time in the House of Lords.

Following the Bill being passed by Parliament the following notice was published:–

GEDNEY ENCLOSURE

Notice is hereby given, that in pursuance of "The Gedney Enclosure Act, 1873" a PUBLIC MEETING of the Lords of the several Manors of Gedney Abbott, Gedney Burlion, Gedney Pawlett, and Gedney Welby, in Gedney, in the county of Lincoln; and the owners and Proprietors of ancient commonable Messauges and Tofts in the parish of Gedney aforesaid, and hamlet of Gedney Hill, in the same county, or such other persons as would on any division and enclosure of the Gedney Commoner's Lands and Sands in the said Act, mentioned be entitled to allotments of land in respect of the said Messuages and Tofts, or in respect of any sale or disposition made of the rights of common belonging thereto respectively (in the said Act and hereinafter referred to as the Lords and Commoners), will be held at the Black Lion Inn, in Gedney aforesaid on the 5th day of January, 1874, at 12 o'clock at Noon, to consider the expediency of giving the consent of Lords and Commoners to the Embankment by the Delegates in the said Act mentioned of all or some part or parts of the land to be reclaimed under the authority of the said Act, and to the borrowing and taking up at Interest by the said Delegates of a Sum or Sums of Money for defraying the costs, charges, and expenses attending the obtaining and passing of the said Act, and the making of the several works to be executed, and the costs, charges and expenses of an incident to any Mortgage or Mortgages to be made by the said delegates under the authority of the said Act, and to carry such Resolution or Resolutions (if any), of the several matters aforesaid, as may be thought fit, at which Meeting the attendance of the Lords and Commoners by themselves, or their Agents, or Proxies appointed in writing, is requested.–Dated this 22nd day of December, 1873.

EDWARD MILLINGTON, & C.M. DERRY, Delegates

January 1874.

Black Lion Inn, Gedney, on the 5th inst., consent was given to the enclosure of the sea marsh, the frontage of that parish, consisting of about 300 acres of land, which is considered to be of superior quality. The embankment is expected to be completed in about six months from the commencement, which will be in a short time.

Gedney Salt Marsh.

The contract for the bank for enclosing about 350 acres of this marsh from the sea has been obtained by Mr. Geo. Clarke, surveyor, of Long Sutton, Mr. T. Clarke, London, and Mr G. T. Adcock, Oxford, and the work will be commenced as soon as materials can be obtained.

Man's efforts at controlling the tide appear to have been about as good as "King Canute's" as the press report of 20th October 1874 illustrates.

October 20th, 1874.

BREAKING OF GEDNEY EMBANKMENT.–On Monday morning last there was an unusually high tide, and the new sea embankment, enclosing about 340 acres, opposite Gedney Drove End, gave way in several places, and the entire marsh was soon inundated to a considerable depth with water. Where the large creeks had been stopped appears to have been the places that first failed. The rush of water when the bank broke, came with a roar, which was heard a considerable distance. On Tuesday the tides were smaller, and not much further damage was effected. At that time a great part of the embankment was injured, and there were at least fifteen open breaks of from five to fifty yards wide.

Snippets from what the papers used to say.

December 1828.

In the night of Wednesday, Mr. Derry, of Gedney, had his premises robbed of 40 fowls, a duck, and a turkey; – on Friday night last, some villains slaughtered a shearling sheep belonging to Mr. Stevely, blacksmith of Whaplode and took away only one of the legs, leaving the remainder of the carcase unskinned in the field; – and on Tuesday night, Mr. Barker of Holbeach, had a sheep slaughtered, and the whole of the carcase stolen. – Considerable rewards have been offered for discovery of the offenders.

January 1896.

The new Vicar of Gedney (the Rev. Canon Atkinson) has been inducted by the Bishop, and on Sunday he read himself in.

June 1896.

Gedney Church. – It is reported that Canon Atkinson is about to start an undertaking to restore the beautiful parish church of Gedney, one of the finest churches for many miles around. The congregations at Gedney have greatly increased.

June 1893.

Fen Farmers and the Potato Trade. – A correspondent writes to the Daily News. – Owing to the state of the potato market in London some extraordinary transactions have just taken place with some of the Fen farmers. Mr. Alderman, a Thorney farmer, sent 35 tons of potatoes of good sample to a London salesman, and after carriage and commission &c., had been deducted, the amount remaining for the grower was 12s. 10d, or less than 4½d. per ton. For five tons a farm at Fleet, near Spalding, secured 7s. 9d., and Mr. Banks, a prominent farmer of Gedney Dyke, near Spalding, forwarded two trucks of potatoes, and he was informed by the salesman that he was indebted to him in the sum of 7d. on the transaction, the amount not covering cost of carriage and expenses.

September 1872.

Most of the Members of the Society of Friends have either left the neighbourhood of Gedney or are dead, and in consequence their chapel, situated near Church End, has been closed for some time; but we understand that it has been engaged by the Primitive Methodists, who we doubt not will successfully exert themselves to form a cause.

October 1872.

The friends' meeting house at Gedney was re-opened last week by the Primitive Methodists. The Rev. V. E. Storr, of Holbeach, preached on Sunday – and on Monday a public tea was gratuitously provided; after which a public meeting was held, when suitable addresses were delivered. The congregations at all the services were good, and the proceeds amounted to about £5.00.

June 1872

The Anniversary services of the Wesleyan Sunday School at Gedney Dyke were held on Sunday and Monday. On Sunday two sermons were preached in Mr. Harrison's barn, by Mr. J. W. Boor, of Whaplode Drove, and on Money the annual tea and public meeting took place. A rival anniversary, professedly emanating, however, from the same body, was held in a marquee near the chapel at the same time. Evidently it is indebted that the rising generation at Gedney Dyke shall no longer go uncared for, which augurs for the future a better and wiser state of things in the village than exists at present.

Gedney Dyke Windmill

Gedney Dyke windmill standing 68 feet high was built in 1836 for a Mr C. I. Rubbins. Being powered by six patent sails it continued working until 1942, and lost its sails in 1947 closely followed by the cap. The mill has eight floors and some of the machinery is still in place.

GEDNEY DYKE, Lincolnshire, near Long Sutton and Holbeach.
To MILLERS and Others.

HACKWORTH and ABBOTT are honoured with instructions to SELL by AUCTION, at the Chequers Hotel, Holbeach, on Thursday, July 14th, 1892, at 3 for 4 p.m., all that well-built Brick Tower Six-sail WINDMILL, with eight floors, driving four pairs of French stones, Dressing Machine, &c., with Yards and well built Brick and Slated BUILDINGS, formerly used as Steam Mill &c., with Yards and brick and slated Stables with granaries over Coach-house, Harness-houses, 2 Horse Hovels with Yards for 4 horses each, Piggeries, Eaggon Hovel, Gear House, and other buildings.

Also all that very desirable and commodious Brick and Slated RESIDENCE, containing 7 bedrooms, w.c., drawing-room, dining-room, kitchen, pantry, store-room, scullery, 2 cellars, large walled-in Garden, Lawns, Orchard, and Kitchen Gardens, and 2 pieces of excellent pasture Land adjoining, situate in the centre of the village, and containing 3A.3R.32P. (more or less).

The Estate is Freehold.
Further particulars will be duly published, or they may be had upon application to the Auctioneers, Holbeach and Spalding; to Messrs. Abbott and Co., Land Agents, &c., 33 King William Street, London, E.C.; or to
J. HARRISON, Esq., Solicitor,
179, Bermondsey Street, London, S.E.

August 28th, 1904.

Gedney Marsh-Stack Fire: – A fire broke out at midday on Sunday in the yard of Mr R. Beba, at Black Barn, in Gedney Marsh, near Long Sutton, and a stack of hay and one of straw were destroyed. The Long Sutton Fire Brigade was sent for, but owing to the lack of water could do very little. The only water obtainable was from a pit three fields off, but this pit was so low and thick with mud that although water was brought in a water cart and poured into a tank the engine could not draw it, owing to its thick state. There were a large number of willing helpers, who worked to keep the fire from reaching the other stacks and the farm buildings, and in this they succeeded. The damage is estimated at £60, which is covered by insurance. It is supposed the fire was caused by children playing with matches in the stackyard.

December 1828.

As Mr. Harvey of Gedney Marsh, was returning home from Wisbech market on Saturday night last, he met with a serious accident, a few yards from Lockings Holt Bar. On arriving at the gate, about eleven o'clock, he procured a candle for the purpose of lighting up the lamps on his gig, and it is supposed that his horse, a spirited animal took fright at them, as he immediately began to plunge, and running the gig into a ditch, fell, and broke his neck. – Mr. H. providently escaped without personal injury.

November 26th, 1899.

Gedney. – Fire: The Long Sutton Fire Brigade was called out on Monday afternoon last to a fire upon the farm of Mr. James Tyler, at Boatmere, in Gedney Marsh. There were seven large stacks of straw consumed, and fourteen pigs were burnt. There was a plentiful supply of water, which enabled the brigade to keep the fire under control and thus save some large and commodious farm buildings. The brigade had to stay the whole of Monday night. Mr. Tyler is fully insured.

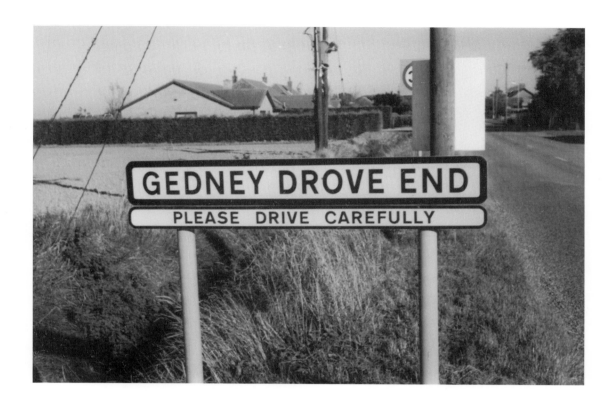

Gedney Drove End with Dawsmere

Gedney Drove End and Gedney Dawsmere are rather unusual as they are really two adjoining localities creating one village, but each locality retaining its own name. The parish is the parish of Gedney Drove End, but the church is in Gedney Dawsmere.

Kelly's Directory of Lincolnshire for the year 1885 calls them "Drove End including Dawsmere" and states that services at Drove End were held in an old Wesleyan Chapel by the Vicar of Christ Church, Dawsmere. The village of Dawsmere was created in the 1850s by two brothers, Edward and Charles Cardwell who bought about 3,000 acres of land in Gedney and Holbeach Marsh in 1852. Prior to that time the area was known as "The Marsh". The name Dawsmere was arrived at, because a creek, so named, flowed from the Wash through the locality.

Gedney Drove End situated about 1 1/2 miles from Dawsmere was at that time nothing more than a collection of small dwellings, some no more than hovels, with no houses of any decent size anywhere close by. These dwellings were occupied by people who were very poor, and many unemployed. The Cardwell brothers village consisted of cottages that were built in pairs, a general shop with buildings, and blacksmith and joiners workshops. There was a Church of England School, recorded as "Gedney Drove End School". Besides this the brothers provided a parsonage, and a site to build the church, together with a large contribution towards the cost of building.

Christ Church,
Gedney Dawsmere
(Photographed 1998).

The Parish of Gedney Drove End and Dawsmere.

Until the year 1856 Gedney Drove End was contained within the parish of Gedney. In that year the new ecclesiastical parish was formed. The newspaper reports of August 1869 and April 1870 take up the story.

August 1869.

Gedney Drove End New Church. – The ecclesiastical district of Drove End was formed in the year 1856, out of the large parish of Gedney, and a clergyman appointed to minister it, but up to the present time the inhabitants have had to meet for public worship in the National schoolroom of the district. It was the anxious wish of the late incumbent, the Rev. W. G. Patchell, to build a church towards which he obtained several large subscriptions; but he was promoted by the late Bishop to another living before he accomplished the work. All arrangements have now been made for building the church, and on Sunday evening last the foundation stone was laid. A form of prayer compiled for the purpose was read by the Rev. R. Powell, the incumbent; and in the absence of the Right Hon. Edward Cardwell, M.P., who had kindly consented to lay the stone, but was prevented from being present by his Parliamentary and official duties, the stone was laid by Mrs. Powell. There was a large attendance of the people of the district, and after the ceremony the usual evening service was held in the school-room, when an appropriate and eloquent sermon was preached by the Rev. J. Jerram, Rector of Fleet. It is hoped that the building, of which Mr. Christian is the architect and Mr. Bennett, of Lynn, the builder, will be completed by the end of the year.

April 1870.

Gedney Marsh. – On Thursday, the 7th inst., the New Church for the Gedney Drove End district, called Christ Church, was consecrated by the Lord Bishop of Lincoln. The weather was all that could be desired, and a very large company assembled. The prayers were read by the Rev. R. Powell, the incumbent, and Rev. W. G. Patchell, of Holbeach St. John's; the first lesson by the Rev. Edward Leigh Bennett, of Long Sutton; the second lesson by the Rev. J. Jerram, of Fleet; the Epistle by the Rev. A. Brooke, of Holbeach; and the Gospel by the Rev. T. D. Young, of Sutton Bridge. The very eloquent and earnest sermon was preached by the Bishop, who took for his text Haggai, 2nd chapter, 2nd verse. During the service the Rev. W. J. Clarke was instituted to the vicarage of St. Luke's, in Holbeach Marsh, and took the customary oaths. Mr. Richard Winter of Long Sutton, presided at the harmonium. After the consecration ceremony a capital lunch was provided by Mr. N. Leggett, of Long Sutton, in the school-room, at which about 100 sat down, under the presidency of Charles Cardwell, Esq. A public tea, supplied by Mr. Lee, of Cawnmer, was afterwards held, when again the room was well filled, and a very enjoyable evening spent by all. The church is erected upon the estate of the Right Hon. Edward Cardwell, M.P., and Charles Cardwell, Esq., and will seat upwards of 200 persons. It is built of local bricks, with ornamental red arches and quoins, from the builder's Clenchwarton bricks, and relieved with a few lines of stone. The whole structure is of a simple but effective character, internally being of brick only, and not plastered. The length of the church is about 70 feet, and 25 feet wide. There is a porch and vestry, but the vestry may be used for children, by drawing back a large curtain, now before it as a screen. The east end is an apse of the whole width of the church, groined with wood ribs, and plaster ceiling. The roof is of a high pitch, with cross-braced rafters, which are all seen, giving a lofty internal effect. The seats, which are of fir, stained and varnished, are of the character known as Pugin seats, or benches; but in the chancel proper, which is separated by a bold wood arch, the seats are of a more ornamental character. The floors of the aisles of the nave are laid with Staffordshire tiles, the chancel with Minton's plain and eucastic tiles, in patterns. There is an appropriate font, a pulpit upon a stone base, a prayer desk and lectern, and oak altar rail with ornamental iron painted and gilded standards, an oak altar table enriched by a handsome crimson cloth; the doors also are of oak, with suitable ornamental scroll hinges. Over the chancel arch there is a bell turret, with a spire, forming a conspicuous and picturesque object among the few trees that surround the church. This is one of the four churches that have lately been built in the Marsh of this district.

Mr. Bennett, of Lynn, was the builder, and Mr. Christian, of Whitehall Place, London, the archietect. The cost of Christ Church is £1,200.

Edward Cardwell, Viscount – Landowner in Gedney Marsh.

Cardwell, Edward, Viscount (1813-1886), statesman, born 24th July 1813, was the son of John Cardwell, a Liverpool merchant. He was educated at Winchester and at Balliol College, Oxford, of which he became scholar and fellow. At Oxford he took a first class, both in classics and mathematics, in 1835. He married in 1838, Annie, youngest daughter of Charles Stuart Parker of Fairlie, Ayrshire.

Among his contemporaries, or those who were nearly his contemporaries, at the university were several members of the special group of statesmen to which he afterwards belonged – Mr. Gladstone, Mr. Robert Lowe, Mr. Sidney Herbert, Mr. Roundell Palmer, and the Duke of Newcastle. He was called to the bar at the Inner Temple in 1838; but he soon turned from the law to public life, and entered the House of Commons as a member for Clitheroe in 1842. In 1845 he was made Secretary to the Treasury.

In 1847 he was elected for Liverpool, but lost his seat in 1852, in consequence of his having voted for the repeal of the navigation laws, and was afterwards elected for the City of Oxford. The Peelites having gradually gravitated towards the Whigs, in 1852 the coalition government of Lord Aberdeen was formed and Cardwell became President of the Board of Trade.

In 1859 Cardwell became Secretary for Ireland with a seat in the Cabinet, and in 1861 he exchanged it for the Chancellorship of the Duchy of Lancaster. In 1864 he was transferred to the Secretaryship for the Colonies.

Under Mr. Gladstone, in 1868, Cardwell became Secretary for War.

On the resignation of the Gladstone ministry in 1874 he was called to the House of Lords as Viscount Cardwell of Ellerbeck.

He died, after a very lingering illness, at Villa Como, Torquay, on 15th February, 1886 and was buried in the cemetery of Highgate.

Viscount Cardwell left no children and in consequence the peerage became extinct upon his death.

Viscount Cardwell's life was almost fully taken up with politics and the running of the estate in Gedney Marsh was left to his brother Charles with whom he was in joint ownership.

Trades and Business People in Gedney Drove End in 1937.

Ball, Jn., cottage farmer.
Banks, B. Y. & A. E., farmers.
Barnes, H. Wm., smallholder.
Barnes, Tom, snr., cottage farmer.
Beba Bros., farmers.
Black Bull Inn (Reginald T. Link).
Blackbourne, Frederick, cottage farmer.
Blackbourne, Harry, smallholder.
Clement, Horace R., fried fish dealer.
Croplet, Geo., butcher.
Cross Bros. (Long Sutton) Ltd., grocers.
Davy Fredk. Jas., shopkeeper.
Disdell, Marshall, cottage farmer.
Everard, Fred Jn., cottage farmer.
Fines, Chas. Sen., farmer.
Fines, Edward, cottage farmer.
Foreman, Robert James, butcher.
Grimmer, Chas. & Jas. S., farmers.
Halifax, Esra, fisherman.
Harrison, Wm., carpenter.
Hutchinson, Rt., farmer.
Hutchinson, Timothy Barron, farmer.
Luke, Jn., insurance agent.
Mackman, Jas., farmer.
Martin, Annie (Mrs.), shopkeeper.
New Inn (Thos. Allen),
Palmer, Noel, poultry farmer.
Payne, Wm., farmer.
Piccaver, J. T. & H., farmers.
Porter, Thomas, blacksmith.
Read, Harold Wm., M.R.C.S.Eng., L.R.C.P.Lond., physician and surgeon (attends Tues, Thurs & Sat at noon).
Reeder, Hy. Herbt., baker.

Rising Sun Inn (Jn. Rt. Twaite).
Ship Inn (Albt. E. Fisher).
Slator, Frederick, smallholder.
Stebbings, Geo. Hy., grocer.
Wain, Harry, boot & shoe repairer.
Walker, Arth. & Jas., farmers.
Wheatsheaf Public House (Chas. Leonard Cliff).

In the 19th century the question of decent drinking water was a serious matter throughout the whole country, and Gedney Drove End was no exception as the following newscutting of April 1877 illustrates.

April 1877.
To the Editor.
Sir, – On reading your Parliamentary Report of last week, I was sorry to see Mr. A. Brown's motion for the compulsory supply of pure water in our villages negatived by 64 to 37. If the measure is not needed anywhere else in the country, it is sorely needed at Gedney Drove End. Very few houses in the village have a good supply of water, and the majority of the people have to drink water taken from a pit in the centre of the village, which is open to the highway and into which horses are taken to wash and cattle to drink, and which in summer becomes so polluted that it is not fit for the beasts to drink, much less a human being. I think with Mr. Brown that no house should be permitted to be inhabited without an adequate supply of pure water. It is a shame that poor people have to pay large rents for places scarcely fit for pig-sties or dog-kennels, having only one sleeping room for themselves and six or eight children, and minus water, being thus deprived of two things essential to health – pure air and water. Surely if philanthropy could not interfer common charity demands something better for the
INHABITANTS of DROVE END.

The following edition printed another letter again illustrating the very poor living conditions:–

Gedney Drove End.
Sir, – A correspondent in your last issue has drawn attention to the sanitary conditions of his village. He has certainly not written too soon on the subject, for a worse state of things cannot exist. There are in this place houses so-called, but as your correspondent states they are not fit for "pig-sties or dog-kennels", and these places (built of mud and thatch) contain large families huddled together in one living and one sleeping room. In one, I am told, twelve persons reside, and these persons have no water supply except that afforded by a hole in the garden, into which, through the porous nature of the soil, is filtered the sewage and contents of privies; or that obtained from the village pond, the colour of which last summer was as "green as a grass field." It is time boards of health were established and sanitary reforms carried out in our villages. Trusting that it will be so shortly, and that Drove End will obtain the benefits they secure.
I am yours, OBSERVER.

Following this letter was another one informing the inhabitants that the Public Health Act, 1875, gives them power to obtain a supply of drinking water by their calling upon their district (i.e. Holbeach Union) Sanitary Authority to do its duty.

No doubt this is what eventually led to Gedney Drove End and other like villages being supplied with a proper pure water supply.

January 1873.
Gedney Drove End. – The annual tea drinking in aid of the clothing club at Gedney Drove End was held in the parish schoolroom at Dawsmere on the 18th inst., when a very large number of the neighbouring community attended. A good sum was realized. The bazaar and Christmas tree, which were held in the same place, were also a great success. The chair was taken by the Vicar, and the evening concluded by a musical

entertainment and readings. During the evening the Chairman in a short and complimentary address, presented the schoolmaster, Mr. Riggott, with a handsome gold watch, as a mark of esteem from himself and neighbours. The music and readings were fully appreciated by an attentive audience, and altogether the evening passed off most happily. The following ladies kindly gave trays on the occasion: Mrs. Foxton, Mrs. Parkinson, Mrs. Brown, Mrs. Main, Mrs. Naylor, Mrs. Dean, Mrs. Dobson, Mrs. Lee, Mrs. Lamin, and the Misses Darley and White. The Rev. J. H. Jowitt, Rev. W. H. James, and the Rev. J. E. B. Welburn assisted in the readings. The musical part was well sustained by the Misses Farley, Butler, Hardstaff, Sewell, Holborn, Goose, and Foxton, assisted by Mr. Riggott.

On Tuesday the 7th inst. there was a meeting at Gedney Drove End to celebrate the extinction of the debt on the Primitive Methodist Chapel. A Christmas tree and "pie" were exhibited, and well patronized. The tea was provided, the tables being filled with visitors three times over. In the evening a musical entertainment entitled "Pilgrim's Progress," was given, the Rev. J. Sheale giving the connective readings, and the Rev. E. Storr presiding at the harmonium. The chapel was literally packed. Considerably more than the remaining debt was realized, and the surplus will probably be the nucleus of a fund for the erection of a new chapel, which is very much needed.

April 1893.

GEDNEY DROVE END
SALE of Valuable LIVE and DEAD FARMING STOCK.

S. and G. Kingston have received instructions
from Mr. JOHN DRING to SELL on Wednesday, April 4th, the whole of his valuable Live and Dead
Farming STOCK and effects, in consequence
of his quitting the farm.
Auction Offices, Spalding and Holbeach.

August 1828.

In the night of Friday the 8th inst. some villains effected an entrance into the premises of Mrs. Reams, who keeps a small public house, called the Wheat Sheaf, and also a little grocer's shop, at Gedney Drove End. They made a hole in the outer wall of the shop and carried off goods to the amount of about £11. Suspicion rests upon four of the labouring bankers employed at Sutton Wash; as four men of that description were seen hovering about Mrs. Reams' premises, and in answer to an enquiry from a person passing by 'What was their business there', they said they wanted lodgings, but the family were in bed; he directed them to another public house a short distance off, which was open, and they went towards it, but made no application for lodgings there. What adds to Mrs. Reams' calamity is the circumstances of her husband being buried the same afternoon.

February 1826.

On Wednesday the 15th inst., at Gedney, Mr. William Housley in his 56th year, formerly landlord of the Bell public-house at that place. He for a long time had been subject to the gout at times, but his death was the effect of a paralytic attack a fortnight previous. He was much respected, and bore his afflictions with great patience and submission to the will of God.

May 1901.

Farmers get Salvage. – Over a hundred large logs of pitch pine timber have been washed up on the marshes at Gedney Drove End. The local farmers have had a busy time securing the wood. Such a haul has never before been made upon these marshes. The coastguard authorities, however, soon learned of the occurrence, and a chief officer promptly arrived at the scene in a motor car and claimed the whole. The farmers are to receive some allowance for salavage, a rare item to appear in farm receipts.

June 1896.

The Rev. G. F. H. Foxton, Vicar of Gedney Drove End, near Holbeach, Lincolnshire, was found dead in a yard attached to the Vicarage on Friday afternoon, June 12th. At an inquest, on Saturday, a verdict of "Death from heat apoplexy" was returned. Deceased was 70 years of age. He graduated at St. John's College, Cambridge, in 1847, and was ordained in the following year to the curacy of Bromsgrove: from 1858 to 1871 he was Incumbent of St. Andrew's Fasque, N.B., and in the latter year was appointed Vicar of Gedney Drove End.

July 1870.

On Wednesday the 13th inst. the members of the New Friendly Society at Gedney Drove End held their 15th anniversary. The members met for business at 9 o'clock and at 11 paraded to Dawsmere church, headed by the Long Sutton brass band, where an appropriate sermon was preached by the Rev. J. O'Reilly, of Fleet. After service they returned to Gedney Drove End, and partook of a capital dinner provided by host Clarke, of the Wheat Sheaf Inn. Afterwards the members marched round the village, the band stopping to play at the principle houses. They then returned, and passed the remainder of the day in a very quiet and enjoyable manner. The club is now in a very prosperous state, there being upwards of 50 members on the books and a balance in hand of over £100.

"Shep White's"

North-West of Gedney Drove End on the edge of the marsh is the remote area known as "Shep White's". This is so called after an old shepherd named Woodruff White, but better known as "Shep White". He lived in a small cottage beneath the sea wall at the sea access point near Thimbleby House, with his large family of six girls and four boys. At high tide sea water would splash over the wall and onto the front steps of Shep's cottage, but it was never known to flow over the wall, and flood the cottage. On the marshes in South Holland the Marsh Shepherd was at one time annually appointed, their wages being paid by a rate of 1s. 6d. for each horse and neat beast and 3d for each sheep grazed onthe marsh.

Shep left his remote home and moved to Penny Hill, Holbeach about 1905 where he had a smallholding. His cottage on the edge of the marsh was pulled down in the late 1950s or early '60s.

This photograph shows the site where "Shep White's" cottage once stood on the left hand side of the road. The road stands on the top of what used to be the sea bank, and to the right of this was the sea marsh. When "Shep" lived here the sea at high tide used to come up to this bank. Today another bank has been built further onto the marsh, so the tide no longer comes in as far as this.

Shep White with his wife and family photographed beneath the sea wall close to his cottage in about 1894.
Back Row.–Left to Right: Henry, Kate, Nell, Emma, Luce, Edward (Ned).
Centre: Woodruff ("Shep"), Jane.
Front Row.–Left to right: Maud, Herbert, Woodruff, Jane (Fanny).

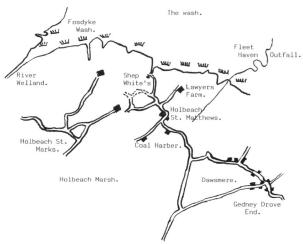

Holbeach Marsh. Showing the area known to local people as "Shep White's" being where the well-known shepherd Woodruff White lived in a remote cottage on the edge of the sea marsh.

The marsh at "Shep White's" in 1999. At high tide the sea flows up the creeks and covers the area. Anybody on the marsh when the tide comes in can easily be cut off. People who are not familiar with the area should treat the marsh with great caution.

Gedney Hill

Gedney Hill

Gedney Hill is a sprawling village and parish in the fens, near to the borders with Cambridgeshire. The main occupation of the area is farming as the soil is very rich and fertile being part clay and part fine loam, with subsoil of clay and silt.

The church of the Holy Trinity, standing on rising ground, is an ancient building of stone, consisting of chancel, nave, aisles, south porch, and an embattled western tower, about 52 feet in height, containing a clock and five bells. This church is a somewhat remarkable structure. There are but three or four churches of similar construction in England. The nave roof is supported by massive octagonal oak pillars, upon which runs a very heavy oak horizontal plate, and against which, on either side of the building, the spars of the north and south aisle roofs rest. The chancel is now much shorter than it has been at some former period. Remains of two ancient doorways and an east window of the 14th century were found during restoration in 1875.

Like all ancient buildings restoration has to be undertaken from time to time, but in 1875 major works had to be undertaken which was completed by the September of that year.

The following notification was published in the local newspaper informing the parishioners of the church re-opening:–

GEDNEY HILL.

The Church of the Holy Trinity will be REOPENED
on Thursday, Sept. 16th. Services at 8 and
11 a.m. and at 6.30 p.m. Sermons by the
BISHOP SUFFRAGAN of NOTTINGHAM and the Rev
CANON HEMMANS, Rural Dean, Vicar of Holbeach.
Public Luncheon at 1.15 p.m.–Consecration
of additional Ground to Churchyard at 3.15 p.m.
All Offerings in aid of the Restoration Fund.

Gedney Hill, 6th Sept, 1875.

Re-opening of Gedney Hill Church.

The Church of the Holy Trinity Gedney Hill, was re-opened on Thursday, the 16th September 1875 with great rejoicings. At an early hour the village was astir, the church bells rang forth their merry peal, and flags were flowing gracefully from many a window, and all was excitement and bustle for the great event of the day. The opening services commenced with Evensong on Wednesday, at which there was a good congregation. The eight o'clock celebration on Thursday was attended by about 40 communicants, the Vicar being assisted in the service by the Rev. C. U. Kingston, of Sutton St. Edmund. The choir was in surplices, and the service was semi-choral. The Bishop Suffragan arrived at the vicarage at ten, and at eleven a procession was formed consisting of the surpliced portion of the choir, the Rev. Canon Moore (Spalding), Rev. Canon Hemmans (Holbeach), Rev. E. L. Bennett (Long Sutton), Rev. C. U. Kingston (St. Edmund), Rev. W. Carpenter (Guyhurn), Rev. W. H. Patchell (Tathwell), Rev. R. Hollis (Whaplode Drove), Rev. G. Clark (Gedney Hill), and the Bishop. The procession thus formed marched round the outside of the church, singing a hymn, entering by the south porch, and so up the centre aisle to the chancel. The Vicar said prayers, and lessons were read by Rev. Canon Moore and Rev. Canon Hemmans. The communion office was taken by the Bishop, and the Bishop also preached the sermon which was listened to with the greatest attention by the congregation which filled the church to the very doors. After the sermon the offertory was collected, the sentences being read by the Rev. Canon Moore, interspersed with soft music from the harmonium at which the vicar's wife presided. Hymn 238 ("Ancient and Modern") was sung as a retrocessional most heartily, and with thrilling effect, the procession just emerging from the south door at its conclusion. The luncheon in the schoolroom was served by Mr. Harrison of Spalding, and was a very excellent order. The Vicar took the chair, supported by the Bishop, the Rev. Canon Moore, and the Rev. E. L. Bennett. Toasts were proposed and responded to amid general enthusiasm, especially the health of Miss Charington, who the Vicar announced had given £1,000 towards the Restoration Fund. The consecration of an additional piece of land to the churchyard cut the speeches rather short, the time fixed for it being 3.15, and the Bishop having to travel to Lincoln after it that night.

At the evening service again held that day the church was full to overflowing, many being unable to obtain seats. The Sermon was preached by the Rev. Canon Hemmans from the word "Freely ye have received, freely give." After the service the bells rang merrily again as the people were returning to their homes, and thus came to a close the most interesting day remembered in Gedney Hill. The offerings during the day amounted to £43.17s.7d., the Bishop of Lincoln sending a cheque for £5 being an ancient structure the church has been thoroughly restored under the superintendence of James Fowler, Esq., architect, of Louth, at a cost of £1,880.

Holy Trinity Church, Gedney Hill (Photographed 1999).

Inside Holy Trinity Church, Gedney Hill, showing the beautiful oak pillars and beams making the building very unusual.

A week after the re-opening of Gedney Hill church the following report was published giving a description of the building, and the various furnishings etc. that was donated to the glorification of this unusual village church.

The church of the Holy Trinity at Gedney Hill is a somewhat remarkable structure. There are but three or four churches of similar construction in England. The nave roof is supported by massive octagonal oak pillars, upon which runs a very heavy oak horizontal plate, and against which, on either side of the building, the spars of the north and south aisle roofs rest. The church has a massive tower rising to a height of nearly 60 feet. The chancel is now much shorter than it has been at some former period, remains of two ancient doorways and an east window of the 14th century work being found built up in the walls which were recently pulled down. A new vestry has been built on the south side of the chancel, and the chancel has been enriched by a very beautiful stained glass window, executed by Ward and Hughes of Soho, London, the gift of the present Vicar, his brother (Mr. Thos. Clark, of Wisbech St. Mary), and Miss Clark, in memory of their father, mother, and a brother, who all lie buried near the spot outside. The central light of the window represents the Crucifixion; the north side light, the Baptism of our Blessed Lord; the south side light, the descent of the Holy Ghost upon the Apostles; while in the two small lights above, the Birth and Ascension of our Saviour are beautifully delineated. The window is a very happy feature in the restored church. The gifts to the church have been both numerous and costly, chief of which are a solid silver Communion service, given by Mrs. S. L. Nussey and Miss Ellen Clark, of Leeds, cousins of the Vicar; the last named lady also worked and gave the two kneeling cushions on the dais. The fine linen Communion cloth is the gift of Mrs. Thos. Clark, of Wisbech St. Mary. The chalice veil and the bookmarks in the Service Book and in the Lectern Bible were the work and gift of Miss Bulmer of Spalding. The altar cloth, which is exceedingly rich and beautiful in design, was given by Miss Clark; and the long kneeling cushion on the altar step was worked by Mrs. Geo. Clark and Miss Bulmer. It is beautifully done; the design is the lily and the passion flower alternately, in medallions on blue ground, the space between being crimson, and it is bordered with small white crosses, grounded to   match the medallions. Two hassocks for use within the altar rail were given by the churchwarden, Mr. Richardson. A splendid carved oak alms dish was presented by S. L. Nussey of Leeds. The alms bags, four in number, were worked and given to the church by Miss Fanny Clark, of Liverpool, a cousin of the Vicar's. They are of crimson velvet, with emblematic design in front, worked in golden colours. The Service Book for the altar, and the Prayer Book for use in the desk, are the gift of Miss Clark. The Bible on the lectern was given by the Sunday School Children, and the carved oak alms chest by Mrs. Heys. Thus has the church been already enriched by many kind friends, and the opening services were marked by a most happy success.

Trades and Business People in Gedney Hill in 1937.

Baxter, Frederick, farmer.
Benson, Wm., motor garage, Hillsgate Garage.
Boor, Leonard, smallholder.
Bridgfoot, Annie (Mrs), farmer.
Bridgfoot, Arthur, farmer.
Buttery, Arth., haulage contractor.
Buttery, Frank, coal merchant.
Cooper, Rd., smallholder.
Coulam Bros., motor engineers.
Cross Keys Public House (Thos. Herbt. Johnson).
Dallaywaters, Jn. jun., wheelwright.
Dams, David James, smallholder & post office.
Dams, Mabel (Mrs.), registrar of births & deaths & vaccination officer for Gedney Hill sub-district.
Drakard, Arthur, farmer.
Drewery, Wm., farmer, Fleet Farm.

Duke's Head Public House (Adderley Cole Seaton).

Edwards, Rt., M.D., M.R.C.S.Eng., L.R.C.P.Lond. physcn. & Surgn.

Fisher, Arth. Edmund, farmer, Fleet Fen,

Fowler, Hrbt., farmer, Fleet Fen.

Fowler, Saml., smallholder.

Great Northern Hotel (Horace Tom Emery), French Drove Station.

Hankin, Ernest, grocer.

Harrison, Walter, farmer.

Henson, George, horse dealer, Fleet Fen.

Hurn, Roland, G., farmer, The Limes.

Johnson, Jn. Wm., smallholder, Fleet Fen.

King, Chas., farmer.

Langlet, Meads, farmer.

Leadbeater, Ernest Harry, smallholder.

Lincoln, Richard, poulterer.

Lynn, Robert & Walter, farmers.

Marshall, Geo.. & Sons, bakers.

Naylor, William, farmer.

Newell, Walter, joiner.

Noble, Walter, farmer.

Parkinson, Alfd. Wm., butcher.

Pell, Jas. Wltr., miller.

Peters, John, smallholder.

Red Lion Inn (Pashler Freeman).

Reed, Horace, chimney sweep, Fleet Fen.

Seaton, Albt., farmer.

Seaton, Arth. Wm., smallholder.

Seaton, Constance (Mrs.), bulb grower, Fleet Fen.

Deaton, Ellen (Mrs.), smallholder.

Seaton, Frank, smallholder.

Seaton, Henry, farmer.

Seaton, Thomas, farmer.

Simmons, Geo.. Wltr., blacksmith.

Stockdale, Percy, blacksmith.

Walton, Wm. Hy., dairyman, Fleet Fen.

Waterfall Isaac, smallholder.

Whiteman, Robert, farmer.

Snippets from what the papers used to say.

1811.

Wanted immediately, a resident Clergyman to serve the Perpetual Curacy of Gedney Hill, in the county of Lincoln. The salary is £70 a year, with a House and Two Acres of Land, rent free. The care of a School is attached to the Curacy. – References will be expected from the Applicants, who may address their letters (post paid) to Messrs. Bellamy, Girdlestone and Bellamy, attorneys, Wisbech.

June 1893.
Extraordinary assault on an Old Man. –

Matthew Cooper, Gedney Hill, carrier, was summoned for assaulting William Cooper, aged 76, also belonging to Gedney Hill. – Mr Percival appeared for complainant. – It appeared that defendant brought complainant in his carrier's cart to Spalding and back, and also conveyed some things of his to Spalding. When nearing home, it transpired that complainant had not sold his goods, and could not pay the fare of 1s. 3d, which was charged. The defendant then, it was alleged, tied him behind his cart whilst they went about half a mile, then he tied him to the wheel, and afterwards bound his hands, and left him in the van until he was liberated by Mr. Isaac Waterfall, who paid the money for him. – The defendant denied cruelty, and said he thought he could detain the complainant until the money was paid. It appeared that he was promised the money in a week's time. – The Bench characterised it as a gross case, and imposed a penalty of £3 and costs.

October 1893.

NORTH ROAD. GEDNEY HILL.
To be Sold by Auction.
By Messrs. Geo. Hall and Son.
Upon the premises of Mr. W. Ellmore (under distress for rent), on Wednesday, October 25th, 1893.
The whole of his Live and Dead FARMING STOCK,
Household FURNITURE, and Effects.

April 1894.

F. Cave, Baker, Gedney Hill, hereby gives notice, that all DEBTS owing to him must be paid on or before the 28th April. All debts outstanding after that date, except by agreement, will be entered in the County Court. 10th April, 1894.

July 1853.
Wedding.

Clark–Richardson. – On July 20th, 1853, at Gedney Hill church, by the Rev. Thomas Clark, father of the bridegroom, Thomas Clark, of Wisbech St. Mary, to Emma youngest daughter of J. S. Richardson, Esq., of Gedney Hill.

August 1902.

Clark. – At Gedney Hill Vicarage, on the 7th inst., after long and severe suffering, borne with great Christian fortitude and patience, Elizabeth wife of the Rev. George Clark, Vicar of the parish, in her 83rd year.

July 1901.

WHITSED-BATES. – At the Parish Church, Old Clee, on the 9th inst., by the Rev. Canon Hutchinson. William John Perkins Whitsed, of Grimsby, eldest son of Mr. William James Whitsed, Gedney Hill, Lincolnshire, to Florence Annie (Florrie), younger daughter of the late Mr. Henry Bates.

July 1902.
Preliminary Advertisement.
Gedney Hill.

Messrs. Saul will offer for sale by Public Auction, in September next, at the White Hart Hotel, Spalding, a FARMHOUSE and PREMISES, a DWELLING HOUSE, GARDEN, and ORCHARD, a DWELLING HOUSE and SHOP, Two COTTAGES, and about 46 acres of LAND, situate at Gedney Hill, in Lincolnshire, the property of the Representatives of the late Mrs. LOUISA BLAND.

Full particulars will shortly appear, and in the meantime apply to the Auctioneers; or T. B. Neale, Esq., solicitor, of 13, New Street, Leicester; or to CHAS ATTER, Solicitor, Stamford.

30th July, 1902.

Gedney

At the White Hart Hotel last week, Messrs Saul offered by auction some freehold and some copyhold houses and land in Gedney Hill and Gedney Drove End. A house and 5a. 3r. 33p. of pasture land in Gedney Hill was withdrawn at £440. A house and shop, copyhold, in Gedney Hill, was passed at £250. A house and four acres of land was passed at £280, and 9a. 1r. 8p. was also withdrawn at £420. Eleven and a half acres of pasture land was sold for £540 to Mr. Pipes, of Skegness; 9a. 3r. 4p. was withdrawn at £440; and 4a. 3r. was withdrawn at £220. Mr. T. B. Neale, of Leicester, and Mr. C. Atter, of Stamford, were the solicitors concerned for the vendors.

1903.

Sale. – At the Cross Keys Inn, Gedney Hill, on Tuesday evening. Messrs George Hall and Son of Spalding, offered for sale by auction a parcel of land situate in Fleet Fen, containing a little over 5 acres. The purchaser was the Rev. G. Clark, Vicar of Gedney Hill. Messrs. Calthrop and Leopold Harvey, were the solicitors concerned.

September 21st, 1895.

Fire Near Spalding. – At Gedney Hill, near Spalding, on Saturday night, a house and blacksmith's shop, occupied by Mr. W. Foster, was completely destroyed by fire. Some stacks in the vicinity were threatened, but despite a scarcity of water the fire was prevented from spreading. The fire appeared to have broken out in the roof, but was attributed by some to a beam passing through the chimney. There were plenty of helpers, and there were some narrow escapes from falling debris. The property was insured..

Gedney Hill Windmill.

Built in the early 1800's this mill had four patent sails, which drove three pairs of stones. The mill was driven by wind until the late 1920's when the sails were taken down. Until the 1940's the mill continued to be used, being powered by an engine.

June 1871.

Remarkable Dream – A Mr. Joseph Tilbury, of Gedney Hill, met with a fatal accident, close to his own door, a few weeks ago. His purse, supposed to have contained from £10 to £14, mysteriously disappeared at the time, and nothing was heard about the money until a few days ago, when a widow (a relative of the deceased) dreamed that the money was hid in a wheel track in a gateway. Strange to say the sum of £5.5s. was actually found in the exact spot indicated by the dreamer, and restored to the family, who hope that another dream may restore the rest of the money,

July 1872.

Gedney Hill Church Struck by Lightning – A terrifying storm of thunder, lightning and rain passed slowly over Gedney Hill between half-past four and six o'clock last Saturday afternoon. At the height of the storm the electric fluid struck the church tower on the western side, knocking out a large piece of the ornamental mullion of the west window and scattering the broken glass and debris about the interior of the church in all directions. The clock in the tower was stopped by the concussion, and the strong solid stone arch of the window was cracked as if it had been a sheet of glass. Fortunately no further damage was done, as the lightning did not appear to have actually entered the church, but glanced off in another direction. Some trees in the neighbourhood were also shivered by the lightning. The fall of rain was tremendous – nearly 4 inches in little more than an hour. The storm ultimately passed away in a N.N.E. direction.

March 28th, 1895.
Holbeach Petty Sessions.

Today (Thursday). – Before R. Merry (chairman), W. C. Worth, and B. L. Brittain, and the Rev. G. I. Leigh-Bennett.

Wm. James Whitsed, farmer, of Gedney Hill and a member of the Holland County Council, was summoned by James Waters Pawson, grocer, of Gedney Hill, for assaulting him at Gedney Hill on the 7th March, the day of the County Council elections. Mr. Ollard prosecuted, and Mr. Stiles defended. The complainant alleged that defendant threatened him, put his fist in his face, and shoved him off a path. The defence was an emphatic denial that anything took place, beyond the defendant warning the complainant not to circulate any misstatements about him. The Bench, after a few minutes' deliberation, dismissed the case, but made no order as to costs.

June 1914.

Heavy rain spoiled many of the annual garden fetes held in the district for various charities, but at Gedney Hill a combined village fete and sports day attracted 1,700 people.

February 9th, 1870.

Clark – A the Vicarage, Gedney Hill, on Monday last, in the 88th year of his age, the Rev. Thos. Clark for 57 years incumbent of that place.

The Rev. Thomas Clark was incumbent of Gedney Hill for nearly 58 years, having obtained the incumbency in March, 1812. At that time the living was worth £70 per annum. Mr. Clark was instrumental in getting it raised (by a decree of the Court of Chancery) to £100 per annum. At this it continued until 1860, when by another decree of the court, without any action at all on the part of Mr. Clark, it was raised to £120, which is its present value. For nearly 50 years he was master of the old Grammar School, which was superseded by the National School opened in 1860. He was a very remarkable man, having few of the infirmities of old age: most simple in his style of living, most temperate, and most regular. Latterly he could take no part in the church duties, on account of the failure in his eyesight. His youngest son has been his curate for nearly 14 years. He was a most kind and indulgent father, and an adviser and friend of very many. He retained most of his faculties up to the day of his death. He went to church in his usual health on Sunday morning, and ate his dinner afterwards, as usual; but in the afternoon he was seized with an apoplectic fit, and he was not conscious again, and never rallied in the least. He died, calmly, about 1/4 before 2 o'clock on Monday morning in the presence of his two sons and his daughter. He was a native of Westmorland, having been born in that county on July 10th, 1782, and he was consequently in his 88th year.

Gedney Hill post office about 1920.

Children gathered on the road near the Cross Keys public house.

North Road Gedney Hill with Benson's shop.

French Drove (Gedney Hill) Station.

Some two miles from Gedney Hill church, but still within the parish was French Drove station, situated on the Spalding to March railway line. According to the Ordnance Survey Map this was also known as Gedney Hill station, and certainly served the village folk, as a means of getting to town.

Farmers in times gone by used the railway to transport their crops, particularly sugar beet and potatoes.

Railway stations frequently had a hostelry of some sort to serve travellers and users of the station. The directory of 1885 gives a John Seaton as keeping a beer house at French Drove station, he was also listed as a coal dealer, which would be very convenient as the coal in those days was transported by rail. In 1885, a Mr. Edward Hoskin was the station master. By 1900 a Matthew Gott was listed as a beer retailer, and by 1919 it was George Johnson. The directory of 1933 lists Horace Tom Emery as a beer retailer at French Drove, but by 1937 the station appears to have gone up-market when the directory gives Horace Tom Emery as keeping the Great Northern Hotel at French Drove station.

The railway line from Spalding to March has long since closed down and traces of its existence are fast disappearing.

The Great Northern Hotel at French Drove station about 1950.

Gosberton

with Gosberton Cheal - Risegate & Westhorpe

Gosberton with Risegate, Clough and Westhorpe.

Pleasantly situated some six miles north of Spalding, and at the junction of roads from Boston and Donington is the village of Gosberton. Close by the hamlets and farms of Risegate, Clough, Cheal, Westhorpe, Belnie and Rigbolt, together with many scattered farmsteads extend the overall community six miles west of the village across the fen. The original termination seems to imply that Gosberton was originally a British village, the later word, ton, denoting that it was afterwards taken possession of by the Saxons. Although the village is now quite some distance from the sea, at one time it came as far as the centre of the village. In the past when digging has been undertaken in the area near the church, seaweed, sand and shells have been found in layers below the surface. It has been recorded that the sea flooded the land in Gosberton in 1292 during the reign of Edward I. Fortunately this is no longer a problem, and the land is now very fertile allowing farming to be the main occupation in the area.

To the south of Gosberton village is the Risegate Eau, a watercourse that was in existence previous to any attempt at reclamation being carried out in the area. In the 19th century this was the main sewer in the district, extending some seven miles in length. The drain has an outfall at both ends, the natural division for the flow of water being about midway at Belney Bridge, the lands on the west side of the bridge draining to the Hammond Beck, and those on the east side to a point about one mile inland from Fosdyke Bridge where it enters the Welland. Standing in the centre of the village the church dedicated to St. Peter and St. Paul is a large cruciform building of stone, chiefly in the Decorated style, consisting of chancel, with south chapel, nave, transepts, south porch and an embattled tower with pinnacles and spire. The tower has a ring of six bells which were rehung in 1928, and the register dates from the year 1656.

The church of St. Peter and St. Paul, Gosberton.

Print of the church of St. Peter and St. Paul, Gosberton, 1842.

Trades and Business People in Gosberton, with Gosberton Cheal - Risegate & Westhorpe in 1937.

Bennett, Rev. Ivor Sterndale, M.A. (vicar), Vicarage.
Kenning, Mordecai, The Woodlands.
Muxlow, Mrs. Acacia House.
Proctor, John M., Hill House.
Shaw, Herbert Nichols, J.P., Bank House.
Smith, Henry, Cressy Hall.
Smith, Herbert Westerby, Conway, Quadring Road.
Taylor, John, West House.
Welby-Everard, Edward Everard Earle, M.A., D.L., J.P., Gosberton House.
Wilson, Alexander S., M.B., The Elms.

Commercial.

Baker, Leslie, grocer.
Baker, Winston Churchill, baker, High Street.
Barclays Bank Ltd., High Street.
Bell, P. H. (Mrs. Maria Enderby).
Bendall, Arth., farmer, Sunnyside Farm, High Street.
Bevis Eliza M. (Mrs.), stationer.
Booth, George, horse breaker, High Street.
Braybrooks, John W., wheelwright.
Brooks, E. H. & Son., bakers.
Brown, Victor, shopkeeper.
Burrell, Walter Fountain, farmer, Bank.
Casswell Frederick Garner, farmer, Monks Hall & farm bailiff to Mrs. R. E. Smith, Cawood Hall.
Cemetery (Chas. Hy. Farr, A.C.I.I., clerk to the burial board).
Chapman, Frederick Brown, farmer, Rigbolt.
Clark, Chas., cottage farmer, Wargate.
Clark, Mrs. farmer, Wargate Bridge.
Clark, Thos, farmer, Boston Road.
Clay, Bertie Casius, farmer, High Street.
Clay, William, farmer.
Cook, William D. & Son, Potato merchants, Bank House Farm.
Cook, William Edward, smallholder, Eau-dyke.
Darby, John William, tobacconist.
Dennis, John William, farmer.
Dobson, J. T. (Gosberton) Ltd., nurseryman, Bank.
Dods, William, coal merchant, Station.
Doubleday, Percy, seed merchant, High Street.
Draper, Jabez, cottage farmer.
Duke of Cambridge, P. H. (Chas. East).
Duke of York P. H. (Arth. Smith).
East Arth., hairdresser, High Street.
Fairbanks, Joseph, farmer, Wargate Bridge.
Farr Chas. Hy., A.C.I.I., local agent of Ministry of Labour; insurance agent & clerk to the burial board, High Street.

Fisher, Walter, butcher.

Five Bells Hotel (Geo. Tinkler).

Fountain, Herbert, G.M., chemist.

Freemantle, Herbert, farmer, Lansdowne House.

Garner, D. jun., butcher.

Garner, David, farmer, Manor Farm.

Garner, F. P., farmer, Wargate Bridge.

Garner, Mordecai, farmer.

Giddings, Douglas, Market Gardener, High Street.

Giddings, Frances (Mrs.), district nurse.

Goodacre, Abel & Son, watchmakers.

Gosling, Samuel, farmer, Cemetery Road.

Green Man P. H. (John William Mumby).

Grice, Samuel, wheelwright, High Street.

Grundy, Harold, Motor car garage.

Hall & Butwright, bakers, High Street.

Hare, Alice (Mrs.), smallholder, Boston Road.

Hill, Comdr., George Walter, (ret.), Market Gardener, White House.

Holden, William, market gardener.

Hutchesson, Harry Thomas, saddler, Boston Road.

Inkley, Jabez Barnes, farmer, Birds Drove.

James, Henry, blacksmith, Boston Road.

Jessop Luke, smallholder, Boston Road.

Kelk Chas., chimney sweeper, Boston Road.

Kenning Mordecai & Son., farmers, Woodlands.

Kenning, Mordecai Franklin, farmer, Wargate Bridge.

McCartney, John Henry, butcher, High Street.

Mann Ada (Mrs.), fried fish dealer.

Marshall Chas. W. private gardener to E. E. E. Welby-Everard, Gosberton House.

Marshall, Mary Lucy (Mrs.), sub-postmistress & vaccination officer to the Gosberton district.

Mastin, Tom, grocer, Cemetery Road & motor cycle agent, Salem Street.

Munton, Frederick, smallholder.

Munton, Wilfred, farmer, High Street.

Muxlow, Percy Roy, farmer, The Bank.

National Provincial Bank Ltd. (agency to Spalding).

Neal, Frederick, cottage farmer.

New Inn. (John William Mann).

Noble, Frederick C., cycle dealer.

Overton, Henry Meredith, tailor.

Paling, Alfred, motor engineer.

Parker, Fred, farmer, Bank.

Parnham, George, blacksmith.

Pinder, Jas. E., builder, Salem Street.

Proctor, Jn. M. & Rt. Edward, farmers.

Rawding, John, fruit grower, Orchard House, Boston Road.

Rawding, Thomas William, farmer, Boston Road.

Reading Room (Thos. Long, sec.).

Rogers, Louis, shopkeeper, Church Street.

Rogers, Walter Swain, farmer.

Sellers, Robert, battery service station.

Smith, Chas. Rt. & Co., farmers, Belnie House.
Smith, Godfrey & Son, wine & spirit merchants.
Smith, Charles Ernest, boot repairer.
Smith, Henry, farmer, Cressy Hall.
Smith, Mark, farmer.
Spalding Industrial Co-operative Society Ltd. (branch), High Street.
Stafford, Harry Sidney, hairdresser, High Street.
Stafford, Thomas, draper, High Street.
Taylor, John (Gosberton) Ltd., potato merchants, West House.
Taylor, John, farmer, Bank.
Taylor, William, builder, Wargate Bridge.
Thorpe, Frederick C., farmer, Sandpit Farm.
Timm, Joseph Herbert, carpenter & joiner, painter & undertaker.
Tunnard, John William, grocer, High Street.
Turner, Edmnd, boot repairer, Church Street.
Ward, Lewis Ernest, general dealer, High Street.
Waterfall, Arthur William, boot repairer, High Street.
Wheel Inn (Ernest Edward Sismey).
Whiting, John William, farmer, Bank.
Whitworth, Edwin Frank, farmer, The Gables, Bank.
Wilson, Alex. S., M. B., Ch.B.Glas. Physician & Surgeon & medical officer & public vaccinator for the Gosberton district, Holland Guardians Committee, The Elms.
Windsor, Alfred Valentine, plumber.
Worthington, William, shopkeeper, Snow Hill.

Gosberton Cheal.

Bendall, George Robert, jnr., smallholder.
Bright, Samuel, farmer.
Burrell, Walter Fountain, farmer, Surfleet Cheal.
Garner, Ambrose, farmer.
Garner, Frank, farmer.
Garner, Mordecai, farmer.
North, Thomas, farmer.
Proctor, Rd., farmer.
Sandall, John, farmer.
Sansam, Timothy Pridmore, farmer.
Tomlinson, C. K. (Mrs.), farmer.
Tomlinson, Fred, farmer, Surfleet Cheal.

Gosberton Risegate.

Blackledge, Rev. Hugh Finch, M.A., vicar of Gosberton Clough, The Vicarage.
Dickings, Mrs. M. E., Kialama.
Doubleday, Percy Millington.
Stanley, Mrs.

Commercial.

Alexander, Walter, smallholder, Fen.
Bates, Bros., thrashing machine owners.
Black Horse Inn (Cecil Leslie Bates).
Briggs, Thomas P., farmer, Fen.
Burrell, Alfred, poultry breeder.
Casswell, Albert, farmer.
Casswell, Albert Edward, smallholder.
Charlton, Herbert Knight, farmer.
Chipperfield, Sidney Charles, grocer.
Cope, Arthur, farmer.
Crosby, Benjamin, farmer, Fen.
Cutforth, Frank, farmer, Chesboul House.
Daniel, Thomas, smallholder.
Dobney, Thomas, haulage contractor, Fen.
Doubleday, Percy M. seed merchant.
Draper, Jn., farmer, Fen.
Draper, Joseph, farmer, Capes Entry.
Duke of York, P. H. (Arth. S. Rylott).
Five Bells, P. H. (Jas. F. Mayfield).
Fountain Thomas, farmer, Capes Entry.
Garner Edward, carpenter.
Garner, Mordecai, farmer.
Goodacre, Reginald, Wireless Dealer.
Haresign Bros., farmers, Clough.
Haresign, Cecil, farmer, Fen.
Haresign, George Alfred, Motor engineer, Clough.
Haresign, Harry, farmer, Fen.
Haresign, Herbert, farmer, Fen.
Harper, Felix, smallholder.
Healey & Dobney, millers.
Holmes Thomas, farmer.
Hutchesson, Edmund, saddler.
Hutson, George, smallholder, Fen.
Inkley, Joseph H., farmer, Fen.
Lane, Herbert, farmer.
Lord Miss, farmer, Fen.
Nelson George, smallholder, Clough.
Nelson, Harold M., farmer, Fen.
Parker, George, haulage contractor, Fen.
Peake, Rse. Miriam (Mrs.), farmer.
Pointon, Mary (Miss), grocer & post office.
Rylott, John Thomas, farmer.
Sansom, Frank, smallholder, Fen.
Searby, Walter David, wheelwright.
Ship, P. H. (Jack Kirlow), Clough.
Skill, George, builder, Collingwood House.
Smith, Robert, farmer, Gosberton Clough.
Smith, Thomas, farmer, Fen, Clough.

Smith, Walter, farmer, Fen, Clough.
Thornalley, John George, baker, The Mill.
Tidswell Bros., farmers.
Twells George, market gardener.
Waite Bros., farmers, Grange Farm, Clough.
Waring Bros., smallholder.
Waring Elijah, smallholder, Clough.
Wilkinson Bros., farmers, Fen.
Witherington, A. J. & Sons, builders, Clough.
Wood, Fred, farmer.
Wood, H., farmer.
Woodthorpe, Jas. J., carpenter.

Westhorpe.

Berridge, George, smallholder.
Brocklehurst, Frank, dairyman, Highfield.
Clark, Harold, smallholder.
Clark, Jn. percy, farmer.
Dickinson, Frederick, cottage farmer.
Draper, George, smallholder.
Faulkner, Frank, smallholder.
Garner, Gilbert, farmer.
Garner, Jn. K., smallholder.
Long, Charles, cottage farmer.
New Crane Inn (George Henry Taylor).
Twell, Jn., farmer.

Betsy Mundy at the Green Dragon Inn, Gosberton.

Barclays Bank,
Gosberton, 1930s

The Wheel Inn, Gosberton,
Spring 1950; Landlord, Ernest
Edward Sismey.

The Wheel Inn after restoration
(photographed about 1955).

The Cemetery.

By the 1880's burial space in the churchyard was becoming scarce. In November 1886 a meeting of the ratepayers was held in the vestry, the Rev. S.B. Sealy, Vicar, presided for the purpose of considering the necessity of providing a new burial ground. After considerable discussion, Mr. J. R. Brittain proposed and Mr. Brian Smith seconded, "That a new burial ground be provided agreeably to the Burial Acts." Mr. H. Garner proposed and Mr. J. W. Chambers seconded, "That the churchyard be enlarged." On the votes that were taken, it was resolved to have a new burial ground. The meeting was then adjourned until Friday, December 17th at 2 p.m. Ratepayers present at the meeting were formed into a committee, with a few other names added, for the purpose of looking out a suitable piece of land for a burial ground. In the meantime the vestry clerk was asked to apply to H. Everard, Esq., to know if he would be prepared to sell a piece of ground in the vicinity which would be considered eligible for the purpose. At the meeting on 17th December 1886 it was reported that through the influence of the Vicar Henry Everard, Esq., has consented to sell a portion of the White Hall Park field, opening out upon Wargate Way, on condition that no chapel be built upon the site, and that the Burial Board make a good fence around the ground. It was noted that it was only a short distance from the church, and the Methodist Chapel making it a very convenient site.

In January 1887 a vestry meeting was held in the parish church which was very well attended, with the purpose of deciding whether a new burial ground should be acquired, and to form a Burial Board. The Vicar presided and reminded the meeting that the churchyard was already too full, and will shortly have to be closed by order of the Queen in Council. It was reported that the churchwardens had been in communication with Mr. Henry Everard, who had offered a plot of land which was considered most suitable, at the rate of £200 per acre, but no chapel was to be built upon the site. Several people present were of the opinion that a piece of land could be obtained at a cheaper rate, but ultimately it was decided to form a Burial Board, and let the body settle the matter. The meeting then proceeded to elect members, the maximum number of nine being decided upon. Mr. H. Garner proposed nine names, the proposal meeting with considerable disfavour. Mr. Bevis seconded the resolution, which was lost by a large majority. After this about a score of names were suggested, but the meeting was unable to determine upon a satisfactory mode of election, so it was decided to arrange a poll of the parish.

The poll was held in the Public Hall, and in April 1887 the Gosberton Burial Board met for its first meeting. Mr. Brian Smith was elected chairman, Mr. Dickinson, vice-chairman, and Mr. Walter Ellis, clerk, together with six other members. Now that the board had been elected they made it clear that they were anxious to obtain a site for the burial ground as near to the church as possible, and tenders were invited for the sale of 2 acres of ground. It was said that the inspector would not pass a ground where the "sock" was less than eight feet below the surface. Doubt was expressed as to whether such a site could be found in Gosberton. No other suitable land was found, so it was decided to accept the offer of Mr. Henry Everard for 2 acres of his land in Wargate Way at a cost of £200 per acre. With regards to the condition that no chapel was to be built upon the site, this must have been waived by Mr. Everard, because in September 1887 the Burial Board met to present an estimate of the probable expense that was likely to be incurred in completing the ground, fencing, planting, and building a chapel. The Board resolved that a sum of money be borrowed for the purpose, not to exceed £1,100 and to be repaid in 30 years. Work on the construction of the cemetery went ahead without any further delay, and by April 1888 it was completed, but the Burial Board and the Vicar were at variance with regard to the consecration of a portion of the new cemetery. The Board decided that the wishes of the church-people for a portion of the ground to be consecrated should be granted, and on it being stated that the Board was liable for the fees it was agreed, by a majority of one, to defray the cost, from £15 to £20. However at a subsequent meeting it was pointed out that the question of liability for these fees was an open one, and it was proposed that those who desired consecration should pay for the rite, and not the whole parish. The motion was carried by a majority of one, and the old minute rescinded. On hearing the result of the meeting the Vicar called a vestry which was largely attended, and the proceedings proved somewhat boisterous. Personalities were exchanged, and the Vicar complained of the manner in which certain persons addressed him. Resolutions were proposed supporting the action of the Burial Board, and it was evident that the meeting contained a majority of that view. The Vicar consequently declined to put any of the resolutions, and adjourned the vestry to the following Monday when there was again a large attendance. The Vicar read a legal opinion which he had obtained, but it did not say positively who was required to pay. The Vicar expressed the hope that the members of the Burial Board would allow wiser counsel to prevail, and reconsider their determination. Some of them might not care for the rite, but they ought to consider the feelings of those who did. The meeting again broke up without any resolutions being put, and it as hinted that the Vicar would take legal proceedings to enforce payment. On the same evening the Burial Board met again, and decided to adhere to their minute, the majority being firm in their resolve not to pay these fees. It was further decided to lock the doors of the cemetery chapel on the day of the Bishop's visit for fear he should enter the building and consecrate it, and thus obtain possession of it for the church party. In May 1888 the first funeral service in the new cemetery was performed over the body of the late Mr. John Epton, by the Rev. S. B. Sealy, Vicar. The first part was taken in the cemetery chapel. About half an hour later the late Mrs. Greetham was interred at the foot of the first grave, the service being conducted by the Rev. J. Carnegie, Free Methodist Minister. At a meeting in June 1888 of the Gosberton Burial Board the question of consecrating a portion of the cemetery again came forward, the Board having several times refused to accede to the memorial of the Vicar and churchwardens praying for such consecration. At this meeting a letter was read from the Vicar, stating that the Bishop of Lincoln had written announcing that he would consent to consecrate the ground on the petition of the Vicar and churchwardens, but his lordship required an assurance from the Burial Board that no obstacle would be placed in his way on arriving at the ground. After a heated discussion, in which strong language was used, it was decided by six votes to three, to have the gates of the cemetery locked should the Bishop visit the ground. The Board further made it clear that as far as they were concerned this was the end of the consecration dispute, and they would receive no more communication on the subject.

The members of the Burial Board have changed many times over the years, and during that time they have had a change of heart. Now a portion of the ground on the north and south side of the footpath that runs through the cemetery is consecrated.

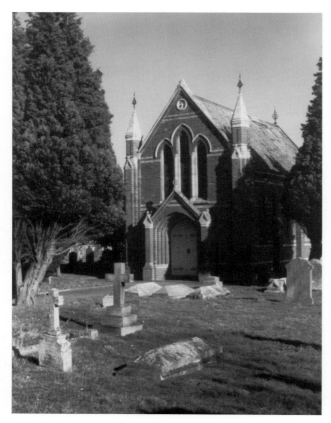

Gosberton Cemetery Chapel.

Rigbolt House.

Rigbolt or Wrightbolt as it was known in earlier times is situated at one of the furthest points in the Gosberton parish. Until the early part of the 20th century Rigbolt House was in Sempringham parish, but boundary changes brought Rigbolt within Gosberton parish. It was established in the late 12th century as a cell attached to Sempringham Priory, At the dissolution many religious houses were demolished except those which might be useful for farm purposes, hence Rigbolt survived the purge.

Blaeu's Map of Lincolnshire dated 1645 shows Wrightbolt as being a religious establishment.

The present day building is a more recent structure. It is certain that there has been several buildings constructed on or near the site of the present building. Records show that one building was destroyed by fire, and certainly an earlier building was moated as traces of a moat are still visible on the grass in front of the present house. Much of the material in the present house certainly originated from an earlier building especially flagstones used for the floors inside.

The Gentlemen's Magazine of 1793 says, "The old part of the house is built of stone, and some of the windows have stone mullions arched over."

White's Directory of Lincolnshire for 1872 states that a farm then called Rigbolt belonged to Mr. Frederick Brown, Earlier records show that the building and land once belonged to the Duke of Ancaster.

The most interesting part of the somewhat little recorded history of this house concerns an old bed, its present whereabouts unknown, and which is supposed to have been slept on at Cressy Hall by the mother of one of the former Kings of England. As to which king or mother, there appears to be some diversity of opinion. Some records say (referring to Cressy Hall). "In this house, Katharine, mother of Henry VIII, was once entertained. The bed whereon she lay was removed to a farmhouse by the Fen Side called Wrightbolt, where Dr. Stukeley saw it." Other records read: "Margaret, mother of Henry VIII, was once entertained at Cressy Hall – the bed she slept on was removed to Rigbolt (Wrightbolt) where Dr, Stukeley saw it."

With regards to the style of the bed, the Gentlemen's Magazine records that it comprised of thirty-six carved oak panels 18 inches by 9 inches in size. It was very large, shut up on all sides with a wainscot, and two holes left at the bottom and, each big enough to admit a grown person. The last reported sighting of the bed was when Mr. Guy a Spalding furniture dealer, took the old oak to make it up into a sideboard, giving the owner a Mr. Cook an iron bedstead for it.[1]

Whether or not any of the remains of this bed are still in existence is doubtful, but it is possible that somewhere there could be a piece of furniture made from a portion of this bed, and the owner not aware of its history.

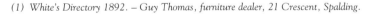

(1) White's Directory 1892. – Guy Thomas, furniture dealer, 21 Crescent, Spalding.

Rigbolt House (Picture from Gentlemen's Magazine, October 1793.

Four Panels of the old Bedstead that was once at Rigbolt (Picture from Gentlemen's Magazine, October 1793).

RIGBOLT, GOSBERTON.
Valuable FREEHOLD ESTATE.
To be SOLD by AUCTION,
By Mr. J. LAMING,
At the White Hart Hotel in Spalding, on Tuesday, 9th October, 1883, at 3 o'clock in the Afternoon, in the following lots, and subject to conditions to be then declared,
Lot 1. ALL that capital FARM-HOUSE, called "Rigbolt House," with the Barn, Stables, and other Out-buildings, and very superior Farm, surrounding the Buildings and lying in a ring fence, containing 212A. 0R. 20P. (more or less), whereof about 56 Acres are Pasture, situate in Gosberton, in the county of Lincoln.
Lot 2. All that COTTAGE and Garden, lying opposite to lot 1, and adjoining Capes Entry, situate in Pinchbeck, containing 0A. 0R. 38P. (more or less).
The Estate was for many years in the occupation of Mr. Frederick Brown, the late owner. The House and Buildings, some of which are newly built, are roomy, substantial, and in capital repair, while the Land is of good quality, well situated, and in a high state of cultivation.
The purchases are to be completed on the 6th of April next, but possession of lot 1 will be given at an early date.
The whole or any part of the purchase-money may be had upon approved security.
For further particulars apply to
Messrs. BONNER and CALTHROP,
Spalding, 17th Sept., 1883. Solicitors, Spalding.

Rigbolt House from across the fields, 1999.

Snippets from what the papers used to say.

Gosberton Seminary.

Miss Beeton very respectfully informs her friends, that she has opened a Boarding and Day School at Gosberton. Having had the advantage of several years experience in scholastic employment, Miss B. hopes to secure the patronage of the public; and by an invariable attention to the duties of her station to promote the moral and intellectual improvement of her pupils.

Gosberton 18th January, 1818.

May 1833.

On Thursday the 15th inst. an inquest was held at Gosberton, by Mr. Mastin, coroner, on the body of John Ingall, the postman from Gosberton to Donington, who was found drowned in a ditch by the road side. As the unfortunate man had been making merry at a wedding, it is supposed he slipped from the path and perished for want of assistance. – Verdict found drowned.

July 1823.

Lately, at Gosberton, Mr. Crosby: it is supposed that he has left behind him more than £50,000, and yet in his life he would hardly allow himself common necessaries. It was his delight to have his apparel always of the meanest kind; a hat at the price of 2s. 6d. was an extravagance. It is said that many persons who did not know him, have given him alms on account of his appearance. Neither of the Elwes's nor even Dancer himself, could be more squalid, or more penurious in a general way, and yet this man kept a good table as far as beef and bacon went, and was always accessible to any poor man that might call at his house; rich, and what he called "fine" men, he detested. – It is somewhat remarkable that on the day before Mr. Crosby's dissolution his house-keeper died, who had been in his service for many years. He had well provided for her, but it is said forgot his poor relations whom he left behind, and who are numerous.

March 1869.

Our ingenious townsman, Mr. James Coxel, has recently invented a new kind of velocipede, where the motive power is obtained by the application of springs, so that by it a person sitting in a kind of easy carriage has nothing to do but occasionally to wind up the spring, while he continues the progress in a rapid and complacent manner. A description and drawings of the model appeared in a recent number of the Mechanic, ** Kelly's Directory of Lincolnshire 1861 – Coxel, James – plumber.

August 1889.

Gosberton – A Juvenile Horse-stealer – On the 22nd inst., John Thomas Norris about 12 years of age, son of a Gosberton labourer, was charged before Captain Gleed with stealing a pony, the property of Mr. Hill of Gosberton, on the previous Wednesday. The evidence went to show that the child, who had on another occasion been found to have stolen a silver watch from the owner's pocket, had evidently premeditated the theft of Mr. Hill's pony, value at £15. It appears that a week or two ago Mr. Rogers, saddler, Gosberton, missed a whip from his shop, and it was found in possession of the prisoner, and that he had taken it in view of his future requirements. On the 21st it was alleged, he entered a field where the animal was grazing, and, having loosened a tether which was fastened to one of its legs in order to catch it more easily, he mounted the horse's back, and, as proved by the lad's own confession rode around Gosberton Bank, on to Spalding Road. P.C. Dain went in search of the offender, and caught him on the Pinchbeck Road, at Spalding, riding the animal, about 9 o'clock at night. The horse was then wearing a bridle – not its own – and the boy, upon being interrogated, stated that "he had been to George Jennings for a quart of sweet nitre,' and that he had also been to Whaplode to see an uncle of his. Both these were false statements; and being questioned regarding the bridle, he said that he had purchased that of Mr. Andrews, saddler, Spalding. Inquiries were made with reference to this, and it was found that the boy went into that tradesman's shop about a fortnight ago, and tendering 2s. 5d. said Mr. G. F. Birch had sent him for a bridle, and he was supplied with one which the horse was wearing. The child acknowledged that during his journey the pony threw him two or three times, and the owner states that he never dared to mount the animal himself. Prisoner was remanded.

October 1898.

The Gosberton schoolmaster will have cause to remember the little love affair which cost him £216 8s. 5d. in the way of damages for breach of promise in the Civil Court at the West Riding assizes at Leeds in December 1897. He is in receipt of an annual income of £66, all told, and out of this he is supposed to pay this comparatively large sum. Up to Monday he had not commenced to reduce the amount, but on that day Judge Short had the circumstances before him at the Spalding County Court, and made the merciful order of 10s. a month, or £6 a year. Six into 216 goes 36 times, so that Mr. William Boothby Jnr. will be quite an old man by the time he is, "all square with bogey." Perhaps when old age is upon him 10s. a month will serve to conjure up memories of his youthful ardour, and, in some degree, compensate for the drag which his first love affair seems likely to prove to him.

June 1871.

Gosberton. – A meeting of the shareholders in the Gas Company was held in the schoolroom on the 7th inst. (Mr. Thos. Cocks in the chair), to meet Mr. Penny, the engineer, who was in attendance with the plans and specifications of the proposed gas works. The plans were approved, and it was agreed to advertise for tenders to be sent in for the erection of the works, which are to be in operation by the 1st Dec. next. Most of the shares being now taken, it was agreed that the company be registered at once; and the following persons were duly elected directors, viz., the Rev. John Topham, and Messrs. Boyer, Cocks, R. Bicheno, S. Baxter, and Bryan Smith. Mr. J. H. Oliff was appointed clerk and collector, and Messrs M. Kenning and H. S. Bichero the auditors. A vote of thanks was proposed to Mr. Cocks for his kindness in presiding at the different meetings.

September 1871.

At a meeting held in the National School, Gosberton, on the 26th, the following tenders for the erection of the gas works were received:–

Swerwin £389, accepted; Milson £400, Dawson £412, Gaunt £399 15s. 4d., Padison £450, Green £577 12s. 6d. and Moor £365.

February 1874.

Gosberton – A nice pillar with gas lamp, has recently been erected in the centre of this village, doubtless to be followed by others in darker and more dangerous localities. It is near the Church, nearer the Wesleyan Chapel. but nearest the Bell Inn, and doubtless the landlord will look upon it as a seasonable favour.

June 26th, 1895.

Gosberton. – A heavy thunderstorm passed over this district on Wednesday night. Great damage was done to crops. Mr. Green had a horse killed by lightning.

January 7th 1896.

Gosberton – The members of the Hand and Heart Pig Club had their annual supper at the Five Bells hotel on Thursday week. Although there have been heavy losses during the year the society has a balance in hand of £52. The membership is now 32.

1870

Mr. Brackenbury, formerly of Butterwick, now of Gosberton, whose success as a grower of potatoes when resident at the former place was literally astounding, he has thrashed the produce of 56 acres of wheat, the yield of which is found to average a trifle over 8 quarters an acre. It would seem therefore that he knows how to cultivate the growth of wheat with quite as much success as that of potatoes. His success is all the more remarkable from the fact of his not having been brought up to the farming business.

BELNIE, GOSBERTON.
7 BEASTS, 3 HORSES, IMPLEMENTS, POTATOES, &c.

S. and G. KINGSTON will SELL, upon the premises of Mr. EDWARD WORTH, situate at Gosberton Belnie, under a bill of sale, To-morrow, Saturday, March 19th, 1881, the whole of the Live and Dead Farming STOCK, FURNITURE, and Effects, comprising—

7 *Beasts.*—Two-year-old steer, two-year-old heifer in calf (time up in May), cow in full profit, rearing calf, 3 burlings.

3 *Horses.*—Brown cart mare (Lively) aged, black cart mare (Beauty) aged, roan half-bred mare 9 years, quiet to ride and drive.

Implements.—2 Scotch carts with raves, horse hoe, iron plough, Howard's potato ditto. iron seed harrows, iron drag, dressing machine, weighing machine and weights, slicer, potato masher, wheels and hecking barrow, patent chaff box, wheelbarrow, waggon jack, 36-stave ladder, 2 short ditto, 8-step ditto, about 20 sacks, stack cloth, tumbril, wood pig troughs, tubs, 2 battens, 3 coops, potato riddles and stand, about 50 skeps, 8 crates, iron bar, cow bin, paraffin cask, steelyards, thatch pegs, swath rake and forks, rakes, hoes, shovels, old wood, &c.

Cart and Plough Gears for 3 horses, light spring Cart, set Brass-mounted Harness.

Potatoes.—Twelve tons of Champions ware and seed, half-ton of ditto seed, 12cwt. of Magnum Bonum seed, 6cwt. of Myatt seed.

Core of Hay, Cob of Oat Sheafs, Stack of Straw, about 8 tons of Mangels, with use of Yards to April 5th ; also the whole of the Household Furniture and Dairy Utensils.

The whole will be sold strictly for ready money, without the slightest reserve ; and the Sale will commence at One o'clock in the Morning.

BELNIE FARM, GOSBERTON.

S. & G. KINGSTON will SELL, upon the premises of Mr. JOSEPH SMITH, Belnie Farm, Gosberton, in consequence of quitting, on Thursday, March 31st, 1881, the whole of the Live and Dead FARMING STOCK and Effects, comprising—

13 *Beasts.*—Red and white cow, time up March 29th ; red Cow, time up April 10th ; roan cow, time up May 22d ; red and white cow, time up Sept. 1st ; red two-year-old steer, 2 two-year-old heifers, 5 burlings, and a rearing calf.

25 *Sheep.*—25 half-bred lambhogs, very fresh.

Pure-bred Prize Berkshire Gilt.

8 *Horses.*—Dark-brown mare (Blossom) 5 years, black horse (Major) 7 years, dark-brown horse (Prince) 10 years, bay horse (Prince) aged, bay horse (Captain) rising 3 years, black mare (Lively) aged, bay filly 2 years (by Ploughboy), and a nag mare 8 years, quiet to ride and drive.

Implements.—Narrow-wheel waggon, two Scotch carts with raves and patent arms by Chapman, Peterborough (nearly new), two ditto with ditto, wood plough, double ditto by Hornsby (new), two potato scarifiers (new), potato hiller by Howard (new), three-horse duckfoot, set of four iron harrows (new), Hornsby's Indispensable reaper (new last year), Samuelson's ditto, turnip cutter by Hornsby (new), pulper, chaff box, sheep troughs and trays, boarded tumbril, pig troughs, tubs, tank, Bedford's patent swath rake, shovels, forks, hoes, rakes, and other tools, old iron, old wood, &c.

Cart and Plough Gears, partly new.

The Horses are quiet and powerful, the Beasts and Sheep are well bred and in forward condition, and a great portion of the Implements are new.

The Sale will be strictly for ready-money, and will commence at One o'clock.

Gosberton

August 10th 1901.

Gosberton – A terrific hailstorm passed over the Gosberton district on Saturday. The hailstones were spoken of as the largest seen in the district for many years, and were described as the size of walnuts. Round about Gosberton, The Risegate and Quadring the storm was seen at its worst. The damage done to cropping is most extensive, the standing corn has suffered most seriously, whilst amongst the potatoes and other root crops the devastation wrought by the storm is clearly to be seen. The effect was described by some of the local agriculturalists as "terrible", and claims are being made upon the insurance companies for the damage done – windows have been broken by the hailstones in many cases, and in one instance, at Gosberton Risegate, 13 panes of glass were broken in one house and many others cracked. A few miles out, however, the storm was scarcely felt at all.

December 1886.

Gosberton: – Feoffee Doles – The annual distribution took place last week, when 42 widows received 5s. 6d. each and bread, and 139 married couples received 4s. 6d. each, and bread, the total given away amounting to £46 17s. 9d.

The feoffees also gave away five good great coats to five poor men, and six good black gowns to six aged women.

The trustees of Mrs. Bankes's charity also gave £6 worth of meat, flour, and coals to 14 aged widows and single women.

1891.

Ladies School. Irene House, Gosberton near Spalding, Principal: Miss Child.
The next term will begin (D.V.) September 23rd.

1891.

Mr. Boyer's School, Gosberton Hall, near Spalding. Established 1848.
Vice-Principal – C. F. Boyer, jnr. Int.B.A.London.
The Winter Term will commence Monday, September 21st 1891.

Miss Child's School,
Gosberton, 1885.

Gosberton Hall.

Moulton

**with
Moulton Chapel
Moulton Seas End
Moulton Eaugate
etc.**

Aspects of Spalding Villages

Moulton is an example of what many consider a village should be. Most roads into the village converge at the small green in the centre, surrounded by the church of "All Saints" on one side, and on the other sides a selection of fine old houses, small shops and the ancient Swan Inn. Standing close by is the old tower mill which can be seen from quite a distance when approaching the village. In summer when the trees are in leaf the area around the village green makes a pretty sight. You could well imagine in times gone by the locals sitting under the trees of an evening, discussing the day's events.

Many years ago the sea was much closer to the village, but with drainage and reclamation the sea is now much more distant.

At one time the village had a station situated on the line from Spalding through to Kings Lynn, but this has long since disappeared, although the road leading to it has kept its name of Station Road, and some of the station buildings are still standing.

Not far from Moulton are the hamlets of Moulton Seas End, Moulton Chapel, and Moulton Eaugate. Overall the parish of Moulton with its hamlets covers a large area, and was said in 1875 to be 16 miles in length.

The village green about 1870.

Above and Below: Scenes around the village green about 1870.

View from Moulton Church Tower. The Axe & Handsaw public house is in the centre of the picture.

View from Moulton Church Tower looking in a northerly direction. Taken in 1889.

Moulton

Left:–The Axe & Handsaw
public House.

Below:–The Bell Inn.

Trades and Business people in Moulton in 1937.

Axe & Handsaw Public House (Jn. F. Bothamley).

Baxter, Jn. L., horse slaughterer.

Baxter, Violet M. (Mrs.), shopkeeper.

Bayston, Chas H., farm foreman to T. W. Tointon Esq., Austendyke.

Beeson, Frederick, farmer.

Bell Inn (Capel Booth).

Bellairs, Frank, cycle agent.

Biggadike, Jn. Thos. jun., miller.

Boston Coal Co. Ltd., coal merchants.

Bransom, Arth., farmer, High Road.

British Legion Club (G. Lungley, Hon. Sec.).

Brown, Sidney J., boot & shoe repairer.

Charlton, Thos. Hy., farmer, Hallgate.

Clark, Tom, butcher.

Coddington, Saml. G., motor car garage proprietor.

Cook, Wm., smallholder.

Crampton, Chas., grocer & post office.

Dent, William, bulb grower, Alton House nursery.

George Inn (Thos. Lee, Hipworth).

Grammar School (Jn. Geo., Westmorland, headmaster).

Grimor, Wm., fried fish dealer.

Hardy, Hy. Geo., farmer, Austendyke.

Holland, Robert, farmer.

King, Claude, A. M. (agent for Soames & Co. Ltd., brewers & spirit merchants, Spalding), Mulberry House.

King, William Harrison, farmer.

Lawes, William, carpenter.

Martyn, Frank de R., M.R.C.S., medical officer, Moulton District, The Goddards.

Mashford, Philip, smallholder.

Mayford, Jas., smallholder.

Morfoot, Rose Ada (Mrs.), smallholder, Hallgate.

Oldershaw, Harry, live stock transporter, Sunnyside.

Parrott W & Son, saddlers & harness maker.

Pickwell Bros., market gardeners, The Limes.

Railway Hotel (Joseph Carter).

Rower, Norman, baker.

Skupham Bros, farmers.

Skupham Rt. Wm., farmer, Station Road.

Smith, G. T. & H. bulb growers.

Sporton Chase. H, & Son, farmers.

Swan Inn (Frederick Wm. Pettit).

Taylor, Jn., bricklayer.

Taylor, John Thomas, farmer.

Taylor, Thos., carpenter.

Thomas, G. Wm., shopkeeper.

Thorpe, Rt., butcher.

Ward, Joseph, farmer & landowner, Moulton Park.

Watson, Reginald, garage proprietor.

Webb & Porter, grocers.

White, J. T. & Sons Ltd., bulb growers.
Widdows, Jn. W. jun., baker.
Wright, Geo., farmer, Hogsgate.

Above: High Street, Moulton about 1870.

Below: Mr. Robert Thorpe, butcher, with his shop, house and family, Moulton Village about 1870.

Restoration of Moulton Church.

Moulton Church before restoration, 1867.

On the 29th January, 1867, the Vicar of Moulton, the Rev. J. Russell Jackson wrote a letter to the Editor of the Mercury drawing the public's attention to a meeting that he and the churchwardens had convened for the purpose of laying before the parishioners a report on the condition of the parish church – of devising a scheme for its restoration, and also of considering the need of a school-chapel at Seas-End. Some twenty of the principle parishioners were present. Proceedings commenced by a statement from the chair as to the events which had led to the meeting. A full report on the condition of the church, and drawings showing the proposed work of restoration (furnished by Mr. Wm. Smith, of 10, John Street, Adelphi, London), were produced; also drawings by the same gentleman, of a school chapel at Seas-End. Resolutions were subsequently passed to the effect that the works should be undertaken, and that Mr. Smith's plans should be generally adopted, and that the parish should be asked to consent to a loan of a portion of the money needed. A committee was formed, and the chairman was requested to convey the thanks of the meeting to Mrs. Johnson, who had kindly promised £500 for the restoration of the chancel. Those present at the meeting earnestly hoped that the building, and restoration work would be carried out. A large majority were of the opinion that the proposed loan was positively needful in order to secure an efficient restoration of the church.

It was much hoped by the meeting that the inhabitants would adopt this scheme in vestry. The Vicar went on to say that the fabric of the church was in a most unsatisfactory condition. Much of the masonry was defective: the roof of the nave was, in places, in a dangerous condition: the floors, were in many places, completely rotten, and the paving was very damp. Besides this the pews were unsatisfactory because of their high backs, and much of the tracery was missing from the windows.

The need was also expressed for the proposed school chapel at Seas-End, as the district was a most important one, both in population and in area; but it possessed no Church of England place of worship, and the week-day school which had opened some few years earlier was limited to such poor accommodation as an upper room of a public house supplied.

This then was the matter that was brought before the meeting. The agreement of the parish was obtained, and the work on the church went ahead with much enthusiasm.

Inside Moulton Church before restoration, 1867. Clerk, William Smith in the foreground.

During restoration the church looked a terrible state inside, but the efforts of the workmen and various tradespeople were to good effect, and by May 1868 the church was ready for re-opening.

The following newspaper report gives an account of the proceedings, and the work that was done.

May 1868.

Reopening of Moulton Church – On Thursday the 7th Moulton Parish Church was reopened, after having undergone extensive repairs and restorations. Several circumstances gave this celebration a wide interest, extending to several counties. The village is exceedingly picturesque; it was a bright morning, and the inhabitants put everything in the best trim. From the lofty and beautiful tower several flags fluttered in the breeze, and the sweet toned bells gave an intimation to the surrounding level that a festival was at hand. The hawthorns and the orchard blossoms, groups of rustics in holiday attire, and here and there a clerical band, interspersed with gay equipages, made up as lovely a piece of English rural scenery as can possibly be imagined. Soon after 11 o'clock a procession of forty clergymen in their white surplices accompanied by the Bishop of the Diocese, passed from the upper school to the church. The Bishop preached the sermon. The church was crowded with strangers. The money for the restoration has been borrowed of the Government, and the ratepayers have consented to pay it off in twenty years with interest, by a church improvement rate on their houses and land; but the sum so raised has been liberally supplemented by voluntary donations. The church has been reseated with open oak seats, the organ has been reconstructed by Corps of Norwich, and is a fine acquisition to the church service; the floor is relaid, the windows restored, a new porch raised, the roof made secure, the chancel restored, and the floor paved with Minton's tiles and white marble; the grave yard has been drained and planted with beautiful shrubs; there is a new font, and the bells have been rehung. The additions to follow, we hear, are heating apparatus, a sixth bell, and memorial stained glass windows. The beauty of the church when thrown open on Thursday called for general admiration. The success of the great undertaking has been greatly owing to the business tact and perseverance of the Rev. J. R. Jackson, the Vicar.

Moulton Church before restoration, 1867. Looking west, Benjamin Skeath Sealow in foreground.

Group of workmen engaged on the restoration, end of 1867, North doorway. Mr. William Brown, contractor in dark suit. Mr. Thorpe, foreman on the ladder. Vicar of Moulton just behind Mr. Brown.

Moulton Church under restoration end of 1867, looking east.

Moulton Church under restoration end of 1867, looking west.

At 3 o'clock a well provided luncheon was set out in a marquee by Mr. Thomas Smith, to which 300 sat down. Lord Kesteven took the chair, supported by the Bishop, W. Erie Welby, Esq. M.P., the Rev. W. Brooke, the Rev. W. Wayett, &c. A. Clark, Esq. the vice-chairman, was supported by Major Moore, of Frampton, the Rev. A. Brook, Vicar of Holbeach, H. Clark, Esq. (churchwarden)), Mr. Smith (architect) &c. – The chairman in giving "the Queen and Royal family," said her Majesty had shown sympathy with the good work going on in this parish; she had contributed £200 towards the church restoration fund, and £100 to the church mission fund at Moulton Seas End. Although the Crown had estates in this parish the money was not paid from that revenue. They would all sympathise with her Majesty in the suffering which the dastardly attempt to assassinate her talented son on the other side of the world had caused. The Chairman next proposed "the Bishop and Clergy,". He had never on any former similar occasion met so large a body of the clergy as were now present. The way in which this great work of restoration had been conducted was a most remarkable proof of the soundness of feeling to the church, and it was worthy of note that so many gentlemen residing at the extreme ends of this fine parish (16 miles in length) had willingly contributed their share to the work, although they could hardly hope to share in the advantages. The way in which the fund had been raised was a remarkable feature in this case; it had not been done by going round with begging letters with which he was so familiar; it was creditable to this spirited parish. He had called it a fine parish, and it was so in every sense, in extent, in opulence, and in its love of independence. He (the chairman) thought the works had been well carried out that they defied criticism. The Bishop, in returning thanks to the toast, expressed his pleasure at the privilege of attending on these occasions, which were in fact the bishop's holidays, for on these happy days he had no cares; he knew all would go on well. They afforded opportunities of worshipping God with the people, and of saying a word to them. Such works were a great cause of gratification; they spoke of zeal and self denial. The affluent gave cheerfully of their abundance, and often those of humbler means, in their abiding love, gave more liberally still. Self denial was shown in many ways. Not a few had very strong prejudices to remove. They were deeply attached to the ugly pew of their early days; they loved it, and even its musty smell was associated with the fondest recollections of their lives. "It was the old seat where in childhood they had sat under a loved parent's care; and the dearest memories were associated with the old pew". Many such said "Your new plans are all very well; my old pew shall go for your improvements, but I like the old pew still." Now I, for one (continued his Lordship) respect such a man for the sacrifice he makes for the good of others. In carrying out these works there are a number of things which bring forth the better feelings of parishioners. During the last 15 years 300 churches have been rebuilt or restored in this diocese. The results have been larger congregations, better church feeling, and more earnestness in religion. At the present time the church was assailed from without and within. Church rates were to go. Well, the people would not allow their churches to go to decay. The church was to be separated from the state in Ireland. Next in England, said some people. This would destroy our parochial system, which gave to every Englishman a right to a seat in his parish church, where the pastor was known to his flock. Then there were parochial vestries, and the people were trained in self government. This state of things would be dissolved, and probably a tyrannical centralization set up in its place. When he thought of these things, he rejoiced in the zeal he saw around him. He was no alarmist, and he took little heed of the passing storms of political life, for they soon cleared off. Major Moore of Frampton, replied on behalf of "the Army and Navy", and observed that Moulton was his native village. In some measures he considered himself a pioneer in this work. When a young man he remembered returning from his studies at Oxford, and his first object was to examine this old church, here pulling down old boarding or pews, or scraping off stucco in search of hidden architectural beauties. Caution and secrecy were necessary in such matters in that day, for if any parishioner had caught him the sound would have gone forth that he was a Roman Catholic, or a Puseyite, or some such bugbear. They had now come to the resolve not to let the Catholics have it all their own way in the beautiful in church architecture; it was not in the revival of this taste that religion would suffer it was rather in that wide-spread carelessness and indifference to all religion or what pertained to it. In revisiting this his native church after many absent years, he was struck with the absence of many faces familiar to his youthful days; they had gone for ever, yet there remained one who had been minister of this parish for a whole generation (the Rev. C. Moore, of Wyberton) bowed down with the weight of 80 years, who was with them in feeling on this day. Another 30 years and more of the present company will have passed away, but not without leaving their mark. The Bishop gave "the Lay Rector, Mrs. Johnson," who had restored the chancel and "the Vicar," who had so actively promoted the general work. The Rev. E. Moore replied on behalf of Mrs. Johnson, and remarked that Whaplode was the first to commence this work of church restoration in this Deanery and its restored chancel was the ugliest appendage he had seen to a church; the sooner it was pulled down the better. In the year 1292, Bishop Sutton, holding a court at Croyland, ordered the Moulton people not to hold their fairs and markets in the churchyard, but rather to set about repairing their campanile, and this was the origin of their most beautiful tower and spire. The Rev. J. R. Jackson, the Vicar, who was cheered very briefly returned the thanks, and acknowledged the services of is churchwardens, especially Mr. Clark, who has assisted him throughout, and the inhabitants and others who had so generously supported him. Mr. Alfred Clark gave "the old and new members of the South Division of the County."

Moulton

Lord Kesteven having replied, Mr. W. Earl Welby observed that this was the first time he had addressed a public audience since his election. He had the greatest pleasure in renewing his acquaintance with this parish, for 500 years his family having resided or owned property in it. Three of them had represented the county in Parliament, and it was a remarkable coincidence, along with a member of the Hussey (Packe) family. He trusted he should be pardoned for absenting himself from his Parliamentary duties for such an occasion as this, in a parish where his ancestors in days of yore have acted a prominent part. It had been a source of enjoyment to him to indulge in the reflections called forth of days lang syne in connection with Moulton. At this stage Lord Kesteven and the Bishop left to catch the train. The remaining toasts were quickly disposed of under the chairmanship of the Vicar. At the evening service the respected Vicar of Pinchbeck, the Rev. W. Wayett, preached the sermon.

Moulton Parish Church, May 1868. Restoration just complete.
The flag staffs are still on the battlements.

Print of the Church of All Saints,
Moulton, 1842.

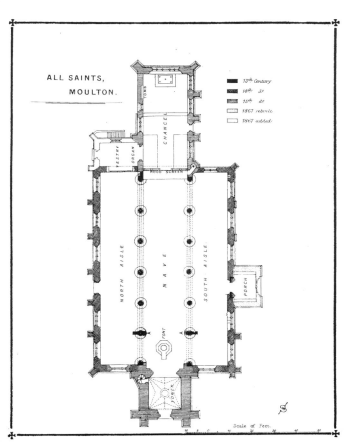

Plan of All Saints Church, Moulton,
about 1870.

Moulton Church after restoration May 1868 viewed from the church yard.

Inside Moulton Church just after restoration, May 1868.

View inside Moulton Church after restoration from the south porch, May 1868.

Moulton Church from north doorway, May 1868.

Moulton Parish Church showing the Sacrarium and new Reredos, taken about 1885.

Moulton Vicarage, 1887.

Moulton Vicarage Paddock after the gale in October 1883. Thirty nine large trees were blown down or so damaged as to need taking down.

The new Vicarage shrubbery after the old one was damaged in the October gale 1883 (Photograph taken in 1884).

Moulton Grammar School.

The Free Grammar School in the village of Moulton was founded by John Harrox, Yeoman, a native of the parish, by his will, dated the 19th of September, 1560; and endowed by him with approximately 275 acres of land which 263 acres are situated in the Parish of Moulton, and the remainder on the neighbouring Parish of Whaplode.

Moulton Grammar School about 1880.

John Harrox lived in the Mansion House which he had purchased from a Mr. Harrison in 1553, and it was in this house in 1561 that the school opened on the 1st August. The first headmaster to be appointed was Mr. Nicholas Belson, and the first scholar was John Jackson. The statutes appointed by the Founder were such as was common to most Grammar Schools; and particularly require Prayers to be said daily in the school, and strict attention to the Religion of the Established Church of England.

During the 278 years of the school's existence, the original house was rebuilt and various buildings added on. The school that was built in 1792 still stands gracefully in the centre of the village, overlooking the village green, and opposite to the church, although it is no longer a school. Moulton Grammar School closed down in 1939.

Seal of Moulton Free
Grammar School.

View from Moulton Church tower showing the Grammar School House. Taken in 1889
when the roof was under repair.

Headmasters of Moulton Grammar School.

1. Nicholas Belson, 1561-1569.
   Was buried at Moulton in August, 1592.

2. George Hall, 1569-1574.
   Dismissed or induced to resign; describes himself in a law suit in 1574 as "a Clerk of the age of 26".

3. .... Hooper, 1574-1581.
   Was appointed on the recommendation of Lord Clynton, who wrote on his behalf from Bolingbroke.

4. John Jobb, 1581-1590.
   Buried at Moulton 19th November, 1590.

5. James Assheton, B.D., 1590-1620.
   Buried at Moulton, 18th September, 1620. He was also Vicar of Moulton.

6. Thomas James. M.A., 1620-1631.
   Described on appointment as of Boston. Resigned the Office in 1631.

7. Jonas Smyth, M. A., 1631-1639.
   Buried at Moulton, 8th August, 1639.

8. George Atkinson, 1639.
   Of Boston; resigned after three weeks tenure of office.

9. Benjamin Stoneham, 1639.

10. Solomon Heaton. Date of appointment unknown.
    Buried at Moulton, 6th January, 1658.

11. William King. Date of appointment unknown.
    Buried at Moulton, 9th March, 1666.

12. John Hunt, B.A., 1667-1670.
    Described as a senior Bachelor of Arts of Sydney College; died or resigned in 1670.

13. James Hayes, M.A., 1670-1709.
    Late Usher of the Free School in Lynn Regis. Resigned in 1709, died in Moulton in 1711, and was
    buried in Moulton Church on the 1st April in that year.
    N.B. Richard Reynolds, Bishop of Lincoln in 1723, was educated at Moulton under Mr. Hayes.

14. William Stanton, 1709-1711.
    Described as "Clerk". Died and was buried in the same week as his predecessor in Moulton Church, viz:
    on April 5th, 1711.

15. Francis Curtis, 1711-1717.
    Clerk. Died in August, 1717.

16. George Boulton, 1717-1722.

17. John Chapman, 1722-1763.
    Clerk, was buried in Moulton Church on the 26th February, 1763.
    N.B. Mrs. Chapman was half-sister to the Antiquary "Cole", who often stayed in Moulton. A brother
    of the Antiquary was a scholar at the School, and died and was buried at Moulton.

18. William Maugham, 1763-1814.
    Clerk, was buried at Moulton 6th June, 1814, aged 88 years.

19. Samuel Elsdale, M.A., 1814-1827.
    Clerk, Fellow of Lincoln College, Oxford; was buried at Moulton, 20th June, 1827, aged 47 years.

20. Charles Moore, 1827-1856,
    Rev. resigned in 1856. Died at Wyberton in 1881, upwards of 90 years of age.

21. Hector Nelson, M.A., 1856-1861.
    Rev. resigned in 1861; became Principal of Training School, Lincoln.

22. J. W. Johnson, M.A., 1861-1867.
    Rev. resigned in 1867, and became Headmaster of Leamington College.

23. J. H. Green, M.A.,1867-1869.
    Rev. resigned at the end of 1868, obtained by the Headmastership of Kibworth Grammar School,
    Leicester, and then Rector of Mowsley in Leicestershire.

24. Brian, Christopherson, M.A., 1869-1873.
    Rev. resigned in 1873, obtained the Headmastership of Newcastle on Tyne Grammar School, and then
    Rector of Falmouth.

25. Reginald T. H. Lucas, ll.d., 1873-1881.

26. Frederick Hatt, M.A., 1881-1894.
   A Layman and B.A. of Cambridge when appointed, but later became a Clerk in Holy Orders and M.A.

27. Alfred Stanley Hatt, 1894-1927.

28. J. A. Holden, M.A., 1928-1931.

29. A.R.M. Tranter, M.A., 1931-1934.

30. E. A. G. Marlar, M.A., LL.B., 1935-1937.

31. John George, Westmorland, 1937-1939.

The Rev. B. Christopherson with his Wife and family.

The Rev. R. T. H. Lucas

Above and Below: Headmaster, Masters and boys of Moulton Grammar School.

Points of Interest from the Prospectus for Moulton Grammar School about 1920.

Moulton Grammar School buildings and grounds.

The School, stands in its own grounds of about 12 acres, pleasantly situated in the centre of the picturesque village of Moulton, within easy distance of Moulton Railway Station.

The buildings comprise Classrooms, Chemical and Physics Laboratory, Dining Hall, Dormitories, Bath Room, &c., and School House.

Adjacent to the School is a Playing Field, with a fine natural turf, specially suitable for Cricket which covers an area of seven acres, and a commodious and fully-equipped pavilion.

Personal inspection of buildings and arrangements is invited. Appointments should be made by letter to the Headmaster.

Course of Education.

The aim of the School is to turn out boys qualified by their knowledge, character, and refinement to make the best of their future career.

Every effort is therfore made:–
(1) To develop the character equally with intelligence.
(2) To foster a spirit of loyalty.
(3) To enforce a high standard of manners and reasonable self respect.
(4) To provide for a wholesome physical development.

The School course is so arranged as to supply a thorough and sound training in the essential subjects of a liberal and practical education. Every facility is afforded to boys at the proper stage to pursue the more advanced or special studies which their future vocation may require.

Boys are prepared for the London University Matriculation Examination, the Preliminary Examination of the Legal and Medical Professions, the Civil Service, and the Cambridge School Certificate Examination, for the last of which the School is a Centre.

During the last few years, boys have gained open Scholarships and Proceeded to the Universities and University Colleges, where their successes have included 1st and 2nd Class Honours (in Physics, Mathematics, History and Law) at the London and Cambridge Graduate Examinations.

Boys have also recently acquitted themselves most creditably in the various Entrance and further Examinations of the Civil, Naval, and Air Services.

Subjects of Instruction:

English: Religious Knowledge.
Reading, Writing.
Grammar, Composition, and Literature.
Geography.
History.

Languages: French.
Latin.

Mathematics: Arithmetic, Algebra, Geometry, Trigonometry,
Land Surveying (practical).

Science: Physics, Chemistry, Biology, Nature Study.

Art & Music: Drawing.
Vocal Music, Piano.

Physical Exercise.

Games.

Every encouragement is given to boys to enter into the organised School Games.

It is interesting to know that Old Boys are now playing for their County Cricket Teams; and one has captained England in the Test Matches both at home and in Australia.

Fees.

Tuition: £3 3s. per term (including Stationery, and use of necessary Text Books).
Piano, £1 1s. per term.

Dinners: Dinner is provided at the school at a charge of 5s. per week of five days.

Boarding: £13 per term (in the Headmaster's House).
Weekly Boarders at a reduced rate (£1 per term less).
Laundry (when required) 15s. per term.

Note: All Fees are payable in advance on the first day of each term.

One Term's Notice of Removal must be given in writing to the Headmaster, failing which, payment of one Term's Fees will be required.

Time Table:
School Time Table.
Mornings:

8.45	Prayers.
8.50-9.30	1st Period.
9.30-10.00	2nd Period.
10.10-10.50	3rd Period.
10.50-11.00	Interval.
11.00-11.40	4th Period.
11.40-12.20	5th Period.
12.20-1.00	6th Period.

Afternoon:

2.15-3.15	7th Period.

Moulton

Boarders Time Table:

7.15 a.m.	Call
7.45	Roll-call.
8.00	Breakfast.
8.45	Morning-School.
1.00 p.m.	Dinner.
2.15	Afternoon School.
3.15	Games.
4.30	Tea.
5.00	Games.
6.00	Preparation.
8.00	Supper.
9.00	Bed.
9.15	Light Out.
9.30	Talking stops in Dormitories.

Organisation:

The School is divided into three Houses, the names of which are those of men famous in the School's history:–

1. Harrox – named after the Founder.
2. Burnstone – Named after one of the first Feoffees, who championed the School's interests through many legal difficulties of its early days.
3. Reynolds – Named after a pupil who afterwards became Dean of Peterborough and Bishop of Lincoln.

A School Magazine – "The Moultonian" is published every term, containing a record of the Term's activities, and other matters of interest to Old Boys, Parents, and Friends.

Science room, Moulton Grammar School.

One of the classrooms, Moulton
Grammar School.

Dining Room, Moulton
Grammar School.

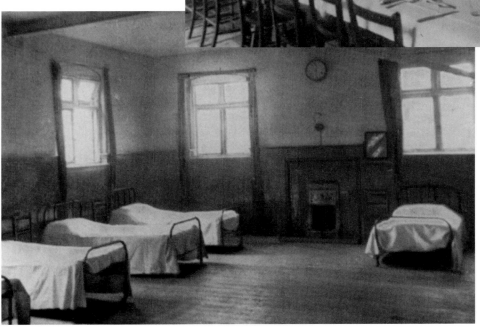

Dormitory, Moulton
Grammar School.

Moulton Village School.

Moulton Village School with residence, built by Mr. Bassett Smith in the year 1878.

Group of school buildings, Moulton village, after the building of the girls and infants school in 1881. Photograph taken in 1884.

In 1881 it was decided to enlarge the village school and the following advertisement was published:

To Builders, Contractors, and others.

Builders desirous of CONTRACTING for the ERECTION of a SCHOOL at Moulton, Lincolnshire, for 104 girls and infants, can inspect the Plans, Specifications, and Bills of Quantities of Mr. Joseph Sawyer, the Board's Architect, at my office in Spalding any day after Thursday, 2nd June next between the hours of 9 a.m. and 7 p.m.

Sealed Tenders are to be sent in addressed to the Chairman of the Moulton School Board, under cover to me, so as to reach me not later than the First Post on the morning of Tuesday the 14th June next. – By Order.

H. Stanley Maples, Spalding.
Spalding, 16th May, 1881. Clerk to the Board.

Moulton Schoolchildren, photographed about 1884.

Moulton Tower Mill.

The tower mill at Moulton stands 80 feet high to the curb, and was originally 97 feet high to the top of its cap.

One of the tallest mills in the country, it was built in 1822 by Mr. Robert King. The sails were removed in 1895 after they were damaged by gales. On the 22nd December 1894 it was reported that great damage was done at Moulton near Spalding, the six-sail mill had the sails and top, weighing ten tons, blown away, the damage amounting to £600. After the removal of the sails a two sack Turner roller milling plant was installed in the adjoining granary, steam power was also applied to the original stones.

Large quantities of milling ceased many years ago, but the Biggadike family who took over the tenancy of the mill in 1924 continued well into the 1990s milling small amounts for local farmers. John Biggadike bought the mill about 1950.

The mill is now owned by a trust, and various interested parties are trying to put plans together to restore and preserve the mill. Only time will tell what the outcome of these plans will be.

Moulton Mill about 1880.

Moulton Mill from
the church tower.

Moulton Tower Mill and in the background the church.

Moulton village and Mill from a sketch by G. W. Bailey. Spalding Gentlemen's Society Collection.

The Mill at Moulton, 1999.

Snippets from what the papers used to say:

February 1818.
A Caution

    Whereas a genteel-looking Woman calling herself MARIA BLANCHARD, who was lately keeper of a School at Moulton, in Lincolnshire, did on the 22nd of December last, shut up her house and school, pretending for the Christmas recess, as is usual for other schools, and gave notice to her scholars, that she should open again on Monday the 12th of January, 1818, but has not yet returned, nor been heard of; and did at the time first mentioned, take away with her a large quantity of the Femail Scholars Works, consisting of different kinds of Irish and other Linens, and sundry articles, entrusted to her care to teach the children as seamstress; and also has got into several tradesman's debt in the neighbourhood. And whereas a way was forced into the house lately in her occupation on Saturday last, and the above things were not to be found, to the disappointment of the children's parents. This is to caution the unwary from trusting her with their children, or their property: and if any person will give notice where she is, to JOHN BAMFORD, one of the Constables of Moulton, by letter, it will be thankfully received, and any reasonable expense allowed by the inhabitants of Moulton, Whaplode and Weston.

    N.B. She is supposed to be in the neighbourhood of Holt, in Norfolk.

December 1883.

    Singular Accident– A somewhat serious accident happened to Mrs. Jackson, wife of the Rev. J. R. Jackson, Vicar of Moulton, on Saturday. The lady had retired to her bedroom shortly after 10 o'clock, leaving Mr. Jackson downstairs. In putting some of the children's toys into a cupboard her hair caught fire from the candle she was holding. Running downstairs screaming, she was met in the hall by Mr. Jackson, who with great presence of mind threw her down upon the hall floor, and endeavoured to smother the blaze with a mat– the only suitable article within reach. The fire burst through the mat, and the lady's position was one of extreme danger, when a servant rushed forward with a large flannel, and the flames were smothered. Mrs. Jackson escaped with slight burns and scorching of head and neck.

October 1888.

    Anthrax – Last week two bullocks died from anthrax in Moulton West Fen, a district where outbreaks of such disease frequently occur: one belonged to Mr A. H. Clark and the other to Mr. T. Chapman.

December 1870.

    The Dryness of the Season. – One day this week two sporting gentlemen were coursing a hare on Mr. Foster's farm at Moulton: for nearly a mile they galloped their horses down the course of the Nene drain, which at this season is supposed to be full of water, but this year it is dry, and being of a silty bottom is firmer to travel upon than the high land.

Newscutting date unknown (about 1880).

    A Romance in Humble Life. – The Rev. J. R. Jackson, Vicar of Moulton, Lincolnshire sends the following instance of a remarkable wedding which took place in this parish church the other day. He says: – Forty years ago a young man named Thomas Griggs was engaged to Elizabeth Goodyear, but alas! a debilitating illness overtook the bride-elect, which so prostrated her that she took to her bed and kept it for eight and thirty years! During this long period of time, assisted by the Guardians, and by a small fund at her disposal, she maintained herself by needle and fancy work. During thirteen years and upwards, I myself knew her in this condition, and never saw her off her bed. In the meanwhile, Thomas Griggs waited patiently for his Elizabeth, but in 1865, despairing of this, he led another young woman to Elizabeth's bedside, and received from her full permission to marry his fresh acquaintance. Thomas forthwith married, but after five years of wedded life, he became and remained a widower until this very day, when Elizabeth Goodyear, restored to health, walked into the parish church of Moulton, and was duly married by me to her old sweetheart. I cannot explain the nature of her prostration, nor her wonderful recovery; but I do know this, that a few months back she became conscious of a slight return of strength, that from feeble efforts to leave her bed and struggle across the room she gained power to pass her door, that the old subject of matrimony was revived by Thomas Griggs, that Elizabeth was willing, that banns were published, and that she is now the wife of her early and only "love". The details of this story are so unusual that I send them, with permission of bride and bridegroom, to your paper. That the remainder of their lives on earth may be prosperous and happy will, I am sure, be the hearty desire of all who read this true and, I think, interesting story.

October 1888.

Foolhardy Feats.– Last week, while Moulton was en fete with the weddings and the harvest festival. Tom Hardy, a labourer, climbed the church spire (160 feet) and brought down from the weathercock a handkerchief tied to it a few months ago by Horace Rower, a sailor, a native of Moulton. These feats have been performed on several occasions in the past. In 1812, Robert Jarvis, labourer, went up the spire with his little child in his arms, and tied it to the weathercock with his handkerchief. He then descended, went to his home, fetched his wife out to look at the child, and again ascended the spire, and brought the little one down safely. Steps will now be taken to prevent a recurrence of such feats.

March 4th 1893.

A Mill Destroyed by Fire. – On Saturday morning, a flour mill at Moulton Seas End, about six miles from Spalding, was completely destroyed by fire, and damage done estimated at over £1,000. About 90 quarters of corn-wheat and barley – was burned in the mill. The cause of the outbreak is unknown, but it is attributed to heat generated by the friction of the machinery. The loss is only partly covered by insurance.

April 1874.

On Wednesday Ben Skeath, the old sexton of Moulton resigned his appointment, at the age of 82 years, he and his predecessor, Ben Skeath having held the office for nearly 100 years. We find from the gravestones in the church yard that Ben Skeath, sexton, died 7th February 1688; also on 12th September 1792 Ben Skeath, sexton died; and in 1799 Ben Skeath, sexton died again in 1828 Ben Skeath, sexton departed this life. The most notable event in the reign of the present "Old Ben" was the exhumation of one of the bodies under his care for anatomical purposes. The parishioners are now being canvassed for a successor to these "grave" duties. It is hoped that a proper surveillance of the church yard will be insisted upon.

September 1891.

Shooting a Dog for Sheep Worrying. – At the Spalding County Court, on Monday before his Honour Judge Stephen James Lunn, a shepherd, sued John Bailey, a farmer, of Moulton, for £5, for shooting his shepherd dog. The shooting was admitted, but the plea of justification was set up. The defendant had had a lamb worried, and had suspected the plaintiff's dog, and on the second occasion when the dog was seen chasing another lamb, the defendant shot it. His Honour held that the defendant was justified in the shooting of the dog, and gave judgement to the defendant, with costs.

The Dun Horse Inn, Moulton Eaugate. January 1949.

The Man and Horse Inn.

On the 12th June, 1827 the Man & Horse was advertised in the local newspaper, to be auctioned at the White Horse Inn, Spalding on the 26th of June, 1827. The advertisement stated that the estate was Freehold and situated in Moulton adjoining the Eaugate Road, near to the South Holland Main Drain. The property was said to be well built with Brewhouse, Barn, Stables, and other Outbuildings, and two Orchards planted with excellent and thriving fruit trees thereto adjoining, and a Homestead of capital Land containing about Eight Acres, now in the tenure of Mr. Richard Hargrave, the owner. Also three Tenements, with Gardens, and Wheelwright's Shop and Blacksmith's Shop adjoining. At the time of the sale these properties were in the several tenures of William Mousley, Henry Faulkner, John Moody, and somebody call Leeton.

Included in the sale was a Parcel of Land on the opposite side of the road, and next to the Moulton River, containing about Half an Acre.

The Man & Horse Inn, Moulton Eaugate, March 1948.

Moulton Chapel

Moulton Chapel

Moulton Chapel is situated 4 miles south from Moulton and 2 miles east from Cowbit church. The road from Cowbit to Moulton Chapel and beyond is almost straight, and is thought to follow the line of a road laid by the Romans during their occupation of Britain. Until 1890 Moulton Chapel was contained within the parish of Moulton, but with its own chapel, dedicated to St. James.

On the 7th day of May 1890 the Chapel had a legal district assigned to it by Her Majesty the Queen in Council, at the Court Of Windsor, so that for all Ecclesiastical purposes it became a district and separate parish from the mother parish of Moulton. The Parochial Church Council minutes also date from 1890.

Moulton Chapel church about 1820 taken from a watercolour painting by Hilkiah Burgess.

When the Chapel of St. James was restored and extended in 1886 Canon Moore said that he was firmly of the opinion that an earlier chapel was situated hereabout, around the year 1259. At this time certain articles were preferred against Sir Thomas de Multon by the Prior and Convent of Spalding, Rectors and Patrons of the Church of Moulton, and by the Vicar of Moulton, for having unlawfully erected a certain Chapel within his Manor, and for carrying on services there without authority. At this time more people started to inhabit the district, and various chapels were erected for the convenience of the people, one of which was the Chapel of St. James in the parish of Moulton. Most of these chapels were built mainly of timber, and thatched with reed. We may fairly assume that the original Moulton Chapel of its day was thus constructed, and in good measure account for the total disappearance of the original Chapel. It was not however destroyed at the "Reformation". More than 100 years before that event it is recorded that Roger Welby, of Moulton, bequeathed by his will dated 1410, a small legacy for the repair of the fabric of St. James' in Moulton, in which he also requested a Mass to be said there on his behalf. Again in 1495 Joan Welby (the widow of Richard Welby), bequeathed a small sum for repairing the Chapel of St. James at Moulton.

Entries in the parish register records the baptism of the twin children of William and Katherine Miller, Curate of the Chapel in 1622, and the marriage of Peter Gresby with Robson Ashbye at Moulton Chapel in 1631. After the Civil War, which ended in 1649 all records of the Chapel of St. James for a period ceased, and it is fair to assume that the Chapel disappeared until the present one was built in 1722.

The present Chapel came into being after Maurice Johnson went riding through Moulton Chapel one Sunday. Noticing a number of men congregated together in idle chat, he enquired of them why they were not at church, to which they replied that their church was four miles off and that was too far to go. He then decided to build them a chapel, which he did, and endowed it with a rent charge of £16 per year upon his estate.

Moulton Chapel west front before restoration, 1885.

Inside St. James' Moulton Chapel, 1885, Moulton

The octagonal Chapel was built of brick with stone dressings, and an octagonal high pitched roof of grey slate, terminated with a leaded spirette, mounted on an open bell turret. The bell bearing the date 1814 was provided by the then incumbent of the Chapel the Rev. Wm. Moore.

In 1886 it was decided to enlarge the Chapel and the following advert was published in the local paper.

To Builders.

Tenders are required for enlarging and re-seating Moulton Chapel Church, near Spalding. The drawings and specification can be seen on application to Mr. John E. Huntsman (opposite the church), between the hours of 9 a.m. and 6 p.m., from June 3rd to June 12th, and the tenders must be delivered free of charge, to the Rev. J. R. Jackson, Moulton Vicarage, Spalding, not later than 12 o'clock on Monday, June 14th, in a sealed envelope endorsed "Moulton Chapel Tender". The committee does not pledge themselves to accept the lowest or any tender.

W. Bassett-Smith, Architect.

Upon completion of the work the Chapel was re-consecrated and the report in the press was as follows:–

25th October 1886.

The chapel of St. James, Moulton Chapel, was re-consecrated on Monday after the restoration and renovation, the presences of the Bishop of the diocese adding additional interest to the occasion. The building had long needed repair, and the work done was as follows:–

New seats and fittings, new floor and pavement, walls fresh plastered, windows glazed, repairs to roof and removal of bell cote, and in addition the east side of the octagonal building has been removed and a small chancel added. The work commenced on July 14th, Messrs. Collingwood and Son of March, being the contractors. Monday's proceedings commenced with celebration of Holy Communion in Moulton Parish Church at an early hour, and at 12 the consecration service was held in the Chapel, Canon Moore, the Rev. J. R. Jackson, and Canon Hemmans assisting. The sermon was preached by the Bishop from St. Luke VII, 45, "Thou gavest me no kiss." At the conclusion of the service a public luncheon was served in a marquee, provided by Mrs. Wadlow, of the Red Lion Hotel, Spalding. E. M. E. Welby, Esq., of Sheffield, presided, and was supported by the Bishop of Lincoln, the Revs. J. R. Jackson, Canon Moore, Canon Hemmans, B. W. Randolph, W. H. James, Riley, Ash, Bennett, Hatt, Bree, Sisson, Sanderson, Pearson, Clarke, Gardener, and Messrs, F. Howard, J.P., H. Clark &c.

The chief toast was that of "the Archbishops, the Bishops, and the Clergy of the Church of England". Dr. King who responded, expressed a hope that the service they had celebrated that day would be the means of inducing a large proportion of the inhabitants of the district to attend service regularly. He gave "the health of the Rev. J. R. Jackson, Vicar of Moulton, and Mrs. Jackson," which was duly acknowledged. Other toasts followed. Two other services were held during the day, also a public tea.

Interior of Moulton St. James after restoration (Photographed in 1888).

Two different views of the church of Moulton St. James after the restoration and consecration.
These photographs were taken by John Millett Coats formerly assistant curate of Moulton parish in the year 1888.

Further improvements were made to St. James in the 1920s when the organ chamber on the south side of the chancel was built, and a vestry on the north side of the chancel was also added.

The last full-time incumbent of Moulton Chapel was the Rev. Reginald Thompson who retired in 1975. He was a colourful character who was often seen riding around the parish on horse back, and also took a turn at refereeing wrestling matches.

In 1978 the benefices of Moulton Chapel, Weston and Weston Hills, and Cowbit were united to form the benefice of Cowbit, the Rev. E. J. Wingfield being the first incumbent of the new benefice.

The vicarage at Moulton Chapel, being no longer required was then sold.

Moulton Chapel Mill.

The tower mill at Moulton Chapel was built in 1865 to replace a post mill that previously stood on the site. It was powered by wind until about 1930 when an engine took over.

The sails were removed before the second world war after gales had damaged them and they became unsafe.

Milling continued into the 1950s with electricity being used as a power source, but eventually the mill fell into disuse as did many more at this time.

Photograph taken in the 1920s showing the Chapel of St. James, the windmill with sails and the Plough Inn just to the right of the picture.

Trades and Business People in Moulton Chapel in 1937.

Achurch Jane (Mrs.) , shopkeeper.
Atkin, Geo. F., farmer, Decoy Farm.
Baker, Allen Victor, bricklayer.
Baker, Jn. Rt., builder.
Barker, Thos. Herbert & Benj., farmers, Engine Bank.
Barnes, Walter R., boot & shoe repairs.
Beba Frank, farmer, Broadwater House.
Beba, Percy, farmer, Chestnut Farm.
Boor, Frederick, farmer.
Bradford, Samuel, foreman to the Richmond Trust.
Burchnell, Raymond Smith, smallholder, Fengate.
Butlers, Jn. Wm., smallholder, Queens Bank.
Clark, Alfred H. & Son., farmers, Crown Hall, Moulton Eaugate.

159

Coates, Jn. Thos., farmer, Bridge Farm, Moulton Eaugate.

Cook, Joseph, farmer, Elm House, Moulton Eaugate.

Cook, Matthew William, smallholder, Moulton Eaugate.

Cook, William, blacksmith, Fengate.

Culy, Edwin, cottage farmer, Woodgate.

Culy, Herbert B., bulb grower, Fengate.

Culy, Rose (Miss), bulb grower.

Dennis, Chas., bulb grower, Fengate.

Fisher, Alfred C. W., bulb grower & dairyman, The Elms.

Fisher, Ernest, farmer, The Sycamores.

Fletcher, Jack, farmer, Fengate.

Footit, Jn., farmer, Moulton Eaugate.

George, J. T. & Co., grocer & post office.

Goy, Alfred Hy., farmer, Moulton Eaugate.

Goose, Frank, farmer.

Grummitt, Joseph, farmer, Bridge Farm.

Grummitt, Rd., farmer, The Willows.

Hammond, Edmund, farmer, Fengate.

Hemmant Bros., wheelwrights, Fengate.

Hicks, Arth, smallholder, Woodgate.

Holmes, Parker, farmer, Fengate.

Huntsman, Jn, farmer.

Huntsman, William A., farmer.

Johnson, Arth. F., farmer, Broadwater Farm.

Johnson, Harry, farmer, Oxcroft Bank.

King, Jack, farmer, Engine Farm.

Leake, Jnthn, smallholder, Woodgate.

Lyons, Jsph, baker & pastrycook.

Mackman, Jsph, chimney sweep, Woodgate.

Man & Horse Public House (Arth. W. Hilliam), Moulton Eaugate.

Moulton Chapel Bulb Co. Ltd., bulb growers.

Nicholls, Geo., farmer, Poplar Farm.

Old Engine Public House (Wltr. Cecil Woods) Engine Bank.

Pack H. (Miss.), fried fish dealer.

Parker, Harry, smallholder, Woodgate.

Plough Public House (Arth. Wright).

Red Cow Inn (Jn. Wood).

Remnant Geo., farmer, Moulton Eaugate.

Rose, J. R., haulage contractor.

Smith, Jsph, Wm., fruit grower.

Stainlsey, Arth. W. Smith., blacksmith & farrier, Moulton Eaugate.

Thorpe, Allan, threshing machine owner.

Thorpe, Bert, farmer, Fengate.

Thorpe, Fred, threshing machine owner.

Thorpe, Harry, threshing machine owner.

Three Tuns Inn (Geo. R. Clark).

Thrower, Ernest, smallholder.

Turnbull, Jsph. (Snr.), poultry farmer.

Twell, Arth. Rt., farmer, Snake Hall.

Vickers, Matilda (Mrs.), farmer.

Vickers, Wm., farmer, Fengate.
Wakefield, Geo., farmer, Moulton Eaugate.
Wheatsheaf Public House (Alfred Bradley).
Wiles, Ernest Wm., farmer, Fengate.
Wright, Emma Ann (Mrs.), retail confectioner, Moulton Eaugate.
Wright, Harry, smallholder.

The Plough Inn,
Moulton Chapel, about
1950.

Snippets from what the papers used to say.

March 1861.

Moulton Chapel. – A Fracas of a disgraceful character to all parties concerned occurred here on the 20th ult. There seems to be a feud between the Chapelites and the Cowbiters of a certain class, and several Cowbit men being in the district on the evening in question, they received a somewhat warm reception, but after a conflict, in which stones, forks, and other weapons were freely used, the Moulton Chapel men appear to have got the worst of the fight, and beat a retreat. An assault case arising out of the above appears in our police news.

January 1965.
Vicar refs. Women's Wrestling.

Moulton Chapel's wrestling referee vicar, the Rev. R. C. Thompson, refereed a bout between women at Halifax on Saturday.

He told a reporter he had agreed to do so, provided the women wore judo costumes. But he stated: "I am very much opposed to women wrestling in briefs I would not in any circumstances whatsoever lend myself to such a display."

October 1940.

One of the last private brewers in Lincolnshire, Mr. G. H. Bradford, died at the Wheatsheaf Inn, Moulton Chapel, the home of his son. The Moulton Chapel brewery established in 1801 by Mr. Bradford's grandfather, was closed by Mr. Bradford in 1927. During the harvest they brewed as many as four times a week to supply three public houses, the 'White Lion', Spalding, the 'Mermaid', Holbeach Fen, and the 'Wheatsheaf'.

Moulton Seas End

Moulton Seas End.

The hamlet of Moulton Seas End or Seaend as it was often known as in earlier times, grew up on a site next to the old Roman Sea Bank, 2¼ miles north of the village of Moulton. The Romans built this sea bank so as to drain, and protect the land between there and the Ravens Bank which they also built some 5 miles south. A large tract of land, containing 2,237 acres in Moulton parish, in common with the marshes in Holbeach and Gedney lying outside the Roman bank, was enclosed from the sea by a bank built in 1660. A further addition of 1,081 acres was made to the parish in 1793 by the South Holland Embankment, when the Red Cow District was enclosed. The inundation of the sea was quite common in earlier times. In 1765 the sea bank was broken by a sudden and unexpected tide which flooded the marsh land, drowning over 2,000 sheep, 7 beasts and 13 horses. Again during the gale and high tide of 1810, a breach was made in the South Holland Embankment which had only been constructed 17 years earlier.

Until the 1950's the sea used to still come in as far as the 1793 sea bank, particularly when there was a high tide that filled the creeks and covered the marshes. The area of marsh close to the Hare & Hounds public house was very popular with people picnicking, swimming in the creeks and collecting samphire when in season. Today much more land has been reclaimed, and the sea is much further off. The sea banks are much stronger and thousands of acres of fine agricultural land are cultivated.

The Windmill.

Seas End like most villages in this area had its own windmill. A tower mill was built in the village in 1810. Not much is known about the mill, and so far no illustrations of the structure seem to exist. The directories of 1885 give Mr. William Twell as the miller and baker. In 1893 a news report tells that the mill was destroyed by fire on the 4th March of that year. Repairs must have been done to the mill, because the directory of 1900 lists William Pocklington as the miller using wind and oil for power. In 1919 William Pocklington was still listed as the miller, but by 1922 the directory does not list a miller. The tower mill was reported to be derelict · in 1923, and by 1953 there were no visible remains of the structure.

Trades and Business People in Moulton Seas End in 1937.

Adcock, Frank, farmer, Carrington Road, Moulton Marsh.
Adcock, Harry, farmer, Carrington Road, Moulton Marsh.
Adcock, Harry, farmer, Moulton Marsh Way.
Ashford, Thos., farmer, Red Cow Drove, Moulton Marsh.
Ashton, Edwd. Rhodes, farmer, Moulton Marsh.
Aspland, Mary (Miss), farmer, Moulton Loosegate.
Baily, Jn. & Son, carpenters, Moulton Seas End.
Buck, Frederick Chas., farmer, Moulton Loosegate.
Buffham, Harold, carpenter, Roman Bank, Moulton Seas End.
Buffham, Hy., farmer, Roman Bank, Moulton Seas End.
Buffham, Jack, smallholder, Moulton Common.
Buffham, Jas., farmer, Roman Bank, Moulton Seas End.
Burwell, J., farmer, Red Cow Drove, Moulton Marsh.
Butters, G. W., farmer, Moulton Marsh Way.
Chatterton, W. Farmer, Moulton Marsh Way.
Chenery Alfred, smallholder, Carrington Road, Moulton Marsh.
Cherrington, Rt., farmer, Charity Farm, Moulton Marsh.
Clark, Barron, potato merchant, The Hollies, Moulton Seas End.
Clark, Sophia (Mrs.), smallholder, Moulton Common.

Coward, John, shop keeper & post office, Moulton Seas End.
Dennis & Sons Ltd., farmers, Seas End Hall, Moulton Seas End.
Dolton, Arth, farmer, Carrington Road, Moulton Marsh.
Dolton, Geo., farmer, Moulton Seas End.
Dolton, Regnld., farmer, Roman Bank, Moulton Seas End.
Earl, Frank, farmer, Moulton Loosegate.
Fletcher, Rt. Mossop, farmer, Moulton Loosegate.
Franks, Israel, farmer, Carrington Road, Moulton Marsh.
Franks, Wm. farmer, Red Cow Drove, Moulton Marsh.
Garner, Harry, farmer, Middle Marsh Road, Moulton Marsh.
Gent, Jsph., farmer, Carrington Road, Moulton Marsh.
Ginn, Geo., farmer, Carrington Road, Moulton Marsh.
Golden Lion Public House (Arth. Hollingsworth), Moulton Seas End.
Gott, Cyril, smallholder, Carrington Road, Moulton Marsh.
Gott, Geo., farmer, Carrington Road, Moulton Marsh.
Gratton, Geo., smallholder, Green Lane, Moulton Seas End.
Gratton, Harry, farmer, Carrington Road, Moulton Marsh.
Gratton, Jn. Jas., farmer, Carrington Road, Moulton Marsh.
Gregory, Saml., farmer, Carrington Road, Moulton Marsh.
Gritton, H. E., haulage contractor, Moulton Seas End.
Hare & Hounds Public House (H. Tear), Moulton Marsh.
Harris, Eliz. (Mrs.), farmer, Moulton Marsh.
Harris, Herbt. Thos., farmer, Moulton Seas End.
Hicks, J. W., shopkeeper, Moulton Wash Way.
Hines, T. W., farmer, Carrington Street, Moulton Marsh.
Hollingsworth Banks, smallholder, Moulton Common.
Jarvis, Jn., farmer, Moulton Wash Way.
Johnson, C. H., farmer, Wood House Lane, Moulton Loosegate.
Johnson, J. H., farmer, Moulton Loosegate.
Johnson, J. W., farmer, Middle Marsh Road, Moulton Marsh.
Kirby, Wm., smallholder, Green Lane, Moulton Seas End.
Kirby, Wm. Thos., farmer, Moulton Loosegate.
Kirton, Emily (Mrs.), butcher, Moulton Seas End.
Lewis, Harold S., blacksmith, Moulton Seas End.
Machin, Alfd., farmer, Red Cow Drove, Moulton Marsh.
Mackman, T., farmer, Carrington Road, Moulton Marsh.
Munton, Jn., smallholder, Carrington Road, Moulton Marsh.
Munton, Thos., smallholder, Carrington Road, Moulton Marsh.
Naylor, Geo. Wm., farmer, Carrington Road, Moulton Marsh.
Naylor, Thos. H., smallholder, Moulton Common.
Patchett, A. B., farmer, Carrington Road, Moulton Marsh.
Patchett, E. P., farmer, Carrington Road, Moulton Marsh.
Pearson, W., Jun., farmer, Carrington Road, Moulton Marsh.
Pocklington Percvl., farmer, Moulton Seas End.
Raynes, Rt., farmer, Carrington Road, Moulton Marsh.
Reed, J., farmer, Roman Bank, Moulton Seas End.
Rhodes, Jn. Wm., farmer, Carrington Road, Moulton Marsh.
Sandall, Jn. E., fruit grocer, Glebe Farm, Moulton Seas End.
Shotbolt, Jn. Rt., farmer, Crown Farm, Moulton Marsh.
Simpson, Sydney Hill, farmer, Carrington Road, Moulton Marsh.

Slator, Fred, Potato merchant, Moulton Seas End.
Sporton, Chas. Hy., farmer, Carrington Road, Moulton Marsh.
Staff, Elijah, farmer, Carrington Road, Moulton Marsh.
Stancer, Alfred, farmer, Carrington Road, Moulton Marsh.
Stancer, Willis, farmer, Carrington Road, Moulton Marsh.
Steel, Groves Gibson, farmer, Carrington Road, Moulton Marsh.
Thompson, Wm., bricklayer, Moulton Seas End.
Twell, Hy., farmer, Moulton Common.
Waite, Wm., farmer, Moulton Loosegate.
White Horse Inn (Leslie Wright), Moulton Seas End.
Wilson, David, farmer, Middle Marsh Road, Moulton Marsh.
Wright, Albert, farmer, Carrington Road, Moulton Marsh.

White Horse Inn,
Moulton Seas End.

Golden Lion Public House,
Moulton Seas End.

Moulton Seas End, Church and Schoolroom.

Moulton Seas End Methodist Church.

Pinchbeck

**with West Pinchbeck and the
hamlets of
Mill Green.
Money Bridge.
Crossgate.
Cuckoo Bridge and
Pode Hole.**

Pinchbeck with Pinchbeck West, and the hamlets of Mill Green, Money Bridge, Guthram Cote, Crossgate, Cuckoo Bridge and Pode Hole.

Situated on the River Glen 2 miles north of Spalding is the village of East Pinchbeck. Due to much residential development the two are almost joined, and it is not beyond the possibility that in the next twenty years it will be difficult to tell where Spalding ends and Pinchbeck commences.

In Saxon times Pinchbeck was a place of much importance, and had attachment with the Abbey of Crowland. The late Canon Moore of Spalding, a respected local historian, maintained that Pinchbeck was a place of note before the Norman Conquest. In the time of Edward the Third, Pinchbeck was classed as a market town, and once had two market crosses. One was situated at the junction of Tydd Road and Mill Green, and it was here that fish from the local sea marshes, and wildfowl from the fens was brought to be sold. The other cross stood near to the Red Lion Inn in Northgate, and it was known as the meeting place for the sale of stock.

Right: The Red Lion Inn at Northgate, photographed about 1950. This establishment ceased trading in 1953, and the last person to hold the licence was Mr. John Cunningham.

This cottage was once the Red Lion Inn. It has kept its name and is called Red Lion House (Photographed 2000).

Fragments of the shaft and stepped based from the Medieval Cross which once stood outside the Red Lion Inn at Northgate.
These are now preserved in the War Memorial Grounds opposite the church.

Trades and Business People in Pinchbeck in 1937.

Andrews, Chas., smallholder, Crossgate.
Baxter, Fred, bulb grower, Weston House.
Bell Inn (Emerson Silas Scott), Church Street.
Benner, Emmanuel, farmer, Glen Side.
Benner, Jas. Edwd., farmer, Redmile House.
Bettinson, Percy Burrell, bulb grower, Northgate.
Bocock, Jas., smallholder, Northgate.
Boothby, Jn. Thos., pig keeper, Rose Lane.
Boston Coal Co. Ltd., Railway Station.
Bratley, Frank, fruit grower.
Bratley, Jn., farmer, Marsh.
Bray, Guy, builder & contractor, decorator & undertaker, Spalding Road.
Breathwick, Ethel Dora (Mrs), tobacconist, Crossgate.
Brewster, Eva Lilian (Mrs.), general stores, Pinchbeck Road.
Brewster, Joseph, Farmer, Cuckoo Lane.

Brewster, Sidney, builder, Pinchbeck Road.
Brocklehurst, M. A., dairyman, Market Way.
Broughton, Herbert, farmer, Pinchbeck Road.
Brown, James F., bulb grower, Rose Lane.
Bull Inn (Miss A. Bainbridge Orbell), Church Street.
Burrell, Walter Brown, farmer, Crossgate.
Burton, Wilfred Robert, L.R.C.P. & S. & L.M. Irel. Physician & Surgeon, Medical Officer, Church Street.
Caesar, Hy., smallholder, Surfleet Road.
Chamberlain, Arth., decorator, Craigwell.
Cheffings, Jn. Wm., baker.
Clark, Rt., smallholder, Crossgate.
Colvin, Geo., fruit grower, Pinchbeck Road.
Cooke, Rt. jun., bulb grower, Otway, Spalding Road.
Coward, Walter, farmer, Bertie Fen.
Crabtree Archibold, J. & Mary (Mrs.), bulb grower.
Darley, Alfred, farmer, Glen Side.
Darley, Benj., farmer, Cuckoo Lane.
Darley, George, farmer, Mill Green.
Darley, George Rt., farmer, Surfleet Road.
Dearnley, Matthew, bulb grower, Mill Green.
Dobney, Amos, smallholder, Northgate.
Dobney, Jn., market gardener.
Dods, Wm., coal merchant, Railway Station.
Faulkner, Ernest William, farmer, Bertie Fen.
Fletcher, Reginald Geo., boot & shoe repairer, Knight Street.
Francis, Cecil, grower & merchant, Graft House.
Freir, Samuel, farmer & land owner, The Yews, Pinchbeck Road, Sharp's Bridge.
Goodacres Filling Station, Surfleet Road.
Gostelow, Harold, farmer, Glen Side.
Green, Valentine Geo, builder, Knight Street.
Griffin, Jas., smallholder.
Grooby, Geo, farmer, Northgate.
Ground, Alfred Gordon, coal & coke merchant.
Grummett, Frank, farmer, Glen Side.
Grunnell, Stanley, smallholder, Mill Green.
Guy, Arth Ernest, smallholder.
Guy, Frank, fruit grower, Knight Street.
Guy, Zillah (Mrs.), shopkeeper, Church Street & Knight Street.
Healey, Frank, smallholder, Boston House, Cuckoo Lane.
Hemfrey, Charles, blacksmith, Church Street.
Hill, John H., market gardener.
Holmes, B., farmer, Glen Side.
Holmes, Thos. jun., butcher, Glen View.
Huntsman, Edmund Coulson, bulb grower, Bertie Fen.
Inkley, Jesse Parkinson, manure agent, Church Street.
Ireland, Harry, fried fish dealer, Knight Street.
Ivatt, Rt., farmer, Northgate.
Johnson, Geo, farmer, Stud Farm.
Lacey, Chas., market gardener.
Ladd George, plumber & glazier.

Lilley, Jn., smallholder.

Lovell, Rt., smallholder, Mill Green.

Mews, Ernest Frederick, poultry farmer, Bertie Fen.

Mews, Percy Hy., farmer, Horse Pit Lane.

Mews, Thos. Wm., farmer, Fenleigh, Bertie Fen.

Moon, Wm., smallholder, Mill Green.

Nickols, R. & E., farmers & landowners, The Marsh.

Nickols, Edward Leslie, farmer, Moortoft Lane.

Nickols, Harry, farmer, Marsh.

Nickols, Ralph, fruit grower, Pinchbeck Road.

Nix, Ruby May (Mrs.), motor engineer.

Palmer, Jn. Hy., rate collector & clerk to Parish Council, Northgate.

Parker, Chas., smallholder, Northgate.

Parkinson, Frank, bulb grower, Cherryholt.

Parkinson, Frank, butcher, Mill Green.

Partington, Ethel (Miss), district nurse, Knight Street.

Pepper, Chas., fruit grower, Cherryholt.

Porter, Wm., farmer, Mill Green.

Power & Burton, physicians & surgeons, Church Street.

Rawding, Ann Maria (Mrs.), smallholder, Northgate.

Rawlinson, Ethel B. (Mrs.), farmer, Northgate.

Red Lion Public House (Walter Wilson), Northgate.

Reed, Jn. Thos., smallholder.

Richardson Bros., nurseryman, Glyngarth.

Richardson, Annie (Mrs.)., farmer, Glen Side.

Richardson, Rupert, fruit grower, Surfleet Road.

Roberts, J. Thos. Jun., smallholder, Northgate.

Rose, Frederick, fruit grower.

Rowell, R. & Son, farmer & bulb growers, Manor House.

Russell, Stanley Major, filling station, Church Street.

Sanders, Jn., cycle dealer, Church Street.

Scragg, Landle Armstrong, market gardener.

Seymour, Charles, engineer & supt. to the Spalding & Pinchbeck drainage board, The Marsh.

Ship Inn (Herbert J. Smith).

Shotbolt, Leonard, farmer, Marsh.

Skerry, Wm. Jas. J., farm foreman to J. T. White & Sons Ltd., Town Farm.

Smith, Hy., farmer, Northgate.

Smith, Wm. S., bulb grower.

Sneath, Edward, fruit grower, Pear Tree House, Money Bridge.

Sneath, George Edward, farmer, Manor House, Money Bridge.

Stassen Ltd., bulb growers, Pinchbeck Road.

Sturman, P., jobbing gardener, Knight Street.

Sykes, Hy., farmer, Mill Green.

Thurston, G. A. & Sons., builders & contractors, carpenters & joiners & motor body builders, Knight Street.

Tipler, Frederick, fruit grower, Northgate Nurseries.

Tointon, Frank Wm., farmer, The Grange.

Turner Brothers (Pinchbeck) Ltd., cattle food manufacturers, Northgate Mills.

Turner, Cecil Frederick, potato merchant, Northgate.

Turner, Wm., boot & shoe repairer, Knight Street.

Vernatts Inn (Ernest Wright), Pinchbeck Road.

Walker, George, grocer, Northgate.
Walpole, Jn. Rt., farmer, Mill Green.
Ward, Rt., insurance agent, Crossgate.
Waring Jas. W., tailor, Knight Street.
Webster, John P., farmer, Glen Side.
Wegg, A. (Miss), dress maker.
Wells, Alfred, draper & grocer, Knight Street.
Woodcock, Jsph. Wm., blacksmith, Knight Street.
Worthington, Mary Jane (Mrs.), confectioner, Church Street.
Wray, A. & E., manufacturers agents, The Bungalow, Market Way.

Knight Street about 1900.

The Bull Hotel, Pinchbeck about 1910. Notice the state of the roads.

From an advert of 1931.

The Ship Inn, situated next to the approach, 1950.

The Pinchbeck village school with the children, about 1900.

Shop at the corner of Church Street, about 1910.

St. Mary the Virgin Church.

The church of St. Mary the Virgin at Pinchbeck dates from the 1350's, but it is thought that a Saxon Church stood on the site before the time of the Norman Conquest. There is evidence in some of the existing foundations to show that a Norman Church certainly stood here, and it had a Nave 80 feet long.

In the 1150's an Early English Church was erected on the foundations of the Norman Church, and portions of this still remain. The early English Church consisted of a Nave of 5 bays, 80 feet long by 23 feet wide, with north and south aisles and transepts.

The Chancel and Chapel as we see it today was built in the 1350's in the Decorated Style. The Tower was added about 1380 in the Perpendicular Style, and now has a peal of 8 bells. During the period 1855 to 1864 extensive restoration was undertaken to St. Mary's Church by the Rev. Canon West Wayet. The architect for the work was William Butterfield F.S.A. His is the spectacular east window with its geometric tracery. He was also responsible for renewing the chancel roof, adding a vestry, and the archway into the churchyard. Much attention was given to the south and east walls which were in a very poor state. All the windows were restored, new floors laid, and the organ gallery removed from the west end. A new altar was provided together with other items of furniture. The Nave was re-opened after restoration on 25th May 1863 when 30 clergy and about 1,000 people were present for a service of celebration.

The restoration mentioned above is one of many that were undertaken before this period, and also since. Buildings of this age and size need almost continual maintenance. This is unavoidable otherwise they would soon deteriorate and become unrepairable.

Standing near to the church is the Vicarage, a fine large building, dated 1772, together with stables and trap house. Evidence shows that an earlier Vicarage also stood on this site, and remains of this earlier building are incorporated in the rear of the present structure.

Pinchbeck Church and Parsonage House, 1820. From a watercolour by Hilkiah Burgess. (Spalding Gentlemen's Society collection.)

St. Mary the Virgin Church, Pinchbeck viewed from Rose Lane, about 1900.

St. Mary the Virgin Church, Pinchbeck viewed from the north/west.

Winter Time scene at Church Corner, Pinchbeck, about 1900.

Winter Time on the Spalding Road out of Pinchbeck, about 1900. Behind the trees on the left is Otway House.

Traffic queued up on the long Spalding Road bend into Pinchbeck.

These vehicles are following the Tulip Field route. In the late 1940's and early 1950's circular route was sign posted around the many fields of tulips, and thousands of people used to drive around the route in buses and cars to view the spectacle. This was before the days of flower parades, and there was many more fields of tulips grown than there is today.

Field of tulips at Pinchbeck. This field is now a housing estate

The Vernatts Inn.

The Vernatts Inn is thought to have been built about 1825. The house was originally called the "Lamb and Flag". A few years after it was built it was re-named the "Parting Pot", but eventually by 1910 it was decided to re-name the inn once again, and this time it was called the "Vernatts Inn" no doubt named after the Vernatts Drain that flows close by. In the days when a toll was charged to pass over Sharpe's Bridge which crossed the Vernatts Drain the inn did much more business. Many people having to pull up at the toll thought it a good idea to refresh themselves before proceedings on their way. Others who were travelling from Pinchbeck and beyond to Spalding would leave their pony and trap at the inn and walk the rest of the journey into Spalding therefore only paying the toll as a pedestrian.

The inn ceased trading in the 1960's and eventually the building was demolished. Today the site is occupied by a garden centre.

The Vernatts Inn photographed in 1950.

Sharp's Bridge.

The Vernatt's Drain has formed a divide between the parishes of Spalding and Pinchbeck since 1642 when the drain was cut by the Adventurers of Deeping Fen. It is almost certain that the early bridges over the drain at this point would have been made of wood. In 1806 the Adventurers contracted Mr. Kirby of Market Deeping to build a new bridge of stone to replace the earlier structure. The cost of the project having a width of 19 feet and no footpaths was £800, and the contractor was given the materials from the old bridge to do with as he wished. Tolls were charged to cross the bridge until 1870 when they were abolished.

With the coming of the motor car, and the increase in the volume of traffic the bridge was considered to be dangerous due to the "hump-back" and the broad-stone parapets.

Holland County Council decided to replace the structure and work commenced in August 1929 under the guidance of the County Surveyor, Major W. A. Rogerson. The total cost of project was £6,744 – of which the Ministry of Transport found £4,833, Holland County Council £1,461, Deeping Fen Drainage Trust £300, and Spalding Urban District Council £150.

On Friday 4th July 1930 Alderman J. W. Gleed, Chairman of the Holland County Council re-opened Sharp's Bridge, it having taken eleven months to complete. The local press reported that "The new bridge is a graceful viaduct, with open baluster parapets coloured sandstone yellow, having a width of 42 feet, 30 feet carriageway, and two 5 feet footpaths.

The Sharp's bridge that was built in 1806 and replaced in 1929.

Pinchbeck Marsh Pumping Station.

In the heart of Pinchbeck Marsh lies the old pumping station. Built in 1833 the engine house contains a 20 h.p. low pressure condensing beam engine with a scoop wheel twenty two feet in diameter. When running at full power the engine needed a hundredweight of coal per hour to feed it, and in return 7,500 gallons of water an hour was pumped into the Blue Gowt outfall, and thence on to the River Glen and Surfleet Reservoir. The old beam engine ceased operating in 1952, and later that year a new electrically powered pumping station came into use, which is still in operation today. At the same time the station was incorporated within the Deeping Fen, Spalding & Pinchbeck Internal Drainage Board.

The old Pinchbeck beam engine was preserved by the Welland and Deeping Drainage Board. In 1988 the Board went into partnership with the South Holland District Council. It was restored, and a land drainage museum was created in the old coal store. The museum was opened to the public in 1989, and now it is open every day from April to October between 10 a.m. and 4.00 p.m. When the engine house was built a house was also built to accommodate a man to attend and care for the engine. In 1909 Mr. Charles Seymour was appointed to the post as Superintendent. He lived in the house, and remained in the post until his retirement in 1952 at the age of 76 years.

A new bungalow was built and the old house was demolished at the same time as the electric pumps were brought into use. In winter the pumping station can appear very bleak, but in summer time the scene is very tranquil with swans swimming on the drains, and fishermen casting their lines from the grassy banks.

Pinchbeck Marsh Pumping Station in the days when the old beam engine was in use.

The old engine house at Pinchbeck Marsh in which the old beam engine is preserved
and a display of drainage is on show (Photographed 2000).

Pinchbeck Marsh Pumping Station.
The modern electric pumps are housed in the modern building on the right of the picture.

Northgate Tower Mill.

Northgate Tower Mill was built in 1848 to replace an earlier post mill. This tower mill had four patent sails driving four pairs of stones, and was powered by the wind until 1922. From 1922 the stones were turned by an engine, and continued until the middle of the 1930's when the tower was gutted, after which the structure was used for storage in connection with a modern mill that was housed in the adjacent buildings. In recent years the mill was known as Turner's Mill, but in the late 1800s James Sellers was the owner, and therefore the mill was known as Sellers Mill.

Glen Side Windmill.

This mill standing on the side of the River Glen between Pinchbeck and West Pinchbeck was built in 1812, and used most of the gearing from a redundant marsh mill that stood in Bourne Fen. The tower had an extra storey added at some time, and was driven by wind until 1931. The last pair of sails was damaged by gales.

Although much of the machinery was dismantled in 1945 it continued to work using modern milling machinery driven by an engine. The mill remained in use until the 1970's. When the mill was in its original working state it was powered by four spring sails mounted on stocks in a pole end, which drove two pairs of stones. The present cap has been fitted in recent years.

Northgate Mill photographed in 2000.

Glen Side Mill from a sketch by George Bailey (Spalding Gentlemen's Society collection).

PINCHBECK.
To MILLERS, BAKERS, and Others.
To be SOLD by AUCTION,
By Messrs. S. and G. Kingston,
At the Corn-exchange, Spalding, on Tuesday, Sept. 29th, 1885, at 3 o'clock in the Afternoon, subject to conditions to be then declared,

ALL that Brick Tower WINDMILL, with capital Dwelling-house, newly-erected Bakehouse and Granary over, Cart Sheds, Stables, Piggeries, Washhouse, other Out-buildings, and Yard, containing altogether 1 Rood (more or less), bounded by the River Glen Bankroad south, and by property belonging to the Rev. George Carter on all other sides.

The Mill is fitted with 2 pairs of stones, flour dressing machine, and all necessary gearing and tackle, and is in thorough working order.

The business of a Miller and Baker has been carried on upon the premises by the same proprietor for the last 28 years, and there is an old-established and good connection attached.

The Sale is in consequence of the death of the late owner and occupier, and Possession will be given at Michaelmas.

The whole or any part of the purchase money may be had on approved security.

To view the property apply to Mr. Fountain Adams on the premises, and for further particulars apply to the Auctioneers; or to EDMUND CAMMACK,
Spalding, 9th Sept., 1885. Solicitor, Spalding.

Advert for the sale of Glen Side Mill September 29th, 1885.

Glen Side Mill (Photographed 2000).

The Church of St. Bartholomew, West Pinchbeck.

The parish of West Pinchbeck situated 4½ miles N.W. from Spalding was made into an ecclesiastical parish on 11th March, 1851 from parts of the civil parishes of Pinchbeck and Spalding. In 1918 the parish boundaries were enlarged by detaching further portions of Pinchbeck and Spalding, and also a portion of Crowland. Included in the parish is the Fen and Pinchbeck Bars where the church is situated. The church of St. Bartholomew was erected in 1849 to the designs of William Butterfield F.S.A. who was one of the most original of the ecclesiastical, and collegiate architects of the 19th century. St. Bartholomew's is built of stone in a modern style of Gothic, consisting of chancel, nave of four bays, north aisles, south porch, and a turret containing two bells.

William Butterfield was responsible for a fair amount of church building and restoration in the Lincoln diocese. The richly coloured chapel of St. Anne's Bede House in Lincoln is a fine example of his work; while in South Lincolnshire he has left his mark in the restoration of the churches of West Deeping, Friskney, Stickney and Pinchbeck.

In 1896 structural problems began to appear with the church, and a meeting was held in the schoolroom. The chair was taken by the Vicar who read an architect's report upon the condition of the church building, together with a description of the work that was considered absolutely necessary as a remedy. The estimated cost, including new stores & c., was put at £300. The Rev. F. F. Wayet, Vicar of East Pinchbeck, next addressed the meeting. After impressing upon those present the necessity of the undertaking, he delivered a message from the widow of the late Canon West Wayet, in which she expressed her wish to contribute £50 towards the required sum. The members of the sub-committee were appointed treasurers, and the Rev. P. L. Hooson, secretary. Messrs James Robinson, William Coulton, and James Holland also addressed the meeting. It was proposed that the work be carried out as a memorial of the 20 years devoted ministry of the late incumbent the Rev. William Hooson M.A.

By the October of 1897 the restoration was completed, and the church of St. Bartholomew at West Pinchbeck was re-opened by the Bishop of Lincoln. It had been found that the building was suffering from subsidence, and the under-pinning of the walls on both sides became necessary to prevent serious injury to the fabric. Other restoration was also carried out and the church was re-decorated. There was a large congregation at the re-opening, the Bishop of Lincoln preached, and the clergy that took part in the service included the Rev. J. Russell Jackson, M.A. of Moulton, the Rev. F. F. Wayet, of Pinchbeck, and the Rev. P. L. Hooson, of West Pinchbeck, Mr. J. C. Traylen, of Stamford was the architect for the restoration work, and Mr S. F. Halliday, of Stamford, the contractor.

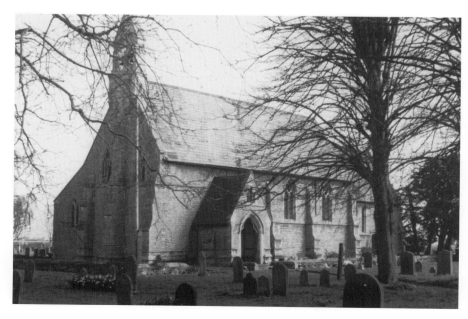

The church of St. Bartholomew, West Pinchbeck.

Northgate Methodist Church.

The early primitive Methodists met for worship in a Meeting House on Six House Bank; probably in one of the original six houses. It was not until September 9th, 1842 that a plot of land situated on Northgate was acquired by the Trustees from a Mr. Edward Marvin for the erection of a new Primitive Methodist Chapel, the first place of worship to be built in the village.

Eight trustees were appointed, and these eight arranged a mortgage on the property of £150, the mortgagee being a Mr. Robert Hardy of Kensington. This debt on the property was finally cleared on 26th May, 1899.

Due to a shortage of space in the Chapel it was decided in 1909 to erect a schoolroom at the rear of the Chapel on the remaining part of the land that was purchased in 1842. A ceremony of Stonelaying was held on 6th May, 1909. The officiating minister was the Rev. C. G. Milson, and the building was completed by the late summer.

The cost of the work was £273 6s. 2d. and the money was raised by means of donations, bazaars, concerts and sales of work. Some of the money required was borrowed, and it was not until the summer of 1919 that the debt on the schoolroom was finally cleared.

On 20th December 1912 the Primitive Methodist Chapel at Northgate was registered for marriages. The first marriage in the Chapel was between William Ellis Pannell and Ethel Rawding. This was conducted on 12th May, 1913 by the Rev. Gervase Hall.

During the First World War there was a considerable increase in the size of the congregation, and it was felt necessary to increase the accommodation, but it was not until the Spring of 1925 that work began with the demolition of the old chapel and adjacent cottages. The new building commenced almost immediately. Mr. J. R. Baker of Moulton Chapel was employed as builder, and the new chapel was similar in design, but larger, to the new Wesleyan Methodist Chapel that Mr. Baker had recently built at Moulton Chapel. The seating capacity was for 240 worshippers, and the builders estimate of the cost was £1,289.

On Thursday 29th October, 1925 the new Chapel was opened and dedicated to the Glory of God. About four hundred people assembled outside the new Chapel to hear the Rev. Gervase Hall introduce Mrs. H. G. Frost of Spalding who performed the opening ceremony.

Life in the Northgate Chapel was very active and music and singing played a great part for many years. The membership was strong, and the Sunday School very popular.

During the Second World War the worship continued as usual, but the premises had to be blacked out. From October 1939 to June 1941 the schoolroom was used as a day school for local and evacuee children from the King's Cross area of London.

Sadly the number of people attending services declined and the decision was made to close the Chapel. The last service was held on the 25th May, 1997 when the membership stood at 19.

Members of the Primitive Methodist Chapel assembled outside the original chapel sometime before it was demolished in 1925.

Northgate Methodist Chapel now closed down (Photographed 2000).

Trades and Business People in West Pinchbeck in 1937.

Alexander, Chas., farmer, Starlode Drove.
Ashby, Wm., farmer, Money Bridge.
Atkinson, Hy. Bernard, farmer, Cuckoo Farm, North Drove.
Barber, Wm. (Mrs.), fruit grower, Small Drove Lane.
Barrow, Sidney, shopkeeper, Six House Bank.
Boothby, John Thomas, farmer.
Branton, George, farmer, Pode Hole Road.
Branton, Harry, farmer, Starlode Drove.
Brooks, Kenneth Wm. Mowson, farmer, Fengate.
Carter, Cyril Storey, blacksmith.
Casswell, L. (Mrs.), farmer.
Chapman, Baker, farmer.
Chapman, Dick, farmer, North Fen.
Chapman, Rd. F., farmer.
Chappell, Eliza Ann (Mrs.), farmer, Riverside.
Chappell, Harold Edward, farmer, Glenside.
Chappell, Joseph William, market gardener, Fengate.
Chatterton, Thos., farmer, Leaveslake Drove.
Christian, Harry, farmer, South Fen.
Christian, Jn. R., farmer, Leaveslake Drove.
Cocks, Harry, farmer.

Cole, Eric M., haulage contractor, Small Drove Lane.

Cook, Leonard, farmer, Leaveslake Drove.

Cook, Walter, smallholder, Holly House.

Cooling, Chas., smallholder, South Fen.

Cox, Cecil, boot repairer.

Cross Keys Public House (Jas. Rd. Brooks), Glenside.

Cuckoo Inn. (Hy. James), Cuckoo Bridge.

Dance, Walter D., smallholder.

Darley, George, farmer, Leaveslake Drove.

Darley, Chas., farmer.

Darley, Jas., farmer, Beck Bank.

Deacon, Herbert G., blacksmith, Starlode Drove.

Dobbs, Albert Frederick, farmer.

Dobbs, Arth. F., farmer.

Dobbs, Cecil W., farmer.

Dobbs, Chas., farmer, Leaveslake Drove.

Dobbs, Harold T., farmer.

Dods, Wm., coal & coke merchant, North Drove Station.

Edinborough, Frank, farmer, Sycamore Farm, Fengate Road.

Fisher, Edwin, insurance agent, Six House Bank.

Fisher, Fred, smallholder, Starlode Drove.

Fisherman's Boy Public House (Esau Ringwood).

Fountail, Thos., farmer.

Garfoot, Harold, miller, Glenside.

Gedney, Benj., farmer, Starlode Drove.

Gedney, Wm., Riseley, carpenter.

Gotobed, Alfred, farmer.

Gotobed, Fred Cecil, haulage contractor.

Gray, Wm., carrier, Six House Bank.

Griffin, Miriam Constance (Mrs.), shopkeeper, Glenside.

Griffin, Tom Boothby, haulage contractor, Glenside.

Grooby, Thos, threshing machine owner.

Hardy, Jsph. (Mrs.), farmer, Forty Foot.

Haresign, Jesse, farmer, Starlode Drove.

Haresign, Wm., farmer, Black Hole Drove.

Hodson, Frank, farmer.

Horse & Jockey Public House (Mrs. Harriett Ann Sharman).

Houghton, Mark, cottage farmer, Six House Bank.

Jacklin, Kate Emma (Mrs.), grocer, River Side.

Kingston, Tom Alfred, smallholder, Glenside.

Leverton, Thos. W., farmer, Black Hole Drove.

Mabbott, Lewis, smallholder, Northgate.

Molson, Ernest E., farmer.

Moon Arthur, potato merchant.

Moon Leonard, grocer.

Morris, Hy., farmer, Fengate.

New Bridge Inn (Geo. Wm. Dowse).

Pannell, Eliza Ann (Mrs.), farmer, West View.

Parker, Thos., farmer, Glenside.

Parson, Tobias Wm., butcher.

Patchett, Josiah, shopkeeper.

Peach, Jn. Matthew, farmer, Glenside.

Peacock Inn (Chas. Clement Swain).

Phillips, Jsph., farmer, Elder Bush Farm.

Riseley Annie (Miss), shopkeeper, Northgate.

Roberts, Jn. Thos., farmer, Starlode Drove.

Robinson Ernest, farmer, Glenside.

Robinson, Jn. A., farmer, Starlode Drove.

Rose & Crown Public House (Fred W. Sporton).

Rylott, Jn. Thos., farmer, Leaveslake Drove.

Searby, Harry, farmer, Cuckoo Bridge.

Shotbolt, Wm., farmer, Starlode Drove.

Smith, Alfred Harold, farmer, Willoughby House.

Smith, Ernest, farmer, Fengate.

Smith, Florence Dora (Mrs.), grocer & tea dealer, Northgate.

Swain, Mrs., fried fish dealer.

Three Horse Shoes Public House (J. Whiting), North Fen.

Tipler, Horatio, dairyman, Six House Bank.

Twell, Jn., farm foreman to F. Richardson Esq., South Fen.

Waltham, Jn., farmer, Leaveslake Drove.

Wheat Sheaf Public House (Michael Healey).

Wheatley Thos., smallholder, Starlode Drove.

Wiles, Evelyn (Mrs.), farmer.

Wiles, Jn. Wm., farmer.

Witherington, Arth. Burton, wheelwright, Starlode Drove.

The Cuckoo Inn

The Cuckoo Inn, Cuckoo Bridge here photographed in 1950, serving the local community for over a hundred years. It is not certain when the inn first opened, but it can be traced back to 1851, and it carried on trading until the 1950's. The building still stands, but now serves as living accommodation

The Peacock Inn

The Peacock Inn, Dozens Bank, West Pinchbeck the photograph on the left shows the building before the brickwork was painted white and on the right after painting.
The inn ceased trading many years ago but in the year 2000 the building is still in use as living accommodation.

The Wheatsheaf.

The Wheatsheaf, at Starlode Drove, West Pinchbeck, here photographed in 1951 stood very close to the Forty Foot Drain. In its early days people could travel to it either by foot or by boat. As people left the area trade diminished and the Wheatsheaf has now been closed down for many years.

The Cross Keys.

The Cross Keys Public House on Glen Side, West Pinchbeck, photographed here in 1948. This public house dates back to the early 1800s, and finally closed its doors in the mid-1950s.

Pinchbeck

Pode Hole.

Situated within the parish of Pinchbeck, 4 miles S.W. of the village is the hamlet of Pode Hole. The name is said to derive from the Anglo-Saxon 'Padded', meaning a toad. Today this community is fortunate to have some light industry to create employment, but years ago the main employer was the Drainage Board, and the hamlet has grown up around the pumping station that stands each side of the main road from Spalding to Bourne. This pumping station is very important as it serves to drain all of Deeping Fen, which is the vast expanse of low land, lying between the Welland and the Glen rivers. It is bounded on the north and west by the River Glen, and on the south and east by the River Welland, and on the south and west by the high lands in Deeping, Langtoft and Baston; it also includes a small tract of fenland, lying between the Car Dyke and Bourne Eau, on the north side of the Glen.

For hundreds of years men dreamt of draining Deeping Fen, knowing full well that if successful the land would be very good for growing crops. Some of these men lost all of their money with the lack of success in draining the fen, but a company of gentlemen who called themselves the 'Adventurers' were a little more successful, and managed to keep some of the Fen drained for several months of the year. One of these gentlemen was a Dutchman called Sir Philibert Vernatti whose name is perpetuated in 'Vernatt's Drain'. The three main drains of Deeping Fen are: North Drove Drain, South Drove Drain, and Counter Drain, all of which converge at Pode Hole where they meet up with the Vernatts Drain. At this junction pumps are brought into use to transfer the water into the Vernatts from the North and South Drove Drains which at this point are a lot lower than the Vernatts. In 1741 two large scoop wheels powered by windmills were erected at Pode Hole, and by 1799 there were three being used to assist the movement of water. In 1800 a report was submitted by four engineers one of which was the famous engineer John Rennie. They suggested extending the Vernatts towards the sea, possibly as far as the Witham, would improve the drainage, but this was rejected as being too expensive, and an alternative suggestion of erecting steam engines at Pode Hole was thought to be more economical. The Commissioners decided to accept this proposal, and after some delay two steam engines were erected at the ends of North Drove and South Drove Drains. These engines were brought into use in 1825 at a cost of around £26,500, and for years they were the largest steam engines used in the fens, remaining in use until 1925 when they were replaced by two diesel engines that had been earlier installed in 1914 and 1920. The steam engines were demolished in the 1950s, but the building in which they were housed is still standing. Today much more up to date pumps have ben installed, and the whole of Deeping Fen is kept well drained by the complex at Pode Hole.

This photograph of a watercolour by Hilkiah Burgess painted in 1832 shows the Inn that was later named 'The Fisherman's Arms' and the newly built steam powered pumping station.

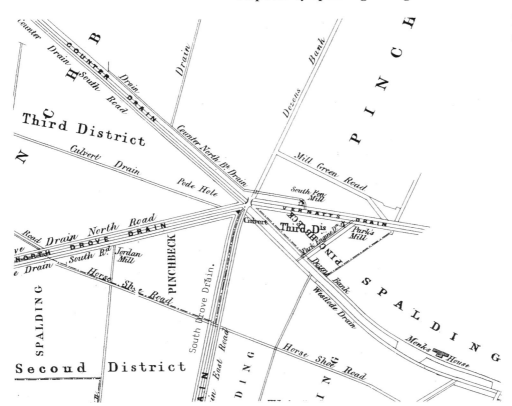

Map showing the area around Pode Hole in 1857.

View of the Vernatts Drain at Pode Hole (Photographed 1999).

Pode Hole pumping station in the centre of the picture with the church of Saint Matthew's on the side of the drain in the early 1900s.

The building at Pode hole that housed the original steam engine (Photograph taken in 1999).

Pode Hole Pumping Station before 1914.

Building the foundations for the new engine house at Pode Hole pumping station, 1913.

The new engine house at Pode Hole. Built to house two diesel engines, 1914.

Inside the engine house at Pode Hole pumping station showing the diesel engines, 1914.

Panoramic view where the North and South Drove Drains reach the pumping station at Pode Hole.
The Fisherman's Arms Public House can be seen on the right hand side of the picture in the back-ground, 1999.

The Fisherman's Arms, Pode Hole (Photographed about 1950).

This public house was known in its early days as the Pode Hole Inn. It was built about 1774 by the Deeping Fen Commissioners to cater for the needs of the large number of labourers employed in the draining of the surrounding fens. It is not known when the name of the inn changed. The old building was demolished and the present Fisherman's Arms was built in the 1950's.

The Fisherman's Arms, photographed in 1999.

Trades and Business People in Pode Hole in 1937.

Branton, Flora Beatrice (Miss), smallholder, Rose Cottage, Pode Hole.

Branton, Wilfred R., smallholder, Pode Hole.

Brighton, Thos. Jn., farmer, Pode Hole.

Chappell, Herbert, builder, Pode Hole.

Dodson, E. A. & Co. Ltd., Road Transport Contractor, Pode Hole.

Fairbanks, B. & W., agricultural engineers, Pode Hole.

Fisherman's Arms Public House (Edward Jefferies), landlord.

Freir, Albert Henry & Sons, wheelwrights, Pode Hole.

Freir, George W., blacksmith, Pode Hole.

James, Harold, grocer, Pode Hole.

Maw, Hy, shopkeeper, Pode Hole.

Nightingale, Horace, motor omnibus proprietor, Pode Hole.

Richardson, Hy. Waller, engineer, Deeping Fen Drainage Board, Pode Hole.

Roe & Son, nurseryman, Pode Hole.

Roe, Albert, wheelwright, Pode Hole.

Roe Buck Inn (Walter Rodgers), landlord, Pode Hole.

Sherrard, Rd. Albert, haulage contractor, Pode Hole.

Simmons & Leavesley, bulb grower, Trent Farm, Pode Hole.

Tierney, D., painter & house decorator, Pode Hole.

The Roebuck Inn, Bourne Road (Photographed about 1950).

Not a lot is known about this inn. It was situated close to Brantons Bridge in Bourne Road. This inn was mentioned in the novel called "Brantons Bridge", written by Carol Ashwell in 1954. She was born in 1907 and in her younger days lived near to the Roebuck.

The site where the Roebuck Inn once stood (Photographed in 1999).

Saint Matthew's Church at Pode Hole.

In the 1860s the population of Pode Hole began to expand, and the Rev. Plumpton Wilson, Vicar of West Pinchbeck in whose parish Pode Hole fell within, felt the people of the hamlet were missing out on church life. He was also concerned that because of the distance, people were not sending their children to day school. A site alongside the South Drove Drain was leased from the Drainage Board, and in 1865 a dual-purpose Church and School was built, and dedicated to Saint Matthew. The building gave the community good service until 1972 when the school closed down, and the pupils transferred to the newly built Monks House school in Pennygate. It was said that the main object of building the Mission Church was to provide a place of worship at Pode Hole. The building was opened on Saint Matthew's Day, September 21st, 1865, and the cost of the building was £349 2s. 8d.

ELEMENTARY EDUCATION ACT, 1870.
Section IX.——NOTICE A.
COUNTY of LINCOLN.
SCHOOL DISTRICT of PINCHBECK.

WHEREAS the Education Department, in pursuance of the Elementary Education Act, 1870, have received the Returns in the said Act mentioned, and made such inquiry as they think necessary with respect to the School accommodation of the District hereinafter mentioned ; now, therefore, the Lords of the Committee of Council on Education have decided, and *hereby give Notice* as follows :—

I. The School District is the Parish of PINCHBECK.
II. The Schools named in the Schedule to this Notice are considered to be available for such District.
III. No additional Public School accommodation appears to be required for the District.

SCHEDULE.

Name and Description.	Situation.	No of Children accommodated.			
		Boys.	Girls.	Infants.	Total.
East Pinchbeck National School.	East Pinchbeck	172		71	243
West Pinchbeck Church of England School.	West Pinchbeck	202			202
St. Matthew's (Pode Hole) Church of England School.	Pode Hole.	74			74
		Total.............			519

F. R. SANDFORD, Secretary.
Education Department, 20th day of November, 1873.
Notice No. 11,207.—Union of Spalding.

Notification of school accommodation for East and West Pinchbeck and St. Matthew's, Pode Hole for the year 1873.

Snippets from what the papers used to say.

April 1882.

Deeping Fen Drainage. – The annual meeting of the trustees was held at the Corn Exchange, Spalding, on Wednesday, Lord Kesteven presiding. The accounts for the past year were produced, and considerable discussion arose with respect to the expenditure for alterations of engines and works at Pode Hole: at the last annual meeting the estimated cost of new boilers and alterations to the engines was £3,000. The accounts produced at this meeting showed that the estimate had been greatly exceeded, and that there are other sums owing to the engineers. The total cost of the alterations to the engines, engine house, foundations &c. (including the new boilers), will it appears be over £5,000 and it was admitted by the superintendent that notwithstanding this large outlay one of the engines is defective and requires a patch upon its cylinder! The total receipts for the year have been £5,928 16s. 2d. and the total expenditure £8,635 14s. 2d. The question of arrears of rates and various other matters relating to this important trust were discussed. The balance due to the treasurer was shown by the accounts to be £4,751 17s. 2d., and it was resolved that a rate of 3s. per acre be laid for the ensuing year.

Pinchbeck

February 1899.

A Big Eel – The water bailiff to the Spalding Angling Association (Mr. Brown) on Saturday captured a monster eel in the North Drove Drain at Pode Hole, near Spalding. While using a pilger he brought up an eel weighing 6 pounds two ounces and measuring four feet four inches. This is the largest specimen ever caught in the district. The skin has been sent away to be preserved.

June 1902.

Obituary – The death has occurred at his residence at Spalding of Mr. George Limmer in his 75th year. Deceased who was a well known resident, had been prominently connected with the Baptist denomination for many years, being one of the oldest members, and one of the founders of the mission at Pode Hole and Spalding Common. The funeral took place on Saturday, conducted by the Rev. J. C. Jones, and a service was first held in the Primitive Methodist Chapel, adjoining the residence of the deceased.

July 1904.

Stack Fire – The Spalding Fire brigade was summoned to a fire on Thursday evening at Pode Hole, two miles distant from Spalding. The outbreak was on the farm premises of Mr. Shotbolt, and fortunately was confined to a straw stack. At one time it was feared that an extensive range of buildings in close proximity would be set on fire, but this was prevented by many willing helpers. The brigade stayed a couple of hours, and then returned home, not being able to render much assistance as the stack burned with great rapidity. There was plenty of water. The conflagration was caused by a child playing with matches. Being half-holiday at Spalding a large number of persons went over from Spalding.

March 1905.

Spalding – Presentation for Bravery. At the Baptist chapel at Pode Hole, near Spalding, on Thursday night a certificate from the Royal Humane Society was presented to Wm. P. Barrett of the Winsover Road, Spalding, for rescuing two drowning boys from the Forty Foot Drain at Pode Hole on the 18th January last. The two boys had got onto the ice and it had given way, and both of them were precipitated into the water. A little girl who saw this ran about 200 yards for help and Mr. Barrett at once ran to the river. When he got there he found one boy coming up for the last time, and the other was lying perfectly still at the bottom of the river. He prostrated himself on the ice and pulled the first boy out by his hair, and then rescued the other by means of a rake. This done he got on his horse and galloped for a doctor. Both boys were restored, one of them having been in the water for a quarter of an hour. At the same time the certificate was presented, the little girl Grassam, who went for help, was given a bouquet of flowers. Both presentations were made by Councillor Martin Taylor of Spalding.

March 8th, 1872.

On Friday last a meeting of agricultural labourers was held at Pinchbeck Bars, Mr. George Bailey presiding. An address was delivered by the Chairman to a large audience in the open air. Mr. George Ball, of Spalding Common, also addressed the audience. At the close, a resolution was unanimously carried that ten hours should be considered a fair day's work and 3 shillings should be asked for the summer season.

On the 7th inst., whilst Mr. Geo. Benner was thrashing with a steam thrashing machine, a man named William Davis, labourer, of Spalding, went to his yard at Pinchbeck and ordered the hands to stop, unless Mr. Benner gave them more money. Mr. Benner at once ordered the intruder off the premises. The man attempted to assault Mr. Benner, but some of the men at work at once took their master's part, and put Davis out of the yard. He then threw off his coat, went into the yard again, and commenced to pull the straps off the machine. Mr. Benner then went for P.C. Dykes, who upon his arrival at once took Davis into custody and conveyed him to the police station at Spalding. Davis was taken before the Rev. E. Moore the next morning and remanded.

27th September 1893.

Fire at Pinchbeck Church. – A storm of short duration, but of great severity, passed over the district on Wednesday afternoon. The lightning was most vivid and the thunder loud, whilst the rain descended in torrents. During its progress, and about five o'clock, the parish church at Pinchbeck was struck by lightning, and the roof which was of wood covered with lead caught fire. Active efforts were made by the Rev. F. Wayet, the Vicar, and a body of workers, to extinguish the fire. Water was taken up the tower in buckets and shortly after six o'clock it was announced that the fire was out; though had the outbreak occurred during the night the result might have been very serious. As it is, it is believed the damage is not very great, and the loss is covered by insurance.

October 1878.

Should this meet the eye of any person living in Sibsey, near Boston, who has in any way tried to INJURE my REPUTATION by scandal, I shall feel obliged if they will consult me before further doing so.
Pinchbeck West, Oct. 4th, 1878. T. J. BURNETT

May 1901.

Mr W. S. Royce, of Komani House, Donington, has just purchased the Grange Farm, near Pinchbeck Station, and the Crossgate Farm, near Pinchbeck Flax Mills, comprising about 700 acres. The estate was formerly occupied by Mr. Plowright, but of late years has been cultivated by Mr. J. W. Rowland.

August 1887.

Interesting Discovery. – A new bridge has recently been erected over the River Glen at Pinchbeck, with a span of 45 feet. It has been reported that a large bridge had once before been erected at the same place, and had been washed away by heavy floods; but the assertion was discredited as there was no evidence to substantiate it. During the construction of the new bridge it was found necessary to deepen the bed of the river at that point, and during these operations the workmen came across the long lost bridge about four or five feet below the bed of the river. It appears that the bridge was erected in the year 1775, and carved stone, supposed to have belonged to the Spalding monastery destroyed in the year 1537, has been found to have been largely used in its construction. Numbers of stone coffin lids have also been discovered.

November 7th 1895.

Opening of a New Baptist Chapel near Spalding. On Thursday a new Baptist Chapel and school premises were opened at the village of Pinchbeck, two miles from Spalding. In the afternoon and evening sermons were preached by the Rev. T. Barrass, of Peterborough, and there was a large gathering of Baptists from different parts of the district. The special services are to be continued during the next fortnight. The Baptist Church at Pinchbeck was formed 51 years ago, and the new and commodious chapel and schools, situate in a more central position than the old buildings, have been built partly as a jubilee memorial.

December 1904.

The Outbreak of Glanders. – Eight Horses Shot – The serious outbreak of glanders which occurred at Pinchbeck, on the farm premises of Mr. J. T. Smith has been dealt with by the destruction of the whole of the eight horses affected. The disease was introduced by a cab horse brought on the farm from London, and the owner has now accepted the offer of the Holland County Council for a hundred pounds compensation. This is the first outbreak of glanders which has occurred in this locality for a number of years.

December 1811.

On the 5th inst. as John Mason was crossing the River Glen, opposite to a place called Guthram Cote, in the Parish of Pinchbeck, in a small boat, the pole or sprit with which he was thrusting the boat forwards stuck so fast in the bed of the river, that the poor man in endeavouring to pull it out upset the boat, and was drowned before timely assistance could be procured. An inquest was held on the body the following day, before Samuel Edwards, gent. coroners verdict, accidental drowned.

Pinchbeck

July 28th, 1815.

Thomas Clarke and Henry Coster, convicted at the Lincoln assizes of a burglary and robbery in the shop of Mr. Thomas Elderkin, at Pinchbeck, suffered the sentence of the law on a temporary gallows erected in the Castle yard at Lincoln. They had conducted themselves since their conviction in a hardened manner, seeming insensible to the awfulness of their situation, thus giving reason to believe that they entertained hopes of either being able to make their escape, or that by the bold agency of the working bankers on the Witham navigation (where about 1,000 men were employed within twenty miles of Lincoln), a rescue might be effected for them on their way to the gallows. To guard against the first an additional watch had been stationed in the castle yard during that night. On the Wednesday evening preceding the execution, two men were discovered lying on the top of the south wall, and shot at by the watchman, when they immediately got up and made their escape. The watch was still further strengthened on the Thursday night, which, with what passed on the former evening, is supposed to have kept intruders off. To guard against a rescue, the magistrates determined that the execution should not take place without the city, as was usual, but, as stated above, had a temporary gallows erected in the castle yard just within the gates, where the execution took place without interruption at 12 noon.

August 1826.

On Thursday the 10th inst., at Guthram, near Spalding, advanced in years, Mr. Lawrence Hardy, formerly landlord of the Horseshoe Public House at that place. He was an eccentric character, but well respected as a cheerful companion. In the vain desire of perpetuating his memory, he requested in his will that a barrel of beer and a quantity of bread and cheese should be given away on the bridge at Pinchbeck, where his corpse was to stop on the way until it was all distributed to the populace; which desire was fulfilled on Sunday last.

August 1826.

Caution to Watchmakers, Silversmiths and Pawnbrokers. – A very daring and extraordinary burglary was perpetrated in the night of Tuesday last at Pinchbeck near Spalding. The parsonage house was broken into at the scullery window; the robber proceeded to the butler's pantry, where he appears to have minutely examined the plate, and selected only such articles as were not particularly marked; he then examined the lower rooms, and in the dining-room he broke open a work table and took out some halfpence, but the desk of the Vicar, containing cash, he left untouched. With very great audacity, he entered the chamber of the Vicar, and took from off a brass hook behind a door a gold watch, chain, and seals, and in passing the foot of the bed he perceived that he was observed by Mrs. Wayet (a rushlight was burning in the room), and he immediately escaped. The following articles are ascertained to have been stolen, and can be identified: – half a dozen silver forks, a teaspoon, three ladles, two gravy spoons, a salad spoon, butter knife, seven dessert spoons, a fish trowel, a gold double-cased watch (makers' names, "Mudge and Dutton") gold chain with round links, and two gold seals (one with a head, and the other with a crest, a bugle horn stringed, above initials "J.W."). The key of the desk was taken away from off the dressing-table.

February 1869.

In our obituary is recorded the death of a man and his wife at Pinchbeck, each aged 77. They lived in one room, and were in bed when the man died. His corpse was taken out of bed and laid on a board at the foot of the bed until a coffin could be provided. The body was then put in, and remained in the same room, his wife being ill in bed, until she died on the 22nd, the day he was buried.

January 1872.

Pinchbeck – On Friday last the church choir had their annual feast of hot roast beef, cake and tea in the school room, which was very gracefully decorated for the occasion with evergreens. The Vicar delivered a short address, and then presented a writing-desk and pencil case to Miss Emily Hill – a gift from the schoolmaster and scholars on her leaving for Lincoln Training College, after being a teacher for five years. A very pleasant evening was spent in singing, reading and dancing. "God Bless the Prince of Wales" and the "National Anthem" were sung at the conclusion.

Monday, March 23, 1908.
A Remarkable Motor Car Accident.

An extraordinary motor car accident occurred during Friday night in the Fens, at Pode Hole, the centre of the drainage system of the district. Here several large watercourses which intersect the Fens pass under bridges, and it was while crossing one of these bridges that the motor car came to grief. The car, a 40 h.p. Napier. belonging to Mr. Marshall Owen Roberts, of Easton Hall, near Grantham, and driven by Alfred Bond, was travelling from Norfolk into Lincolnshire, and should on Saturday have gone to France. In taking an awkward bend the car, instead of turning to the right, seems to have swerved to the left. It caught the masonry of the bridge, which is over a foot thick, carried away about seven feet of it, and was left overhanging the parapet by about 5 feet. The car was of course, very considerably damaged. Beyond a shaking the driver received no injury, and he was able to retain his seat and scramble back onto the bridge. The car remained balanced on the parapet for some hours before it could be hoisted back.

The breach in the wall of the bridge   The damaged car and the undamaged driver.

May 1954.

A surprise windfall of £2,000 for the erection of a new Village Hall at Pode Hole was contained in the will of Mr. G. S. Bromley, of "The Willows" 290, Bourne Road, Spalding. With the £500 already in the hall fund work was expected to start much earlier than expected.

MADRAS FARM, PODE HOLE, PINCHBECK.
S. and G. KINGSTON have received instructions to SELL, upon the farm of Messrs. PHILIP and GREENHAM SHOTBOLT, at Pode Hole, near Spalding, on Friday next, Feb. 9, 1883, 13 BEASTS, viz., roan cow in calf (time up Feb. 28th), red ditto (time up March 7th), red ditto and calf, drape cow, 8 burlings ; 10 HORSES, chestnut mare (Rose) 6 years, in foal ; bay horse (Punch) 9 years, black horse (Sweep) rising 5 years, by King Tom, out of a Sweep mare ; bay horse (Star) rising 3 years, brown half-bred horse aged, chestnut mare (Flower) aged, in foal ; brown yearling cart filly, black ditto, chestnut colt foal, brown pony, 8 years, in foal ; also the whole of the IMPLEMENTS, capital Whitechapel Cart, set of plated Harness ; Three SHEEP and Twelve PIGS ; small lot of Sharp's Improved Blue PEAS, 5 Tons of CARROTS ; the Foldyard KEEPING, with use of yards to April 6th ; and the following Sheep Keeping, viz., 16 Acres of new Seeds, 10 Acres of Grass, the Bank Frontage opposite the farm to April 6th, 1883, and about 10 Acres of Coleseed (light crop) to the 13th of March.
The Beasts are well-bred Shorthorns, the Horses are very powerful animals, and the whole well deserving attention.
The Farm is one mile from North Drove Station, and three from Spalding.
Sale to commence at One o'clock.
Auction and Valuation Offices, Spalding, Jan. 27, 1883.

Notification of a farm sale at Madras Farm, Pode Hole, 1883.

Pinchbeck

July 1899.

Interesting Service at Money Bridge.

On Sunday evening week, at the Congregational Church, Money Bridge, Pinchbeck, an advent of special interest took place in the form of a Floral Service, which was held on behalf of the hospital. The whole of the Saturday was devoted by a number of workers to beautifying the chapel, and preparing for the event of the next day. The building was beautifully decorated. Shortly after 6 p.m. on Sunday, the scholars met in front of the chapel, accompanied by their teachers and superintendent. The scholars were then formed into a procession, headed by a long motto board. All the children carried exquisite bunches of flowers. The procession marched up the right bank of the River Glen, and met the West Pinchbeck Brass Band, which then headed the procession and played a beautiful selection of music. On arriving at the chapel, it was found to be already well filled, and as the children filed up the aisles to lay their floral offerings on the platform, they found a large company to admire the charming spectacle. With the arrival of the children the people crowded in with great rapidity. The large gallery was filled, and the wide aisles were also thronged. Mr. Everard Baguley, from the Congregational College, Nottingham, conducted the service. The singing was accompanied by the band. The preachers text was from St. John's Gospel XV., 22. The packed congregation listened with absorbed attention. At the close of the sermon, the choir sang an anthem during the taking of the collection, and before giving out the closing hymn, the preacher in a few heart felt words, thanked the band for their kind voluntary attendance, also those who assisted in the decorating, and those who had given so liberally from their gardens. After announcing that the collection for the Johnson Hospital had realised £2 5s. 8d. – which has since then been enlarged – the congregation sang, and after the benediction the crowd began to leave the building, whilst the band played outside. For 30 years, such a sight has never been witnessed in the neighbourhood.

The Congregational Church at Money Bridge.

Photograph showing what little remains of the Money Bridge Congregational Church in May 2000.

Surfleet

Surfleet.

Four miles north of Spalding on the A16 lies the village of Surfleet sitting prettily on the banks of the River Glen stretching some two miles from the church to the Reservoir. In the past the name has also been spelt Surflete and Surflet. The termination of the name Fleet, denotes that this was once a tidal creek or stream.

Print of the Church of St. Lawrence, Surfleet, 1842.

Church.

Close by the River Glen stands the Parish Church dedicated to St. Lawrence. The plan of the church consists of the usual Nave with Side Aisles, a South Porch, a Chancel, and a Spire Steeple. With the exception of parts of the interior, and the South Porch, the architecture is wholly Perpendicular Gothic.

Surfleet Church, early 1900s.

Approaching the village from either direction along the A16 one cannot help but notice the severity of leaning on the church spire (it is 6 feet out of the perpendicular), and it is hard to imagine that this tower houses a peal of twelve bells all in ringing order. The Chancel is small in comparison to most churches of this size.

There are several monuments within the church. One is: – "In memory of Henry Heron, Esq., died 10th September, 1730, Aged 55." Another… "Here lieth Sir Henry Heron, Knight of the Bath, of Cressy Hall, in this parish." Interred August 9th, 1695, aged 76. Here lieth the remains of Dame Ann Fraiser, daughter of Sir Henry Heron, Knight of the Bath. Died 25th August, 1769, aged 92. Another sacred to the memory of Theophilus Buckworth, Esq., younger son of Everard Duckworth, died February 17th, 1801, aged 63 years.

Trades and Business People in Surfleet in 1937.

Atkinson, Chas, farmer, Surfleet Marsh.
Barnett, Thos., smallholder, Station Road.
Barnsdale, Geo. & Sons, builders, Station Road.
Bealby, C. W. & Sons, farmers, Bridge House, Roseleigh & Welland House Farms.
Bealby, Chas., farmer, Cheal House.
Bell, Hy., market gardener, Cheal.
Brand, Oliver Ernest, farmer, Orchard House.
Briggs, Hester (Miss), tobacconist, Station Road.
Bristow, Wm., farmer, Station Road.
Brown, Jn. Rd, boot & shoe maker.
Busey, Arth., smallholder, Station Road.
Cave, Edith & Mary E. (Misses), shopkeepers, Station Road.
Cave, Frederick, farmer, Reservoir.
Cave, Fredk, nurseryman, Station Road.
Clay, Hy. Wm., farmer, Bird's Drove.
Cooper, William Wright, nurseryman, Station Road.
Coxen, Fred, farmer.
Crown Inn (Wm. Battram).
Dodds, Wm., coal merchant, Station.
Dyson, Leslie, motor engineer.
Flowers, Jsph, bricklayer, Station Road.
Forman, Alfd. Sidney, market gardener, Reservoir.
Frohock, Edwin Jn., farmer, Reservoir.
Garner, Ambrose, farmer, Cheal.
Garner, Benj., farmer. Cheal.
Glenny, Fredk, farmer, The Laurels.
Graham, Arth, shopkeeper.
Great Northern Hotel (Chas. Harrison), Station Road.
Gresswell, Rt. Wm., smallholder, Thary Farm.
Hackford, Jn., blacksmith.
Holmes, Sidney, farmer, Cheal.
Jackson, Wm., nurseryman, Station Road.
Jessop, David, farmer, Bird's Drove.
Lamming, Geo., blacksmith, Station Road.
Lane, Jn. Sansom, farmer, Marsh.
Ley, Bert G., grocer.
Machin, Geo. Wm., farmer, Marsh.
Marshall, Tom, smallholder, Seas End.
Moon, Wltr, smallholder, Bird's Drove.
Muxlow & Webster, farmers, Aorangi House.
Payne, Thos. Jn., smallholder, Belnie Lane.
Prior, Arth., builder.
Rawding, Chas., carpenter.
Rawlinson, Edwd, farmer, Marsh.
Reynolds, Chas. Altr., farmer, Station Road.
Reynolds, Jn. Rt., farmer.
Rhodes, Albt., farmer, Station Road.
Richardson, Fredk., farmer, Hungate Lane.

Robinson, Harry, farmer.

Rodgers, Arthur, boot & shoe repairer, Station Road.

Rogers, Wltr. Swain, smallholder, Bird's Drove.

Rowbottom, William, market gardener.

Shepherd, Florence (Mrs.), shopkeeper, Seas End.

Ship Inn (The) (Geo. Wm. Parker), Reservoir.

Skells Rd. Daws, bulb grower.

Smith, Wm. M. & A. M. (Miss), farmers, Station Road.

Spalding Golf Club (E. R. Hugh, hon. sec.).

Stanley, Geo. Wm., farmer, Newlands Lane.

Stevenson, E., farmer.

Sykes, John, market gardener, Marsh.

Sykes, Thos. E., nurseryman.

Temple, Fred, farmer, The Red House.

Tidswell, Jn. Alfd., smallholder, Bird's Drove.

Tidswell, Wm. Cecil, smallholder, Bird's Drove.

Tooley, Wltr, farmer, Newlands Lane.

Twell, Sydney, farmer.

Waltham, Chas, farmer, Marsh.

Welby, Herbert, fried fish dealer.

Whitworth, E. F., farmer.

Williams, Jas. P., shopkeeper & post office.

Wilson, Ronald Gordon McLean, farmer & market gardener, Iceni Nurseries.

Wright, Jn., farmer, Colbeach House.

Station Road, Surfleet, about 1920.

Bridge over the River Glen at Surfleet.

There does not appear to be any record as to the date when the first road bridge was placed over the River Glen at Surfleet, but we do know that the present bridge, constructed in 1884 was the first iron structure. Prior to this all the bridges were of a wooden construction. This present bridge was not free of controversy as the following newscutting of October 1884 shows:–

"Surfleet Bridge: – The new bridge over the Glen at Surfleet is now completed, and is a very substantial, but costly structure, and is, we hear, likely to lead to some litigation, owing to the manner in which it obstructs houses. The bridge is carried over the river by iron girders under the roadway, and two massive iron arches over the roadway. These are carried on either side several yards beyond the waterway, almost blocking up the entrances to some of the houses, immediately in front of the houses alluded to. In a clear open space the bridge itself would look well enough – a neat, if not a handsome structure, but standing where it does it dwarfs the houses in appearance, and in itself has a big, clumsy, and heavy look about it".

Fraiser Rooms.

Situated in the church yard is a very old brick building called the 'Fraiser Rooms', so named after Dame Ann Fraiser of Cressy Hall, in the parish of Surfleet. Dame Ann Fraiser founded a school in this building, and endowed it by deed bearing the date October 13th, 1764; in which deed it stated Dame Ann Fraiser had lately built a school-house in the church yard at Surfleet; and endowed it with a salary for the maintenance of a master. She invested £600 in the Turnpike Road leading from Donington to Spalding, the interest of which was to be applied to the maintenance of the master, for which he was to instruct twenty children of the poorer sort of the inhabitants of Surfleet, in reading, writing, and arithmetic, and supply them with sufficient paper, pens and ink; he was also to take no money either for entrance or firing from their parents. The parishioners were to keep the school in good repair.

Fraiser Rooms.

Mr. Timothy Cuney was the first master. He was succeeded by Mr. Thomas Meredith, a butcher, who only stayed a few months. The school continued until 1878 when a new building was erected on the Seas End Road. Mr. John Cadman, Headmaster of the Fraiser School, carried on as Headmaster of the new school, where he stayed until the beginning of the First World War.

Dame Ann Fraiser died at Cressy Hall at the age of 92, 25th August 1769. She was the daughter of Sir Henry Heron, Knight of the Bath, relict of Sir Peter Fraiser, Bart., and was well known for her many good works.

Today the Fraiser Rooms which were restored in the year 1900 are used as the Parish Hall.

Surfleet School in 1993.

Surfleet Reservoir and the River Glen.

Weekend holiday bungalows have stood on the banks of the River Glen at Surfleet reservoir since the 1920s, and to this day the Reservoir is still a very attractive weekend resort. Before the year 1739 water flowed from the River Glen straight out into the River Welland and on to the sea. Consequently the water level varied considerably and left the river banks quite unattractive. The first sluice was constructed at Surfleet between October 1739 and April 1740 by order of the Honourable Adventurers of Deeping Fen according to the model and directions of Messrs. Smith & Grundy. (In April 1736 John Grundy senior and Humphrey Smith were jointly appointed 'Surveyors and Agents' (i.e. engineers) to the Adventurers, Owners and Proprietors of Deeping Fen). This first sluice had a 12 foot waterway with pointed doors 7½ feet high.

By the 1870s the Trustees of the Deeping Fen realised that a larger more modern sluice was required at Surfleet and in 1877 the following advertisement was placed in a local newspaper inviting Tenders for the work to be carried out:–

To Contractors and Builders.

The Trustees of the Deeping Fen General Works of Drainage are prepared to receive Tender for the Erection of an Outfall Sluice for the River Glen at Surfleet Reservoir, near Spalding. Plans and specifications may be seen at our office on and after 4th January next. Tenders are to be sent to us before or on 1st March next. Security for due completion of any contract will be required, and the proposed security may accompany the Tender. The Trustees do not bind themselves to accept the lowest of any Tender.

By order of the Trustees
Bonner and Calthrop, Clerks,
Spalding, 24th December, 1877.

A short time after the closing date for Tenders the quotations were published in the Newspaper:–
New Sluice. The Tenders for the new outfall sluice to the River Glen, about to be erected at the reservoir, were as follows:–

Monday, London – £15,830.
Webster, London – £13,500.
Broadhurst & White, March – £12,775.
Coker, Isle of White – £12,430.
Barwell, Spalding – £11,700.
Cook & Bennett, Downham Market – £10,730.
Wormsley, Derby – £9,800.

The Trustees accepted the Tenders of Messrs. Cook & Bennett of Downham Market, and a piece of land on the farm occupied by Mr. Everitt Coulton was purchased on which to build the new sluice. Work on the project went ahead with due speed and on November 5th 1879 the new sluice was officially opened, as recorded by the newspapers:–

'Opening of the New Glen Sluice'. – On Wednesday morning the new sluice at the reservoir was opened by Lord Kesteven in the presence of several of the Drainage and Welland Trustees and a small number of spectators. The ceremony was a very quiet one, no speeches being made nor any display. The contractors, Messrs. Cook & Bennett, were congratulated upon the conclusion of their arduous task. The work appeared to have been done in a most substantial and satisfactory manner.

The New Sluice at Surfleet Reservoir – During the dry season of some ten years ago we were so often told that wet seasons had for ever forsaken this island that many had come to believe it, but a succession of wet seasons dispelled the illusion and convinced the most acceptable that the danger of floods is as great as ever. The old sluice at the mouth of the River Glen, built 140 years ago, was no doubt considered ample for its purpose at that time, and its cill was most likely placed as low as the tide in the Welland would allow the

Glen waters to escape. But since the channel of the Welland has been carefully trained, an increased scour has taken place in its bed, and a much better outfall secured, leaving the cill of the old sluice several feet above low water, so that the improved outfall was of no advantage to the district drained by the Glen. Hence the necessity for a new sluice was strongly felt; and it needed only to be known that the old sluice was fast becoming unsafe to lead those gentlemen having charge of this important district to decide upon the erection of a new one. After due consideration it was decided to place the new sluice in the same channel as the old one, but a little further inward towards the land, a temporary cut being first made to conduct the Glen waters round the site of the new sluice to the outlet as before. The design of the new sluice was well worked out, and the result is a very neat substantial structure, which will not suffer by comparison with any sluice in the district. It consists of two 15 feet openings, and the cill is placed 6 feet lower than the cill of the old one. The roadway over the sluice is formed on the top of the brick arches and enclosed between parapet walls. The sea doors which exclude the tide are of English Oak, and present a massive appearance. The land doors, which are intended to keep the Glen waters from escaping, except by permission of the sluice keeper, are a combination of oak rails covered with boiler plates and strengthened with iron ribs or rails. The mode in which these doors work is rather a novel one, and may be considered almost in the light of an experiment. The foundation upon which the structure stands is sand or silt, which being enclosed with sheeting piles and further protected by several transverse rows of the same, is thought to be the best upon which such a structure can repose. Not the least indication of subsidence is visible in any part of the work. The walls which have concrete bases, are of brick and stone combined, and are faced throughout either with Bramley Fall Stone or Blue Bricks set in cement.

The engineers under whose joint oversight the work has been done are Messrs. Kingston (of the Welland), Harrison (of the Deeping Fen), and Lancaster (of the Black Sluice). Messrs Bonner & Calthrop were the solicitors, and Messrs. Cook & Bennett the contractors. The first stone was laid by Lord Kesteven in February last, and the sluice was formerly opened by him on the 5th November 1879. There remains the dams to remove and the embankment across the temporary cut to be made; after which the old sluice will be taken up, and all the advantages of an improved outlet be given to the district.

Surfleet Reservoir before any of the weekend holiday bungalows were built. The first bungalow was built by Mr. George Samuel Kingston in the 1920s. Mr. Kingston also played a large part in the organisation of the first water sports at the Reservoir.

Surfleet Reservoir in 1993.

The Outfall side of the
sluice at Surfleet Reservoir
about 1920.

The Outfall side of the
sluice in 1993.

Surfleet

The River Glen at the point where it flows into the Welland, at high tide.

The River Glen has over the years provided some excellent recreational facilities. Today holiday bungalows line its banks at the reservoir, and fishermen seek sport with the fish of this ancient river. In the 1930s Surfleet Reservoir was very popular with families who came from all over the area on warm summer Sunday afternoons, and Bank holidays. Many coming by bicycle, and some even by train to picnic on the river banks. In those days Surfleet had a railway station. Rowing boats could be hired. Swimming Galas were held, and many children learnt to swim in a shallow piece cut out of the bank specially for that purpose.

Swimming Gala in the early 1930s, Surfleet Reservoir.

Swimming Gala at Surfleet Reservoir, 1930s.

Surfleet

The River Glen at Surfleet had its attractions even in the Winter when the skaters of the area took advantage of some sharp frosts, as the following article from a newscutting of the 15th November 1895 shows.

"Surfleet. An open match in which some of the principle Spalding and Cowbit skaters competed, took place on the River Glen, at Surfleet yesterday week, the distance being about one mile, with three turns. The ice was in fine condition, and there were 16 starters. The race was run in the old style, in heats, and the following were the results:–

First round:

W. Holmes, Pinchbeck beat Alwood, Spalding; Tidswell, Spalding beat Brown, Surfleet; J. Davis, Spalding, beat Christian, Pinchbeck West; A. Robinson, Pinchbeck West beat W. Gulson, Surfleet; H. Atkin, Cowbit beat T. Atkin, Pinchbeck West; Elsom, Cowbit beat H. Kirby, Spalding; Flowers, Cowbit beat Iverson, Spalding; and B. Gardiner, Spalding beat Walter Tyrrel, Cowbit.

Second Round:

Tidswell beat Holmes; Davis beat Robinson; H. Atkin beat Elsom and Gardiner beat Flowers.

Third Round:

Davis beat Tidswell and Atkin beat Gardiner.

Final:

Atkin beat Davis.

Winners:

1. H. Atkins, Cowbit.
2. J. Davis, Spalding.
3. B. Gardiner, Spalding.
4. Tidswell, Spalding.

Several local races were also run off.

The Vernatt's New Sluice at Surfleet Seas End. The first stone was laid 9th May 1857 and the sluice was opened 5th October 1857. Designed by W. Lewin of Boston. Some of the ironwork on the sluice was cast by C. D. Jennings, Iron Founder of Spalding. The Vernatt's River at this point flows into the River Welland, and thence out to the sea. At this point the Welland is tidal.

The Wesleyan Methodist Chapel.

The corner stone of the Wesleyan Methodist Chapel was laid in June 1869, by Mrs. Temple, of Surfleet, and Mrs. Fountain, of Boston West. The ceremony commenced by singing, and the reading of scriptures, and prayers followed. The Rev. S. Dixon, superintendent of the circuit, then delivered a brief address, stating the circumstances that had led to the meeting of that day. He then handed to Mrs. Temple, in the name of the trustees, an elegantly chased silver trowel, and she having used it, declared the first stone to be well and truly laid "in the name of the Father, the Son, and the Holy Ghost". Mrs. Fountain having laid the second stone, an address was delivered by the Rev. F. Kellett, of London, and a collection was made, which was succeeded by the laying of bricks by numerous friends anxious to pay for the privilege. A large number of friends from Spalding and adjacent villages afterwards took tea in a marquee erected in a field kindly lent for the occasion by M. J. Aitken, Esq. At 7 p.m. the Rev. F. Kellet preached an eloquent and long to be remembered sermon. from Hebrews Chapter 2 verse 10 to a numerous and highly appreciative audience. The total proceeds of the day's services amounted to upwards of fifty guineas. The building is expected to cost £300, and will seat 150 persons, ample provision for free sitting having been made.

Services ceased to be held in the chapel sometime after the Second World War, and for some years after this the building became a garage selling car tyres.

Photograph of the building that was the Wesleyan Chapel. Taken in 1993 when the building had no particular use.

Methodist Church, Station Road, Surfleet. Built in 1856.

Surfleet Post Mill from a watercolour by Hilkiah Burgess (Spalding Gentlemen's Society Collection).

Surfleet Post Mill. Built 1509; demolished 1909.

Barbarous Murder by Hooton on Surfleet Common.

The murderer Hooton was a daredevil sort of fellow, an auctioneer, residing in this locality. Having some knowledge of a Mr. Stockdale, a rich old bachelor, residing in Yorkshire, he visited him in the Winter of 1769, and persuaded him to come into Lincolnshire and bring his money to purchase corn in Spalding market, where it might in that day be bought to great advantage. Much against the better judgement of his sister, the man of money resolved to try his fortune in the Lincolnshire Fens. His cash was sewn up in various parts of his dress, and he accompanied Hooton on horseback, their last stage being the Robin Hood Inn, Boston, where the formidable nature of Hooton's whipstock (it had a heavy iron hammer) attracted the observation of the landlord. They proceeded on their journey, and on arriving at the Fosdyke Inn, the tide was flowing so that they were not able to reach Moulton Common, where it is supposed the murder was intended to be perpetrated. They turned to the right, down the banks of the Welland, and upon reaching a nook on Surfleet Common poor Stockdale was beaten upon the head until he died. The body was found, and taken next morning into Surfleet Church. In the course of a day or two the offices of justice were on the murderer's tracks. They found him concealed in the house of a relative, at Sutton St. Edmunds. He was hid in a cupboard, and before being charged he protested his innocence.

Hooton's trial was at Lincoln Castle on 6th March 1769 where he was found guilty, and sentenced to be executed. On the Monday after the trial Hooton was brought out of the castle on a cart at about 11 o'clock in the morning. He was executed in public before a large crowd who had come from miles around to see this man suffer death. Later his body was hung on a gibbet on the site of this foul deed, and the hideous relic swayed in the night wind for some years before the bones fell and eventually disappeared.

Snippets from what the papers used to say.

May 1718.

May 15 – To be run for at Surfleet bridge in the County of Lincoln, on Monday in Whitsun-Week; a Saddle of Thirty Shillings Value, by any Horse, Mare, or Gelding: And a Hat of a Guinea Value to be run for by Foot Men. On Tuesday a Plate of Four pounds Value, by any Horse &c. that is 14 Hands high, to carry nine stone, run three heats, the winning horse, &c. to be sold for six pounds; and for every inch above 14 Hands to carry half a stone weight, and to abate half a stone for every inch under. On Wednesday a Plate of eight pounds, by any horse &c. carrying ten stone weight, run three heats, four miles each heat; the winning horse &c. to be sold for fifteen pounds, the second horse 7c. to have a plate of forty shillings; each horse &c. to be entered on the Race Days, between the hours of 9 and 3 on each Race Day; where the articles are to be seen at Mr. John Erle's, at Surfleet Bridge. If any disputes shall happen to arise, it shall be decided by the Clerk of the Race, with the Majority of the Subscribers.

September 1871.

A Waterspout – A violent storm, accompanied by a Waterspout, passed over the neighbourhood of Surfleet on the 27 ult, and did great damage, as well as performing several extraordinary vagaries. Corn and hay stacks were reft and scattered broadcast, tiles were stripped from roofs and descended in dangerous showers, a tree 20 inches in diameter was wrenched from the earth, and a 3 inch plank was blown over the Ship Inn to a spot 200 yards from its starting point. The column of water which rose from the Vernatt's Drain was of large size, and moved with great rapidity, and at a considerable height. We hear of no personal injury.

September 1805.

Sept. 8. – At Surfleet, near Spalding, a poor woman, on turning down her bedclothes, found a large snake, 3 feet long, which had unwittingly been her bedmate the preceding night. The reptile was immediately secured; and Mr. James Heardson, of that place, possesses it.

Surfleet

1900.

Surfleet – The Rev. H. L. James, Vicar of Surfleet, is adopting a novel method for getting a congregation for his Sunday afternoon service at the Parish Church. He has commenced running a small steamer on the River Glen in order to bring up children and adults who reside some distance from the church to attend Divine Service. It is understood that the steamer will be run on Sunday Afternoons during the summer.

January 1893.

A 100-acre Farm in the market. – At Spalding on Tuesday evening. Messrs S. and G. Kingston offered for sale by auction a valuable freehold estate of over 100 acres, situated at Gosberton and Surfleet Fen. Bidding was brisk up to £3,960, but no advance was made, and the property was withdrawn.

October 1873.

Surfleet – A very pleasing event took place at this village on the evening of the 23rd inst., when about fifty-four persons sat down to an excellent supper on the occasion of the presentation of a testimonial to Mr. Richard Liddall, late station-master, and who has lately removed to Tattershall. The company included some of the leading farmers and tradesmen in the neighbourhood. Mr. Liddall was stationed at Surfleet ten years, and was respected by all classes, Mr. Wm. Cocks, seedsman, of Donington, occupied the chair, and Mr. Robinson, of Surfleet, the vice. After justice had been done to a very excellent supper, provided by Mr. Plumtree, of the Railway Inn, Mr. Kay, farmer of Quadring, in a complimentary speech presented Mr. Liddall with a purse containing £22. Mr. Liddall suitably acknowledged the gift.

May 1878.

Surfleet – Charles Rudkin, the parish sexton was charged by Elizabeth Barnett, of Surfleet, with assaulting her. The complainant said that a vault had been made in the churchyard, and the earth therefrom had been carted away by Mr. Allen, the Churchwarden, and put upon his land. She (the complainant) went to Mr. Allen's land, and picked out of the soil several human bones, which she put in a bag and showed to several of her neighbours. The defendant met her, and without saying anything to her, dragged the bag from her, pulling her down upon the road, and dragging her some distance, finally taking the bag away from her. Defendant admitted the charge, but considered he had a right, as sexton, to do what he did. The magistrates considered the case proved, and fined defendant 5s. and costs. The Chairman said the Magistrates considered that a public indecency and scandal had been committed, and that no one had a right to remove the remains of the dead out of the churchyard, and they should order an investigation into the whole matter.

February 1895.

Distressing Case near Spalding – A distressing case is reported from Surfleet, near Spalding, where a family named Baxter, living in the centre of the village, had no fire in the house for four days last week, and there was very little food for the man and his wife and six children, one being a baby only a few days old. Upon hearing of the case a neighbouring farmer (Mr. Alfred Smith, a guardian of the poor) had one of his sheep killed and dressed, and sent in whole to the family. Mr. Baxter was formerly a farmer, and at one time was in a good position.

August 1970.
Historic Ship Inn Sold.

After centuries of ownership by a drainage board the historic Ship Inn at Surfleet has a new owner.

A happy Mr. Arnold Bussey confirmed on Monday his tender had been accepted by the Deeping Fen, Pinchbeck and Spalding Internal Drainage Board, and he would be taking over as landlord on October 1st.

Mr. Bussey who had been tenant of the inn for just over two years had feared he would have to move.

It was put up for sale by the Board earlier this year when Watney Mann, the brewers, announced they were giving up the lease.

The inn, which stands at one end of the Vernatt's Drain, is believed to have been one of the very few public houses in the country owned by a drainage board.

The Fisherman's Arms formerly the Pode Hole Inn, which stood at the other end of the Vernatt's Drain was also owned by the board until a few years ago.

It is thought that the Ship and the Pode Hole Inn were both built about 1642 and were the idea of Sir Philibert Vernatti, a Dutchman employed by the Adventurers, a group of gentlemen who got together to drain this part of the Lincolnshire Fens.

"I am delighted the board accepted my tender and I don't have to move," said Mr. Bussey.

The Ship Inn, Surfleet Seas End (Photographed in 1996).

Weston

with
Weston Hills.

Weston or to give it its full title Weston St. Mary is a village and parish situated on the road between Spalding and Holbeach. The parish is quite large, stretching from the River Welland in the north-west to its boundaries with the parish of Cowbit. Contained within the parish is the hamlet of Weston Hills with its chapel of ease built in 1888 and dedicated to St. John.

The church of St. Mary's at Weston was described in June 1890 as a beautiful and interesting small cruciform church, consisting of a nave, aisles, clerestory, south porch and chancel of an Early English period, early Decorated transepts, and a Perpendicular tower. The east end of the chancel is beautifully designed although simple and rather severe in character, consisting of three lancets between four slender buttresses surmounted by a cusped pointed oval light, copied from one at St. Mary-le-Wigford's, Lincoln. The arcaded clerestory and porch, with its fine outer arch and doorway within, are worthy of examination. The aisle arcades within consist of five bays supported by low clustered pillars, some having circular, and some octagonal central pillars, surrounded by supplemental slender pillars, and surmounted by caps from which spring boldly carved conventional foliage of various designs. The chancel arch of the same period is richly moulded, and the font also is beautifully enriched with carving. This church owes much to one formerly its Vicar, who was chiefly instrumental in carrying out its restoration in the best way possible and wherein his body now rests together with that of his devoted and truly Christian wife, the late Canon and Mrs. Moore, subsequently the well known Vicar of Spalding.

WESTON St MARY'S CHURCH AND SCHOOL.
Lincolnshire

Weston St. Mary's Church, 1998.

St. Mary's, Weston.

Print of St. Mary's
Church, Weston,
1842.

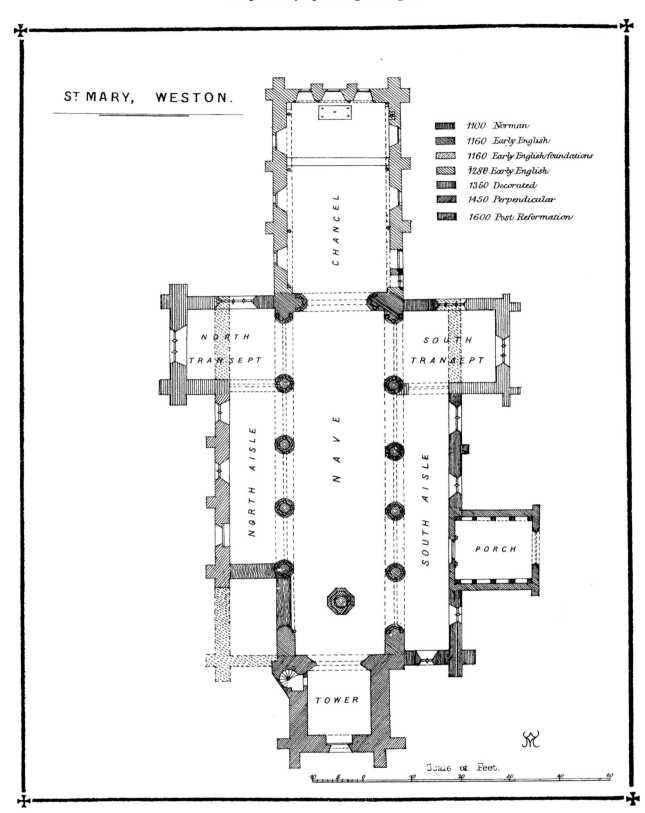

ST MARY, WESTON.

1100 Norman
1160 Early English
1160 Early English foundations
1280 Early English
1350 Decorated
1450 Perpendicular
1600 Post Reformation

CHANCEL

NORTH TRANSEPT

SOUTH TRANSEPT

NORTH AISLE

NAVE

SOUTH AISLE

PORCH

TOWER

Scale of Feet.

Plan of St. Mary's Church, Weston, about 1870.

Trades and Business People in Weston in 1937.

Abbott, Arth., farmer, Gate Farm, Holbeach Road.

Birch, Wm. Harold, farmer.

Carter, George Edward, cycle agent.

Caudwell, George, farmer & landowner, St. Lambert's Hall.

Chequers Inn (Wm. L. H. Dillworth).

Coley, Jn., smallholder.

Courtman, Jn. C., shopkeeper, Cowhirne.

Dae, Samuel, farmer, The Walnuts.

Dillworth, Geo., smallholder.

Dring, Walter, farmer, Woad Farm.

Elwes, Chas. H., haulage contractor.

Eyett, Joseph, farmer.

Fletcher, Frank P., Clerk to Parish Council.

Fletcher, Rt. Mossop, farmer & landowner, Wimberley Hall.

Gate Inn (J. R. Butler), Holbeach Road.

Gibson, Jas. Atkin, farmer, Holly House Farm.

Gibson, Jas., bulb grower, Delgate.

Gregory, Charles S., smallholder.

Hutchinson, Barnet, farmer.

Hutchinson, Cecil, potato merchant, Holly House.

Hutchinson, Rose (Mrs.), shopkeeper.

Hutchinson, Wm., farmer.

Manton, Harry, haulage contractor.

Mashford, Jn., smallholder.

Mawby, Jn. H., farmer, Broadgate House.

Mawby, Thos. Onn., farmer, Methwold House, Spalding Marsh.

Pogson, Harry, farmer, Delgate Bank.

Reeve, Bertie, farmer.

Reeve, Jn. Jas., farmer.

Sly, Hy. Herbert, farmer.

Spalding Bulb Co. Ltd., bulb growers, Wykeham.

Stubbs, Frank, tobacconist.

Tointon, Rowles Heath, farmer.

Ward, Walter, smallholder.

Wegg, Bert W., carpenter.

Westland, A. K. M. (Mrs.), shopkeeper.

The Gate Inn, Holbeach Road, about 1950.

The Chequers Inn, Weston 1930s. The name of this Inn was changed to The Carters Arms in May 1997.

Wimberley Hall, Weston.

Wimberley Hall situated in Stone Gate, Weston was thought to have been built in the 17th century. In the 1930s this house was owned by Mr. Robert M. Fletcher who was one of the principal farmers and landowners in Weston. The house was demolished in 1965, and the site now has a modern house standing upon it.

Land Workers during the First World War on Mr. George Caudwell's farm at St. Lamberts Hall, Weston.

At this time Mr. Caudwell had about 80 women working on his various farms in South Lincolnshire.

Methodism.

At one time the Methodists had three chapels within the Weston Parish. In Weston village a chapel was built by the Wesleyans in 1844, but was taken over by the Wesleyan Reformers in 1854. This chapel was destroyed in 1883, but was re-built and subsequently re-opened for worship on the morning of July 12th, 1883. The last service in this chapel was held on August 25th, 1968, and it was then sold to a Mr. Dunmore for £260. Various objects from the chapel were dispersed around the circuit. The clock was given to the Broad Street, Spalding, chapel. The communion set was given to the minister for use in private homes. It was suggested that 5 chairs that were given to the chapel be handed over to the village hall. The chairman's chair together with Hymn Board and Numbers went to Moulton Seas End. At Weston Hills there were two chapels. The building by the Primitive Methodists of the chapel in Broadgate was commenced in February 1854. It was enlarged in 1868, and on 25th April 1976 the last service was held. This chapel that has long since been demolished stood on a site next to where the present village hall stands.

The Wesleyans first built a chapel in 1813, and this was thought to have been taken over by the Free Methodists in 1854. This was demolished and a second chapel was erected in 1871/82 in Austendyke Road. The last service in this chapel was held on the 25th August 1969, and the building has long since been demolished, and houses have been built on the site.

There is no longer any Methodist places of worship in the Weston Parish, and members have to come into Spalding for services.

Weston St. John's Chapel of Ease.

From a report of 1890

"The Chapel of Ease to the Parish Church of Weston St. Mary which was consecrated under the Dedication of "St. John the Evangelist," on November 9th, 1888, by the Lord Bishop of Lincoln, is not only complete, but is now free from all debt.

Early in the year 1888, it became evident to the Vicar that the time had arrived when if possible an effort should be begun to make better and more adequate arrangements for a service being held, than had hitherto been possible in the School Room, situate very nearly four miles distant from the Parish Church. For fifteen years an afternoon service had been held in this School Room, but all Parishioners had to come of course to the Parish Church for the Sacraments.

Many plans for a licensed Room, a Chancel to be added to the School, &c. were proposed, thought over and finally rejected.

It was whilst these plans were still under consideration that the Vicar received an Easter Offering of £5 from Canon and Mrs. G. Venables as the commencement of a fund, to be called "The Weston Hills Effort Fund". This was placed in the Bank on April 11th, and by June 30th £200 was in the Bank, and a considerable sum in addition was promised.

A plan was then proposed for the Bishop's sanction; by which it was intended to build a new Church or Chapel immediately behind the School Premises, on a site to be purchased for that purpose. The building to have a Consecrated Chancel to insure its continued use by future Vicars, and for the administration of the two Sacraments: but to have an unconsecrated Nave in which a Lay Reader might legally hold services.

After due consideration by the bishop, this scheme was sanctioned under the advice of the Chancellor of the Diocese, careful terms and restrictions being imposed as to the time of building the two portions; and the separation of the Chancel from the Nave by an iron screen.

On September 14th, 1888, the Brickwork was commenced and though there were still from time to time difficulties to overcome, as to the purchase of the site, as to the means of access, as to the size of the Chancel, and the erection of the Chancel complete before the Nave walls were more than a few feet high; still matters went forward. On November 9th The Chancel (at that time made into a complete building by the erection of a boarded partition at the arch which would presently lead into the Nave) was consecrated by the Lord Bishop of Lincoln, who afterwards celebrated the Holy Communion therein, and then admitted H. S. Maples Esq., Solicitor of Spalding as the licensed Lay Reader for work in that part of the Parish. The chancel being only 12ft 6in by 12ft 2in there was only room for, The Lord Bishop of the Diocese, his Chaplain, his Secretary, The Rural Dean (Canon E. Moore of Spalding), The Vicars of Moulton and Weston St. Mary, H. Stanley Maples, Esq., and Messrs T. Diggle and W. Grummitt, Junr., the Churchwardens of Weston St. Mary, at these services.

After the Consecration of the chancel the work of building the Nave was proceeded with as quickly as the weather allowed.

On February 7th, 1889 the completed building was opened, and the sermons in the morning and evening were preached by the Rev. Canon G. Venables, Rector of Burgh Castle.

From that time, there has been an afternoon and evening service every Sunday: a morning service at 9.15 a.m. on Wednesdays, and occasional evening services on week days.

A celebration of the Holy Communication has ben held on the Second Sunday in the month at 8.00 a.m. and on some other occasions.

The Sacrament of Baptism has been administered to nine infants.

There have been very good congregations, and the evening services have been taken by the Lay Reader,

On November 7th the Anniversary of the Consecration, an effort was made to pay off the remaining debts, and so successfully made, that after all payments were completed a small balance was left in Hand.

In accordance with the original scheme a sum of £100 has been invested in the 2½ per cents. in the name of four Trustees (the Bishop of the Diocese kindly consenting to act as one) to form a nucleus for an Endowment Fun. (The living does not just now produce £250 nett per annum.)

In giving an account of the sums so generously offered for the carrying out of this work, the Vicar wishes to state, that in some cases they have been given on more than one occasion. A cheque was sent by T. M. S. Johnson, Esq. for the offertory on the opening day; one sum of £20 was given from another source in the offertory on Easter Day, 1889, and on the occasion of the Consecration and again on the opening Day sums of money collected chiefly by Mrs. Sanderson from 104 Parishioners were placed in the offertory. The names of these donors are not given in the accompanying List.

Again as on the occasion of the Restoration of the Parish Church in 1885, the Vicar has to express his deep sense of the loving kindness and mercy of Almighty God, shewn to him and the Parishioners by the way in which the work has been so successfully carried out, and by the generous gifts which have been so freely and so generally bestowed from all sides.

Acknowledgement must be made of the care and attention bestowed by Mr. J. T. Irvine on the designing of unusual details; of the many useful and helpful suggestions made by the (late) Reverend Canon E. Moore; and of the satisfactory nature of Mr. S. Dawson's work.

Many persons have given much help whose names are not recorded here, but so it must always be. God knows all who work for Him. That this work has been carried out and completed in about 18 months is a matter for great thankfulness and rejoicing. Laus Deo! To God be the Praise!

The following is a List of the Offerings made to the Chapel of Ease of St. John the Evangelist, Weston.

"Altar, (formerly in the Chapel of Moulton St. James) Vicar & Churchwardens of Weston S. Mary.
Altar Vessels. (Silver, in oak case). A Friend.
Altar Service Book, &c. The Vicar.
Altar Frontals. Miss M. Sanderson.
Marble Slab for Credence. Canon E. Moore.
Leather Case for Vessels. Mr. Simpson, Spalding.
Font, Bowl of (originally lying unused in Kent). The Vicar of Great Yarmouth.
Holy Bible for Lectern (Russian Leather.) Mrs. Gedney.
Prayer Book for Prayer Desk (to match above.) Mr. R. Appleby.
Stove, Vicar and Churchwardens of Moulton.
The Kneelers and Pede Mats were worked by Ladies in the Parish.
Bell. Mr. S. Dawson.
Messrs. Bonner & Calthrop, and Messrs. Maples & Son gave the Deeds with no expense, but payments for stamps. A gift amounting to over £10.
Mr. Appleby printed "the Appeal" issued by the Vicar, gratis.
Offerings, gifts and money thus reach a total of above £700.

As regards the balance in hand; something is required for gravel for the Church Road, and it is proposed to add £5 to the Endowment Fund, and to use another £5 as the commencement of a Fund for a new musical instrument. The present Harmonium presented by Mr. Gedney, has done very good service for fifteen years in the school, and is still fit for use there, but we believe the Parishioners desire a larger and more powerful instrument in the present building."

Above: St. John's Church,
Weston Hills.

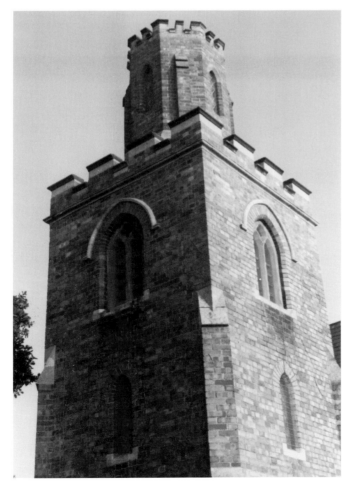

Left: The ornate tower of St. John's Church.

234

Trades and Business People in Weston Hills in 1937.

Adams, Carl Geo., farmer, Delgate.
Admans, Harry Seth, farmer, Broadgate.
Allmand, Geo., smallholder, Broadgate.
Armstrong, Wm. E., farmer, Station Farm.
Banks, Jn. Wm. E., farmer, Delgate.
Barnett, Rt., smallholder.
Bates, Stanley, farmer, Magpie Holt Farm.
Batterham, Tom, smallholder, Broadgate.
Bell Inn (Thos. Ward).
Blackburn, George Henry, smallholder.
Blachburn, Hy., smallholder, Broadgate.
Bollons, Jsph., farmer, Foots Lane.
Brown, Geo., farmer.
Burt, Chas. W., farmer, Bridge Farm.
Burton, Joseph, smallholder.
Carter, Geo., smallholder, Broadgate.
Casson, Fred, farmer, Broadgate.
Charlton, Jn. Thos., farmer, Broadgate.
Clark, A. H., farmer.
Clarkson, Chas. W. & Geo. M., bulbgrowers.
Clayton, Walter F., farmer.
Cook, Jn., farmer.
Cook, Jn., smallholder, Fendyke.
Cordley, Fred, smallholder, Broadgate.
Cowlen, Ben, Jnr., smallholder.
Crosby, Benj., farmer, Broadgate.
Crosby, Wltr., farmer.
Crosstuck, Geo., smallholder, Delgate.
Culy, H. B. & Son, bulb growers,
    Moulton Chapel Road.
Culy, Ernest B., smallholder.
Culy, Sidney L., bulb grower,
    Moulton Chapel Road.
Dean, Victor Fred, farmer.
Dring, Walter, farmer, Blenheim.
Ealham, Jn., smallholder, Broadgate.

Earl, Frank, farmer.
Eliff, Wltre, smallholder.
Fletcher, Fred, farmer, Delgate.
Gale, Chas., smallholder, Delgate.
Goodrum, George, bulb grower.
Goodyear, Arth. T & Son.,
    motor haulage contractor, The Hollies.
Hall, Arth., smallholder, Delgate.
Halgarth, Joshua, smallholder, Broadgate.
Harlock & Lill, shopkeepers, post Office.
Harris, Rd., smallholder, Delgate.
Hepworth, Wltr., farmer, Bridge Farm.
Jenkinson, Albt. Edwd., farmer, Broadgate.
King, Saml., carpenter, Moulton Chapel Road.
Laming, Stanley G., farmer, Weston St. Johns.
Lill, Jack, smallholder, Broadgate.
Lythell, T. R. & J. W., farmers.
Ostler, Charlie, farmer.
Pick, George, farmer, The Beeches.
Pogson, Harry, farmer, Broadgate.
Rains, Rd. Stanley, farmer, Delgate.
Seymour, Rt., bulb grower, Broadgate.
Sharp, David, tobacconist.
Sly Bros., farmers, Turfpits Farm.
Smith, David, bulb grower, Asholt.
Spriggs, Job, cottage farmer, Broadgate.
Stainsby, Arth., blacksmith.
Stockdale, Ralph, market gardener.
Todd, Hardy. W., baker.
Turnbull, Edwd., smallholder.
Turnbull, Tom., farmer.
Wade, Jsph., farmer, Magpie Fen.
Waterfall, Jn. Wm. farmer, Broadgate.
White, Hy. W., farmer, popular House.
Witherington, Edward, farmer.
Wright, Arth., farmer, Whittington Farm.

Weston Hill Post Mill.
Demolished 1919.

Newscutting October 1919.

Hunley Mill, Weston Hills, almost the last of the old Wooden Post Windmills, has been taken down during the last few days. The old mill, which latterly had been in the tenure of Mr. W. H. Todd, miller of Weston Mills had seen nearly 500 years service.

Note:

Some of the timber rescued from this windmill when it was demolished was later cleaned-up and used to make a display case in the museum of the Spalding Gentlemen's Society.

The scene in 1998 showing
where the Post Mill once stood.

Weston Hills Post Mill from a sketch by
George Bailey. Spalding Gentlemen's
Society collection.

Weston Hills Post Mill from a watercolour painting by Hilkiah Burgess. Spalding Gentlemen's Society collection.

The Schoolhouse and Chapel, Spalding Marsh.

In the north-west of Weston St. Mary's parish is the area called Spalding Marsh, and Wragg Marsh. This land was reclaimed from the sea in 1793 when the South Holland embankment was constructed. To this day the occupation of almost everybody living in the area is connected with agriculture, although the population is far smaller than it was fifty years ago.

In 1872/73 Mr. John Savage, who lived at The Park, Moulton, had erected on a piece of his land in the Marsh a Wesleyan Methodist Chapel, with schoolroom, teacher's house, stables and other various outbuildings for use of the inhabitants living in the area. The buildings were designed for use as Day and Sunday Schools, and Public Worship. Inside the schoolroom is a plaque giving the date of presentation of the building to the inhabitants as January 1873, but the building was opened for public worship on the 10th March, 1873. The cost of the buildings including the value of the land was put at £860.

The day school that was held within the building gave good service to the children of the district, providing them with their educational needs for about seventy years, but with the decline in the number of people that were required to work on the land the school was closed down. It was on the 6th April, 1950 that Holland County Council Education Department ceased their tenancy of the premises.

Although the Day school had ceased, the schoolhouse continued to be occupied, and services were still held on a Sunday. The congregation was very small, and members were asked if they would attend services at the Broad Street church in Spalding, but this did not meet their approval even when it was suggested that a bus be provided to take them into Spalding each Sunday. It appeared that the Spalding Marsh Church was becoming a problem to the Trustees. At the annual meeting of the Spalding Marsh Church Trustees', held at Broad Street on 26th January 1959 under the chairmanship of the Rev. J. Wilson, concern was expressed over the house adjoining the Church as Mrs. Hollsworth had now vacated the premises, and the tenancy was vacant. It was suggested that as the Spalding Bulb Company had interests in the district they should be approached with a view to renting the house for one of their employees, and if they were not interested to advertise the letting of the house in the local press.

Soon after this time the tenancy of the house was taken on by Mr. & Mrs. Sismey, and although Mr. Sismey died some years past, Mrs. D. Sismey remained in the house until 27th March, 1999.

The chapel eventually had to close, and the last service was held in 1963. At a meeting held on Friday 31st July, 1964 it was reported that Conference approval for the sale of the Spalding Marsh property had been obtained. Negotiations had resulted in a sale to Wragg Marsh Farms Ltd. for the clear sum of £1,000. The trust continued to operate for some time to dispense the funds due to be received from the investment of the £1,000 received from the sale of the century.

The last Annual meeting of the Spalding Marsh Methodist Trust was held at Broad Street, Methodist Schoolroom on Tuesday, 18th October, 1977 when the trust was disbanded.

The Schoolhouse and Chapel, Spalding Marsh 1998.

Last Spalding Marsh Trustee's.

George Raymond Hastings, The Island, Cowbit Road.
Jack Douglas Mann, 28, Avebury Gardens, Spalding.
Cyril Henry Bester, 122, Spalding Road, Pinchbeck.
Charles Walter Lemmon, Norwich.
Frederic Charles Bratley, "Doric" Cley Hall Drive.
John Harold Worley, 6 Prospect Crescent, Swanage, Dorset.
Alfred Spencer, 26 Priory Road, Spalding.
Leonard George Bacon, 15, Knipe Avenue, Spalding.
John Reginald Green, 42 Halmer Gate, Spalding.
Vera Wooldridge, 13 New Road, Spalding.

Snippets from what the papers used to say.

Show of Rams.

Mr. Robert Fisher informs his friends and breeders of sheep in general, that his Show of Rams will commence on Monday the 10th of September next, at Weston; on which, or any future day during the season, he shall be happy to see those gentlemen who will please to favour him with their company.

Weston, near Spalding, Lincolnshire, Aug. 1821.

Presentation plaque inside the old chapel schoolroom.

THIS BUILDING PRESENTED BY
JOHN P. SAVAGE ESQ. OF MOULTON
FOR THE BENEFIT OF THE INHABITANTS OF
SPALDING MARSH AS A SCHOOL
AND PLACE OF WORSHIP.
JAN.ᵞ 1873.

Inside the derelict schoolroom, 1997.

Weston Tithe rent Charge.

Attendance as heretofore will be given at the Chequers Inn in Weston on Wednesday the 7th instant, to receive the TITHE RENT CHARGE due to the impropriator 1st instant, when is expected and required that the same be punctually paid.

Spalding, 19th Oct., 1869. CHAS. HARVEY.

To Builders.

Tenders are invited for the ERECTION of SCHOOLS and a TEACHER's RESIDENCE at Weston Hills, in the parish of Weston St. Mary. The plans and specifications may be seen on application at the School, Weston St. Mary. Tenders to be sent to the Rev. J. H. Nowers, Weston Vicarage, near Spalding, endorsed "Tender for Schools," not later than Tuesday, 29th March.

The lowest or any Tender not necessarily accepted.

Weston St. Mary, 28th February, 1872.

13th February 1873.

Weston Hills. – On Thursday evening, the 13th inst., there was a large gathering of parishioners and friends to celebrate the opening of the New School and Teacher's residence, just erected in this part of the parish of Weston St. Mary, at a cost of about £600, nearly £400 of which sum has been raised by voluntary contributions.

Tea being over, readings and recitations were given by the Vicar, and Messrs, Watkinson and Blackman; and vocal and instrumental music by Mrs. Blackman, Mr. Hufton, and other amateur friends.

To Builders and Contractors.

Tenders are required for RE-BUILDING St. LAMBERT'S HALL, Weston near Spalding, for Lord Kesteven –

The plans and specifications may be seen on application to the undersigned. – His lordship does not bind himself to accept the lowest or any Tender.

W. H. Mills, Architect.

Spalding, July 5th, 1878.

March 1894.
Singular Collapse of a Prosecution at Spalding.

At an Inland Revenue prosecution at Spalding on Tuesday, Arthur B. Hilliam, farmer, of Weston, was summoned for shooting partridges without having a game licence. The case was one which occupied a good deal of attention, the defendant being one of a shooting party of well-known sportsmen. The shooting was on his own occupation. After the case for the prosecution closed, a legal point was raised that the order of the Inland Revenue Commissioners sanctioning the proceedings had not been put in evidence. The order was then produced, but it was contended that it was too late, as the case was closed.

The Court held the objection was fatal, and dismissed the case.

December 1903.
£160 For A Pound of Potatoes.

Further high prices continue to be made in the Spalding district for special varieties of seed potatoes, which are occupying very prominent attention in agricultural circles. Mr. William J. Atkinson, of Weston, near Spalding, has just sold a pound of the famous Eldorado potatoes for £160, and a second pound for £150. Previously the highest figure at which Eldorados had been sold in the Spalding district had been £100 per pound.

A Weston Discovery.

Some workmen dug up, in the precincts of Weston St. Mary's Church, on Saturday an immense bone. It was supposed to be the rib-bone of the remains of some monstrous animal of former ages. It is probably the remains of some monster of the deep; for, in ancient records, it appears that the lords of the sail in this parish of Weston stipulated with their tenants to have all the "grand fishes" which might be cast upon the land by the ocean tides.

April 24th, 1855.

1906.

Weston "Pen-Fold" Demolished.

The old wooden parish pen-fold which used to stand at the corner of the late Mr. Ashton's stackyard at Weston, but which has not been used for many years past, has just been pulled down to make room for a new fence. This was the only pen-fold remaining for many miles around Spalding.

September 1899.

Spalding Police Court.

Tuesday, before the Rev. J. Russell Jackson, M.A. (Chairman), Rev. J. T. Dove, M.A., Rev. G. S. Leigh-Bennett, Dr. H. T. Stiles, Mr. W. J. E. Hobson, Mr. T. Atkinson, Mr. R. Rose, Mr. R. Merry, Mr. F. Howard, Mr. G. F. Barrell, Mr. W. J. Thompson & Mr. J. T. Atton.

Assault in Weston Church.

Fryer Smith, sexton, of Weston Parish Church, was summoned by Elizabeth Aldrich, wife of Fleetwood Aldrich, of Weston, for assaulting her son Ralph William Aldrich, aged 11, at Weston, on the 20th ult – the boy, it appeared, laughed in church, and the sexton struck him on the face. The result was that his nose bled profusely, that he became faint from loss of blood, and a doctor had to be called in.

Dr. Jackson described the injury the boy received which appeared to be serious owing to the difficulty in stopping the bleeding. He learned that he had had a fall the previous day, and he thought that, but for that the injury would not have been so severe. At the suggestion of the Chairman, the matter was settled out of Court, the complainant paying all the expenses, the doctor's bill, and 5s. for the boy's loss of time – in all £1 12s. 6d. The defendant stated that the boy's conduct in church had given him a great deal of trouble, but he was cautioned by the Bench not to strike boys in church in future.

July 1877

Weston – A cyclist's church parade was held here on Sunday last, and the village was thronged with hundreds of cyclists and others. The Holbeach Cycling Club had the arrangements in hand, and cyclists from Holbeach, Spalding, Wisbech, Long Sutton, Bourne, Revesby, Baston, Sutton Bridge, and Horncastle to the number of 300 were present. The Rev. J. H. Spokes, the Vicar preached an appropriate sermon to a crowded congregation, and the Holbeach Victoria Brass band accompanied the singing. After the service the cyclists were entertained to tea by the Vicar in the schoolroom. The vicarage grounds were thrown open to the public, and the band played selections on the lawn. The parade was a decided success.

November 1861.

Spalding – Extensive Fires. – A stack-yard of Mr. Charles Capping of Spalding Marsh, was last week the scene of two fires, it is feared both being the acts of incendiaries. The first broke out on Saturday morning, when two stacks of straw, one of oats, a gig house, sociable and harness, calf and some fowls, were destroyed. The fire-engines were despatched to the scene, and after great exertions the fire was extinguished. On Saturday evening, however, another fire broke out in the same yard and a stack of wheat, the produce of about 70 acres, was destroyed. The engines were the means of saving the remainder of the property, all of which was insured in the Phoenix Fire Office. Suspicion pointed to two of Mr. Capping's servants a male and a female as the perpetrators of the above acts, but on Tuesday last they were examined before the magistrates at a special petty sessions and discharged.

Whaplode

Aspects of Spalding Villages

Whaplode is a large scattered village situated on the road between Spalding and Holbeach. Before the closing of the railway from Spalding to Kings Lynn, Whaplode had a station, but this has long since closed down. The church dedicated to St. Mary is a stone building in the Norman, Transitional and Early English periods, consisting of a chancel, clerestoried nave with seven bays, aisles, north transept, north and south porches, and a mighty tower in the south east containing bells and a clock. In the interior the crowning glory is the fine altar tomb of stone, bearing the effigies of Sir Anthony Irby and his wife Alice. On the base of the tomb are the figures of five children kneeling. Above is a canopy supported on ten columns, and the whole tomb is surrounded by railings.

The church yard is grassed and well kept with fine trees, and remains of a 14th century cross.

The church of St. Mary, Whaplode, about 1870. This photograph was taken before the trees that are in the churchyard now were planted, making it almost impossible to take a photograph like this.

Print of the church of St. Mary's, Whaplode, 1842.

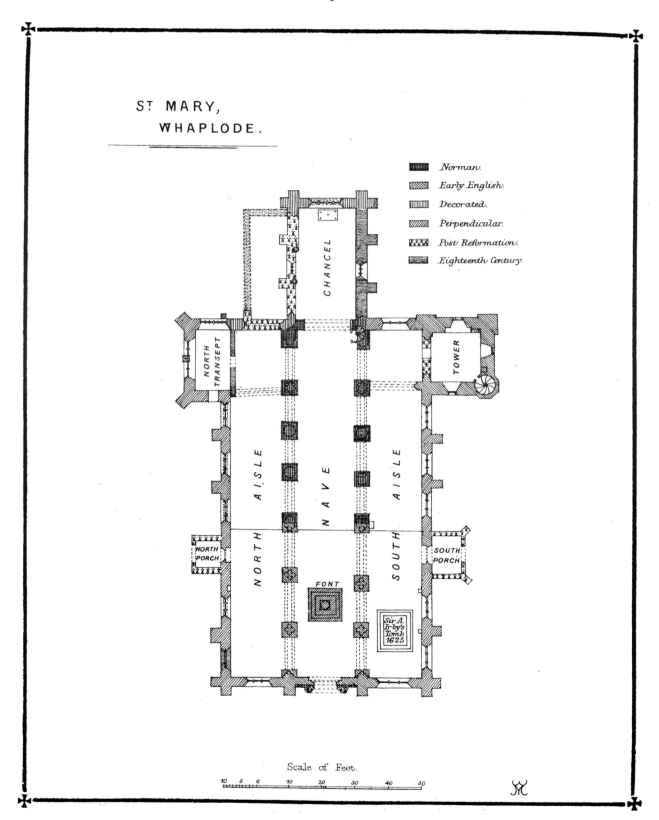

ST MARY,
WHAPLODE.

Norman.
Early English.
Decorated.
Perpendicular.
Post Reformation.
Eighteenth Century.

CHANCEL

NORTH TRANSEPT

TOWER

NORTH AISLE

NAVE

SOUTH AISLE

NORTH PORCH

SOUTH PORCH

FONT

Sir A.
Irby's
Tomb
1625

Scale of Feet.

10 5 0 10 20 30 40 50

Plan of St. Mary's Church, Whaplode, about 1870.

The Vicar of Whaplode and the Governors of Oakham and Uppingham Schools.

In the year 1900 the Rev. J. W. Rhodes, Vicar of Whaplode began a lengthy dispute with the Rectors of the parish regarding the maintenance of the chancel of Whaplode St. Mary's. The tithes collected from the parishioners goes toward the support of the Oakham and Uppingham schools, but the Vicar contended that the Rectors or Governors were liable for the repair of the chancel of Whaplode parish church. Some repairs have from time to time been carried out by the tithe owners, but the Vicar described these as "the most miserable tinkering". He estimated that the cost of adequately restoring the chancel was £3,000. In September 1900 the Vicar called a meeting of the tithe payers. After the gathering was addressed by the Vicar the following resolution was adopted: – "That we, payers of the great tithe at Whaplode, having heard the statement from the Vicar of Whaplode concerning the failure of the Rectors to fulfil the obligations on which they hold the great tithe, hereby express our indignation at their conduct, and pledge our whole-hearted support to the Vicar in his efforts to induce the Rectors to fulfil those obligations." The income from the tithe at this time stood at considerably over £1,000 a year.

In May 1901 a petition to the Bishop of Lincoln was signed in Whaplode with reference to the tithe question, which was before the Holbeach County Court a few days earlier when the Rev. J. W. Rhodes, Vicar of Whaplode, was sued by the Governors of Oakham and Uppingham school for the non-payment of the rectorial tithe of Whaplode, of which they are the owners. The Vicar's objection was that the plaintiffs had no right to the tithe, as they had failed in their obligations to maintain the chancel of the parish church. The petition then signed set forth that, while anxious to avoid any public scandal, the petitioners desired to make clear that they were united in their determination to support the Vicar of Whaplode in his efforts to induce the rectors to make some attempt to carry out their covenanted obligations. The moderate request made by the Vicar that the rectors should place £100 per year aside for 20 years to accumulate for rebuilding the chancel cannot, said the petition, be construed into an unreasonable demand, and especially in view of the fact that the tithe has yielded £1,600 per annum, the smallness of its original cost, the long years of neglect, and the extremely damaging efforts to shift upon the parishioners the undoubted obligations of the rectors. The Bishop of Lincoln was asked to use his influence to bring about an amicable settlement.

In June 1901 the press reported as follows: –

Whaplode – The Vicar and the Tithe – A crowd of people assembled in Holbeach Market Place on Saturday evening to witness the sale of six pieces of household furniture, belonging to the Rev. J. W. Rhodes, Vicar of Whaplode, which had been distrained and removed for sale under an order obtained through the Holbeach County Court, to satisfy a claim for the tithe rent charge and costs due to the Governors of Oakham and Uppingham schools. Punctually at seven o'clock, Mr. C. E. May (Auctioneer), accompanied by Mr. Robert Gee (County Court Bailiff), appeared upon the scene, and the proceedings commenced.

The first lot offered was, according to the sale bills, a gent's low back arm chair, with rush seat, and this was purchased by Mr. B. W. Kent for 11s. Lot 2, a fancy bamboo table, with flaps, was purchased by Mr. R. W. Oldershaw for 2s. 6d. Lot 3, a mahogany circular card table with cloth covered top, led to some spirited bidding, and was eventually secured by Mr. B. W. Kent for the sum of 22s. Lot 4, a gent's high backed arm chair, with wood seat, again caused some brisk bidding, this also being bought by Mr. Kent, for the sum of 37s. 6d. At this stage the auctioneer intimated that the required amount had been realised, but Messrs Wright and Dickinson stated they had the Vicar's authority to have the remaining goods sold, and the sale accordingly proceeded. Lot 5, a lady's bentwood rocking chair with cane seat and back, was knocked down to Mr. Kent for 5s. 6d., and the last Lot, a French Iron bedstead, four feet wide (way past its prime), was bought by Mr. George Harris for 2s. 6d. The total amount realised was £4 1s., so that there will be a balance to hand over to the Vicar when the claim and expenses are paid.

The petition that was sent to the Bishop of Lincoln gained no support for the Vicar's stand against the rectors. The Bishop regretted the misunderstanding which had arisen, but supported the proposal of the parishioners to take in hand themselves the restoration of Whaplode church at an estimated cost of £1,000. His Lordship enclosed a contribution of 10 guineas. The Vicar considered the Bishop's reply a painful rebuke and informed him that the parishioners could not proceed with the proposed restoration effort. The question of the Vicar of Whaplode paying the tithe eventually proved to be utterly illegal. A document was discovered in a lawyer's safe. This Tithe Apportionment Deed specially exempted the Vicars from tithes. Therefore the Rev. Rhodes and his predecessors from whom the tithe had been taken for more than forty years should not have had to pay. Had the Vicar been able to prove this earlier his furniture would not have been distrained and sold in public auction.

In May 1907 the Rev. Rhodes wrote in the Parish Magazine, saying the efforts on behalf of the chancel had been successful. The clergy of the Rural Deanery had memorialised the Bishop of Lincoln to intervene, and he assured them that he would endeavour to do so.

Some time after this the Vicar announced that the Rectors had at last taken a favourable view of the appeal made to them with regard to the renovation of the chancel, and an assurance had practically been given that the work would be carried out. For this satisfactory settlement of a long quarrel, the Vicar said, the Bishop was responsible.

Trades and Business People in Whaplode in 1937.

Andrew, Jsph. Edwd., insurance agent, Red House.
Ashton, Jn., farmer, Stennetts Farm.
Baker, Fredk., nurseryman, The Nursery, Spalding Road.
Barnes, Chas., smallholder, High Road.
Beba, Albt. Edw., farmer, Hurdletree Bank.
Beeson, Fredk., farmer.
Bell & Bowl Public House (Edwd. Daly).
Benton, Bernard, farmer, Millgate.
Bettison, Thos, farmer, Highfield Farm.
Biggadike, Arthur Edward, farmer, Sycamore.
Biggadike, Frank, bulb grower, Rosedene, Hill Lane.
Biggadike, Fred, snr., smallholder, The Bungalow, Cobgate.
Biggadike, Geo. Wltr., bulb grower, Westholme.
Biggadike, Jn., farmer, Crown Holdings.
Biggadike, Jn., smallholder, Hockley House.
Birchnell, H. S., smallholder, Southernwood, Whaplode Fen.
Blue Bell Inn (Mrs. Beatrice Gott), Whaplode St. Catherines.
Bollons, Arth. Herbert. jun., smallholder, Mill Gate Road, Fen.
Bollons, Wltr., farmer, Vailima.
Bowers, Thos., farmer.
Burchnell, Geo, haulage contractor, Ravens Bank, Whaplode St. Catherines.
Burchnell, George Smith, farmer, St. Catherines Bridge.
Cade, Wm., threshing machine owner.
Cartledge, Ernest, butcher, Double Street.
Castle, Leonard Jn., farmer, The Laurels.
Castle, Wm., florist, Victoria Cottage.
Catling, Thos., fruiterer, Mill Lane.
Cemetery (Walter Diggle, keeper).
Clark, A. H. & Son, farmer.
Clarke, Chas. Burton, carpenter, High Road.
Clarke, Frank, farmer & bulb grower.
Clarkson, J. H., farmer, Randalls Bank.
Clay Bros., farmers, Holly House, Hop Lane.
Congreve, C. A., farmer, Crown Holdings.

Congreve, Jsph., farm bailiff to Harold Kingston, esq., Whaplode Bank.

Coward, Geo., farmer, Sholtsgate.

Croker, Bert, smallholder, Cranesgate.

Croker, Ernest W., farmer, The Ramblers, Whaplode St. Catherines.

Croker, Frank, farmer, Whaplode St. Catherines.

Crosby, Albt. Edwd., farmer, Hurdle Tree Bank.

Dennis, Frank, grocer.

Dennis, Wm., poultry farmer, Roseleigh.

De Pear, J. C., farmer, Briar Farm.

Dickinson, Hy., smallholder, Church Street.

Dickinson, Jsph, bulb merchant.

Dring, Frank, farmer & landowner, Double Roof.

Dun Horse Public House (Percy Davis), Whaplode Bank.

Fletcher, William, cottage farmer, Crown Holdings.

Foreman, John, cottage farmer.

Fowler, Geo H., farmer, Quick Lane.

Freeman, E. A., farmer, Ash Tree Farm, Whaplode Fen.

Freeman, Edwd. Ellis, smallholder, Whaplode St. Catherines.

Giddens, Eric Ronald, farmer, Cranesgate Farm.

Graham, Geo., smallholder, The Vineries.

Green, Harvey John, motor engineer, High Road.

Green, Percy, plumber, Station Road.

Grundy, Norman John, farmer, Ash Tree Farm.

Hall, Geo., farmer, Cranegate, Whaplode Fen.

Hall, Geo. C., farmer, Mill Gate.

Hammond, Stephen, farmer, Westgate House.

Harpham, F. & A. E., farmers, Crown Farm.

Harpham, Arth. S., smallholder, The Hollies.

Holbourn, Ernest Edwd., farmer, Brikburg, Mill Lane.

Hotchkin, Geo., farmer, The Limes.

King, Jas. M., farmer.

Kingston, Harold, farmer, Whaplode Bank.

Lamb & Flag Public House (Frek. H. Biggadike), High Road.

Laming, Percy Allen, farmer, Hurdletree Bank.

Lawson, Jn. H., farm foreman to T. R. Pick, esq., Irby House.

Lawson, Wltr. Hy., bulb grower, Avondale.

Layen, Sidney, farmer, Randalls Bank.

Love, Chas, farmer, Cranesgate Road, Holbeach St. Johns.

Manyard John, farmer, Fields Farm.

Mimmack, John Wiseman, farmer, Jekells Bank.

Mitchell, John Rupert, blacksmith.

Morfoot, Geo, cottage farmer, Toll Bar Cottage, Spalding Road.

Neal Frank, fruit grower, Park Coates Farm.

Neal Walter John, farmer & fruit grower, The Gables.

Nicholls, Thos. Martin, carpenter.

Pope James, farmer, Cranesgate.

Pope, Percy, farmer, Cranesgate Road, Holbeach St. Johns.

Porter, Jn., farmer, Shotsgate.

Prior, Dorothy W. (Mrs), fried fish dealer, Station Road.

Ram Inn Public House (Herbt. Ayes).

Reed, Jas. & J. D., farmers.
Roberts, Jsph, cottage farmer, Peacock Cottages.
Robinson, Louis Harold, farmer, Hitherhold Farm.
Rose, Arth. Rd., farmer, Cranegate Road.
Rouse, John, farmer, Great South Holland.
Scott, Arth. Wltr., jobbing gardener.
Scott, Geo. H., market gardener, Station Road.
Seaton, Edwd. Harold, cycle agent.
Seymour, Arth. Jas., farmer.
Sinclair, W. A. & Son Ltd., millers.
Sleight, Herbert M., insurance agent.
Sly Bros, farmers, Mill Gate Farm, Fen.
Smith, Eric, farmer, Cranegate, Holbeach St. James.
Smith, J. T. farmer, Cranegate Road, Holbeach St. Johns.
Star Inn (Rt. Grimwood).
Starr Eliza Edith (Mrs), shopkeeper.
Stockdale, Gilbert, farmer, Ravens Bank Fen.
Stokes, Geo. Hy., boot repairer, Double Street.
Thompson, Lloyd, farmer, Guy Wells.
Vincent, Mary Ann (Mrs.), grocer & post office.
Watson, Alfd. Hy. Jason, farmer, House Farm.
Welch, Wm, farmer, Field's Farm.
Wheeler, Jack, boot repairer, Station Road.
Wilson, Jn. R., farmer, Arbour House Farm.
Wright, G. N. & A. bulb growers, Irby Hall.
Wright, J. & Son, bakers.
Wright, Wm. Bernard, farmer & landowner, Hurdletree Bank.

The Bell & Bowl Public House, about 1950.

The Ram Inn, Churchgate, Whaplode, about 1950.

Snippets from what the papers used to say.

January 1891.

Triplets at Whaplode. – The wife of Mr. Allen Decamps, carpenter, Whaplode, near Spalding gave birth on the 22nd to triplets, two boys and a girl, who are still alive. Decamps who now has eight children, will apply for the Queen's bounty.

1820.

March 10. – Two horses, the property of Mr. William Cook and Mr. Hircock, of Whaplode, Lincolnshire, having rubbed open a door of a barn belonging to the latter person, ate so immoderately of some wheat which lay on the floor, that both died soon after.

August 1897

A Lady School Attendance Officer's Methods – The School Board of Whaplode, near Spalding have a lady school attendance officer, named Mrs. Bourne, and at the last meeting of the Board some interesting and amusing facts transpired as to the novel methods adopted by her. It was reported that not only did she hunt up the would-be truants, and herself escort them to school, in some cases as many as six or eight times a week for a single child, see to its toilet, and then take it on to school. The board commended the attendance officer for the energetic way in which she discharged her duties.

Whaplode

October 14th, 1898.

About six o'clock on Friday morning the premises of Mrs. Lucy Naylor, of Whaplode, were discovered to be on fire. Fortunately plenty of help was at hand. The fire was confined to the chaff-house, wagon hovel, and calf shed, which were destroyed, together with a number of implements. Two in-calf heifers were so seriously injured that they had to be killed. The loss is covered by insurance in the County Fire Office. The cause of the fire is unknown.

June 1870.

A very interesting meeting was held at Whaplode on Monday last to celebrate the 101st birthday of one of the old ladies – Mrs. Ann Atkinson – in the Almshouses. Tea was very kindly given by the Vicar's lady, and presided over by Miss Franklin, the Vicar's daughter. Mrs. Atkinson retains all her faculties quite clearly. There were also present, her two daughters, aged respectively 73 and 58; her great grandson, aged 36; an old pensioner, aged 84, who served at the battles of Vittoria and Salamanca; and five old ladies, whose united ages amount to 367 years.

1823.

Absconded, and left his wife and Family chargeable to the Parish of Whaplode, in the County of Lincoln, Thomas Walker, labourer, 5 feet 4 or 5 inches high, stout made, marked with the small-pox, sandy hair, his right knee stiff and had on when he went away a light fustian corn jacket and breeches. Whoever will apprehend the said Thomas Walker, and lodge him in any of his Majesty's gaols, shall receive Two Guineas reward from Ashley Palmer, Overseer of Whaplode.

4th February 1896
The Vicar of Whaplode and the Church Bellringers. –

At Spalding Police-court on Tuesday, three summonses were returned for the hearing arising over a dispute between the Rev. John Collin, Vicar of Whaplode, and the bell-ringers of Whaplode Parish Church a matter which has attracted a good deal of attention in the district. The ringers with the consent of the churchwarden proposed to ring a muffled peal in memory of a deceased parishioner, but the Vicar objected. The ringers persisted, and as a result of what then transpired, three of the ringers were now summoned by the Vicar for riotous, violent and indecent behaviour in the church, and the Vicar was summoned for assaulting one of the ringers. The matter was now settled by an expression of regret on the part of the ringers that they should have persisted in the action in the face of the objection of the Vicar, and the withdrawal of the whole proceedings. It was stated that whilst legally the churchwarden had the custody, the incumbent had control of the bells. Under the settlement each party to the proceedings bore their own costs. There was a crowded court to hear the case.

November 1897.

The Rev. J. Collin, Vicar of Whaplode, announced on Sunday that he was about to leave the village and that a clergyman from the neighbourhood of Liverpool would succeed him. Mr. Collin has held the living since 1883, and is now going into Hampshire. This will make six new clergymen in the neighbourhood in about two years.

Show of Rams.

J. Codling respectfully informs his friends and the public that he intends showing his Rams, at Whaplode, on Monday the 4th September next, at Eleven o'clock in the forenoon; at which time, or on any future Monday during the season, the company of his friends will be esteemed a favour.

Whaplode, August, 1826.

December 1828.

In the great Christmas market in Smithfield on Monday the 15th inst. were noticed a large lot of fine sheep of the true Lincolnshire breed, bearing a great resemblance to what that valuable breed was 50 years ago; and two very large and well-fed oxen of the Lincolnshire breed, the property of Mr. Joseph Rogerson, grazier of Whaplode. The oxen were bred by Mr. John Codling, of the same village. Our correspondent observes that such stock are worthy of notice, and do credit to the old county.

27th February 1900.

On Thursday, a special treat was arranged in connection with the Wesleyan Band of Hope. In the afternoon, a public tea was provided and was attended by the members of the Band of Hope and a considerable number of adult friends. At 7 o'clock, a public meeting was held in the chapel. In the unavoidable absence of Mr. J. S. Patchett, the chair was occupied by Mr. C. H. Mashford. Recitations were given by members of the Band of Hope, and a solo rendered by Miss Wiles. The address was given by Mr. J. B. Thornley (district superintendent of the United Kingdom Alliance). Mr. Thornley received a hearty welcome on this the occasion of his first appearance at Whaplode. There was an excellent audience.

21st May 1850.
Sweep's Wedding at Whaplode.

At Whaplode, on Monday week, Mr. Francis Muckalo, chimney sweep to Rachel James; and at the same time Charles Fiddler, sweep to Sarah Muckalo, daughter of Mr. Muckalo, master sweep. The pathway to the church was carpeted with soot-cloths and bags; over which at intervals were placed sundry hand-brushes, scrapers, and bunches of gay flowers.

May 1894.

On Monday morning, there was a sharp frost, which cut off some of the early potatoes, damaged others, and blackened the whole. Those just out of the ground are cut off, and lie with darkened heads; those more advanced have had their leaves all shrivelled up, the stalks being saved by the abundance of leaves. Farmers were congratulating themselves on their prospects on Saturday and Sunday, and now the crop is blighted. The later potatoes which were up have suffered the most. At four a.m. yesterday (21st May), the slates, grass and woodwork were covered with rime.

Whaplode Wesleyan Methodist Church. Built 1838. Photographed 1999.

Whaplode Drove

with
Dowsdale & Shepeau Stow.

Whaplode Drove is a sprawling village. Together with hamlets of Shepeau Stow and Dowsdale it gives the impression of having very little past history, but upon delving deeper it appears that the area was inhabited in Roman times, and possibly even before then.

In 1860 the churchyard was enlarged. During the construction of a dyke to enclose the new portion, about half an acre in extent, a large quantity of Roman pottery was met with, together with coins of VESPASIAN (A.D. 69-79), ANTONIUS PIUS (A.D. 138-161) and others. Besides this in 1938 a rather crude Romano-British altar was found in the churchyard which is now kept in the church porch. The altar is made of stone from the Northamptonshire area, and was probably used in the worship of pagan gods.

It is thought that the Whaplode Drove area became uninhabited in Saxon times. This could be due to the flooding of the land caused by neglected drainage.

By the middle of the 13th century the village again started to become established after the land between Whaplode village and Postland was reclaimed in stages. The first stage was accomplished with the building of Hurdletree Bank. This was followed by Jekil's Bank, and finally in 1241 the common bank was built. The latter bank followed the line of the existing road between Shepeau Stow and Holbeach Drove.

There has been a church in Whaplode Drove since the early part of the 14th century when the Abbey of Croyland built a chantry to serve the local inhabitants. For hundreds of years the village had been served by a church built of wood. In 1821 the present church dedicated to St. John the Baptist was built by Jeptha Pacey and William Swansborough. Until the year 1902 the village was contained within the parish of Whaplode. On the 15th August of that year Whaplode Drove became an ecclesiastical parish formed from the civil parish of Whaplode. In 1907-8 the church was restored at a cost of £1,000 when a new chancel, organ chamber and porch was added, with seating for 200 persons. The chancel and the new portion of the church were consecrated by the Bishop of Lincoln October 8th 1908. The organ was bought from the Vicar and Churchwardens of Surfleet church; one of the two silver chalices presented by Queen Elizabeth in 1569 to the parish, disappeared for over 100 years, until 1912, when it was discovered in Rippingale Church; it was returned in 1927.

At one time there were three Methodist Chapels within the parish. The Methodist Chapel at Whaplode Drove was built in 1862 with seating for 120 persons. A schoolroom was added in 1902 for 80 children. At Shepeau Stow a chapel was erected in 1867. At Dowsdale their first chapel was built in 1841. In 1897 a new chapel was built with seating for about 150 persons, and the old chapel was then used as a schoolroom. A further extension was added in 1938. Despite the isolation of this chapel it was still in use for worship in 1998, but Whaplode Drove and Shepeau Stow have closed down. The village of Whaplode Drove and surrounding area was in the past well served with public houses. In the old directories of Lincolnshire the following names appear:–

The Romano-British altar that was found in 1938 now kept in the church porch.

The Shoulder of Mutton.	The White Horse.
The Bottle & Glass.	The Black Horse.
The Red Last.	The Mill.
The Ram's Head.	The Peacock.
The Red Cow.	The Dun Cow.

and at Dowsdale, The Wheatsheaf and the Duke's Head. Today all the public houses have ceased trading, the last to remain in business was the White Horse.

The Church of St. John the Baptist, Whaplode Drove. To the left can be seen the porch and the right the chancel that was added in 1907-8.

Dowsdale Methodist Chapel.

The Dowsdale Methodist Chapel that was built in 1897 to the right of the picture can be seen the 1938 extension that was added. In 1841 Mr. J. Leatherhead gave this site for a chapel. The first of which was built in that year. The 1897 building here shown was built on to the first building, part of which can still be seen attached to the rear of the present main building.

The Mill at Shepeau Stow.

Shepeau Stow mill here photographed in 1998. Records show that this mill was here in 1800, and the lower section could date earlier than this. The mill was powered by four patent sails which drove two pairs of stones above ground level, and another pair on the ground floor. A sail was lost in the early 1920s but milling continued by engine for some years. By 1935 the cap was missing, and today the mill is in a ruinous state.

Trades and Business People in Whaplode Drove in 1937.

Barker, Herbert, butcher.
Baxter & Guion, farmer.
Baxter, Arth., carpenter.
Black Horse Public House (Hy. King).
Boor, Jsph. Wm., farmer, Aswick Grange.
Bottle & Glass Public House (Arth. Gilbert Judge).
Brand, Wm., motor engineer.
Burchnell, Wm. Hugh, baker.
Burdett, Jn. Thos., smallholder.
Cooper Bros., smallholders.
Cragg, Ansell, farmer, Dowsdale.
Crockett. C. (Mrs.), fried fish dealer.
Day, Geo., farmer, Dowsdale.
Day, Jn., blacksmith, Shepeau Stow.
De Pear, Chas. Herbt., farmer, Briar House.

Duke's Head Public House (Thos. Noble), Dowsdale.

Farrow, Herbert Walter, bulb merchant, Elder House.

Farrow, Jn. Herbt., smallholder, Laburnum Cottage.

Fisher, George, saddler & harness maker.

Fisher, Wm., shopkeeper.

Fletcher, Benj. Nathnl., farmer.

Ford, Eliz. (Mrs.), farmer, Shepeau Stow.

Ford, Herbert, farmer, Shepeau Stow.

Form, Wm. Hy., farmer, Dowsdale.

Goose, Edwd., farmer, Hagbeach Farm.

Grummitt, Jas., farmer, Bridge Farm.

Grummitt, John, farmer.

Grundy, Norman Jn., farmer, Whaplode Bank.

Hankin, Ernest, grocer.

Harrison, Albt. Alex., farmer, Crown Farm.

Hemmant, Susannah (Mrs.), draper & post office.

Hemmant, Wm. B. Carpenter, Shepeau Stow.

Judge, Wm., builder.

Kingston, Harold, farmer.

Lawson, Annie (Mrs.), farmer, Mill House.

Login, Frank, threshing machine proprietor.

Monckton, Albt., smallholder.

Money, Thos. & Son, farmer.

Money, Harry, saddler, Shepeau Stow.

Perkins, William, baker.

Pont James, smallholder.

Porter, Danl., haulage contractor.

Red Last Public House (Chas. Wltr. Davis), Shepeau Stow.

Rouse, Jn., farmer.

Seaton, John, farmer.

Shoulder of Mutton Public House
    (Wltr, Footett).

Strickland, Isaac, farmer.

Taylor, Jn., farmer.

Walton, Geo. Edwd., farmer.

Waterfall, Geo., smallholder.

Wheatsheaf Public House
    (Wltr. Freeman).

White Horse Public House
    (Wm. Edwd. Jas. Spinks).

Whitwell, Jn. Herbt., farmer.

Williams, G. G. Ltd.,
    motor engineers.

Wright, Bert, haulage contractor.

The Dukes Head Inn, Dowsdale. Summer 1951.

The Wheatsheaf Inn, Dowsdale. Summer 1951.

The Bottle & Glass Public House, Whaplode Drove.

The Red Last Inn, Shepeau Stow.

Goodbye to The Bottle and Glass, Whaplode Drove.

A family association for three generations with a village public house ended on Whit Monday evening 1963 with the closure of the Bottle and Glass, Whaplode Drove.

The event was marked by a presentation of an electric fire to Mr. and Mrs. Jack Judge, the host and hostess at the Bottle and Glass.

The gift, donated from snookerette funds, was handed to them by Coun. H. W. Farrow, the "father" of the village and of East Elloe Rural Council.

Coun. Neil Judge presided at the ceremony, supported by snookerette captain John Willcox. Vice-captain Albert Rouse thanked Coun. Farrow. Friends from the White Horse and Gedney Hill Cross Keys, and guests from Peterborough and Halifax joined Bottle and Glass patrons in making the best of a sad occasion.

While agreeing with a comment that rural England lost something of its charm whenever a public house sign was taken down, the guests joined in singing "Land of Hope and Glory".

Both bottle and glass were put to good use in what proved not too dismal a farewell to a Whaplode Drove haven of refreshment for many a son of the soil.

Snippets from what the papers used to say.

July 1881.

The Whaplode Drove Church school festival was held on the 14th inst. in the picturesque garden adjoining the parsonage, and through the kindness of the Rev. R. Hollis and Mrs. Hollis the children attending the Board school in the village were allowed to participate in the treat. Soon after 1.00 p.m. about 200 children assembled near the parsonage, where the Croyland Brass Band played some lively tunes. Having formed a procession they marched to the church, where a short service was gone through, followed by an instructive address by the Rector. After service the children were taken to the adjoining paddock, where a booth had been erected, and they were then regaled with tea and plum cake. Various sports were subsequently provided for them. Tea for visitors, of which there were from 200 to 300, was laid out al fresco under the magnificent trees surrounding the lawn. Dancing on the lawn to the strains of the band was freely indulged in, and at dusk the grounds were brilliantly lighted up with a large number of Chinese lanterns. The Rev. R. Hollis, Mrs. Hollis, Miss Eason and others were indefatigable in their exertions for the comfort and enjoyment of those present. The company present in the evening was estimated to number at least 700, yet not the slightest damage to the grounds of flowers was perceptible on the following day.

July 1894.

Sad Fatality at Whaplode Drove. – The Coroner for the Spalding district (Mr. J. G. Calthrop) on Monday night held an inquest at the Red Last Inn, Whaplode Drove, touching the death of Alfred Wilcox, aged 17, who was run over and killed in the hay field on the Friday previous. Evidence was given by three witnesses, from which it appeared that on the day in question the deceased was working on the farm of Mr. Geo. Griffin, at Postland. Hay was being carted, and Wilcox was riding a horse attached to a wagon. The animal, from some cause or other, ran away, and the rider was thrown to the ground, the wheels of the wagon passing over his body. He sustained serious internal injuries, which terminated fatally on Sunday night. Wilcox told a witness named Mason that when the horse ran away he decided to jump off, and get hold of the animal's head, but whilst endeavouring to do this he fell, and went under the wheels. Dr. Crowden of Gedney Hill, described the injuries inflicted, and the jury returned a verdict to the effect that the deceased was accidentally killed.

July 1877.

Notice is hereby given, that a separate Building, named the Wesleyan Chapel, situate at Whaplode Drove, in the parish of Whaplode, in the county of Lincoln, in the district of Holbeach, being a building certified according to law as a place of religious worship, was on the Seventeenth day of July, 1877, duly Registered for Solemnizing Marriages therein, pursuant to the Act of 6th and 7th Wm.4, c.85.

Witness my hand this Seventeenth day of July, 1877.
ROBERT MILLNS. Superintendent Registrar.

August 1823.

As Mr. Wm. Eson, of Whaplode Drove, was returning from Spalding market between 11 and 12 o'clock on the night of the 4th inst., he was met near Moulton Chapel by three men (supposed to be Irishmen), who pulled him off his horse and robbed him of his watch and 30s, in silver.

1827.
Mr. John Goglar.

June 21, Mr. John Goglar, grocer and draper, of Whaplode Drove, Lincolnshire. He had long been celebrated for an eccentricity of character, which continued to predominate to the last moments of his existence. More than twenty years back he named a stone, called Old Kate's Stone, as the one he wished to place over his grave; his coffin he purchased about three months before his death. Some of his bequests are in unison with the eccentricities of his life; for, after bequeathing an unusual annual sum to the Peterborough

Dispensary and to the School of Whaplode Drove, he gives the further sum of thirty shillings to be sent in plum cakes, to be marked, "J.G.W.D." and twenty shillings for ale to be given to the poor of Whaplode Drove on Christmas Eve for ever. Upwards of 400 persons, after following him to the grave, assembled at the school-room, where about 800 cakes and a hogshead of ale were by his desire. Dealt in that old fashioned measure which once his cheerful heart called pleasure.

November 1904.

New Primitive Methodist Chapel at Whaplode Fen – The foundation stones were laid last week of the new Primitive Methodist Chapel at Whaplode Fen, in the Spalding circuit. The total proceeds amounted to £50. Dr. Pigott, of Grimsby spoke both afternoon and evening, and congratulated the friends on their efforts, speaking of the church as a social, religious and educative factor in modern life. The new chapel, which is being built by Mr. W. Jepson, of Spalding, is to cost £210.

June 1870.

Whaplode Drove Races and Gala. – Encouraged by last year's experiment and with a strong belief in the sporting inclinations of hundreds in the district, the promoters of this yearly gathering in the Fens have been again successful in carrying out a good day's sport. The weather on Monday was specially congenial for a gala day, and great numbers of visitors of all classes, from far and near, found their way to the little village, both by road and rail. The band of the Peterborough Rifle Corps was in attendance, and added not a little to the pleasure of the day. The day's proceedings were closed with a display of fireworks.

The following stakes were run for::

The Whaplode Drove Stakes, for horses not exceeding 14 hands, open to all England; about 1 mile; heats: Mr. Thom's Red Pepper – 1st; Mr. Wilkin's Metty – 2nd; and Mr. Holmes's Wasp – 3rd. Six ran. The Whaplode Drove Cup, value £8, for horses the property of gentlemen residing within 25 miles of Whaplode Drove; about 2 miles: Mr. J. Hays's Grace Darling – 1st; Mr. C. Wright's Lizzie – 2nd; and Mr T. T. Whincup's Louie Stapleton – 3rd. Eight ran. The Farmers Stakes; entrance 15s; £6 added; about 2 miles. Mr. J. Hayes's Grace Darling – 1; R. Fleshborn's Attamante – 2nd; Mr. C. Wright's Lizzie – 3rd. Eight ran. The ladies Purse, value £2, for ponies not exceeding 13 hands; about half a mile; heats: Mr. Wilkins's Metty – 1; and Mr. Terrington's Creeper – 2. Five ran. The Consolation Stakes were won by Mr. Fleshborn's Attamante, beating three others.

June 1811.

On Friday last a quantity of bread, deficient in assize weight, was seized at a shop in Whaplode Drove, and a fine of £3 16s. imposed on the seller. The bread and the fine (after deducting the constable's expenses) were distributed amongst the poor of Whaplode, in the church there, on Sunday.

1893.

To Brewers and Publicans and Others.
Spalding and Whaplode Drove, Lincolnshire.

To be Sold by Auction.
By Messrs S. &. G. Kingston.
At the Red Lion Hotel in Spalding on Tuesday 21st November, 1893.
at Three o'clock in the Afternoon.
In Whaplode Drove.
Lot 4. All that old established fully licensed Free Public House, called "The Black Horse", with Blacksmith's Shop, Stable, Granary, and other Out-Buildings, Yard, Garden, and 5A. 3R. 3P. (more or less) of very Rich Arable Land adjoining and belonging thereto, situate in the centre of the village of Whaplode Drove, in the occupation of Mrs. Sarah Money as undertenant of Messrs. Soames & Co.

Messrs. H. H. and L. C./ Harvey, Solicitors.
Spalding and Holbeach.
Spalding, October 23rd 1893.

It was reported that the Black Horse, Whaplode Drove did not sell in the auction of the 21st November 1893.
Eventually the public house was sold for the sum of £500.

Although the Black Horse Public House, Whaplode Drove was eventually sold this was not the end of the story as the newspaper report of October 1895 hereby tells us of the case that was before the courts:

Smith (Alfred), brewer, Surfleet, v Kingston (s.), auctioneer and estate agent, Spalding – Claim £50 for misrepresentation in the sale of real estate, – Mr. Page of Lincoln, was for plaintiff, and Mr. H. H. Harvey of Spalding, for defendant, – The plaintiff purchased a Public-house at Whaplode Drove (The Black Horse) for £500 the matter being negotiated through Mr. T. H. Osbourne, of the firm of Osbourne and Mercar, of Piccadilly, London. Mr. Kingston, the defendant, was trustee of the estate of which the property in question formed a part, and Mr. Osbourne was one of the beneficiaries under the will, and the plaintiff contended that in the sale he was acting as Mr. Kingston's agent. The plaintiff purchased the property in November 1894, and his point was that he was promised possession on 6th April, 1895, but the tenant, Mrs. Money, declined to go out, and an action for ejectment failed. The plaintiff alleged that through not securing possession he had suffered a loss of £40 and £50 for the year, and the proceedings to gain possession had cost him £26 further. In reply the agency was denied, and Mr. Osbourne was called and stated that he had acted entirely on his own account in advertising the property and quite independent of the defendant, but it appeared that there had been an understanding that Mrs. Money would give up possession at Lady-Day last. Some legal points were raised, but it was also contended that the plaintiff had not suffered any loss, or need not have done so, as the tenant had offered him an order of beer and spirits, and had been willing to deal with him exclusively. The Judge found that the action for misrepresentation must fail, as the defendant was not responsible for the statement, and that if he had been, it was nothing more than a mistake, as it was believed that the tenant would give up possession. In the signed contract attached to the condition of sale were the usual words that on completion of the purchase the buyer would be entitled to possession or to the rent and profits, and Mrs. Money the tenant, had paid her rent to Mr. Smith the plaintiff. Judgement was given to the defendant with costs.

A MAP OF
DEEPING FEN
in the
COUNTY OF LINCOLN:
The several Lands and Commons, Survey'd
by Vincent Grant, about the Year 1676.
The several Rivers & Drains are carried
down to their Outfalls.

By JOS FEATHERSTONE. 1763.

A Scale of Five Miles.